LOVED
BEYOND
COMPARE

A JOURNEY OF MIRACLES AND RESILIENCE
DURING A WICKED WAR

I0519339

DR. JANE AMANA EKONG

LIVING WATER PRESS

Loved Beyond Compare -
A Journey of Miracles and Resilience During A Wicked War

Copyright 2023 © Jane Amana Ekong

Published by:
Living Water Press
Box 429, Mossbank, Saskatchewan, Canada, S0H 3G0

The scripture quotations in this book are
used with permission, specifically:

NIV – the Holy Bible, New International Version, Copyright © 1973, 1978, 1984, 2011 by Biblica, Inc. (All rights reserved)
NLT – the Holy Bible, New Living Translation, Copyright © 1996, 2004, 2015 by Tyndale House Foundation. (All rights reserved)
ESV – the Holy Bible, English Standard Version, Copyright © 2001 by Crossway. (All rights reserved)
The Message – The New Testament in Contemporary English, Copyright © 1993 Eugene H. Peterson (All rights reserved)

ISBN: 978-1-990863-455 (Paperback)
ISBN : 978-1-990863-479 (eBook)
ISBN: 978-1-990-863-462 (Hardcover)

To contact the author: https://linktr.ee/Loved.Beyond.Compare

Dedication

I dedicate this book to my Family.

First, to my Heavenly Father who gave me life, cared for, protected, and sustained that life through all its changing scenes. Without His intervention time and again, I would not be here today. I owe all that I am to Him. To Him be the glory now and forevermore.

To my Mom and Dad, Chief James, and Madam Arit Amana, you were the best. You taught me about life, about values, about what is temporal and what is eternal. You were selfless in going to all necessary lengths to provide whatever I needed to succeed. Best of all, you introduced me to God and taught me to love and trust Him. You led by example and left me with a rich heritage of love, godliness, and service. Thank you.

To my siblings, especially my two elder siblings who co-parented me:

To my elder sister Adiaha, thank you for allowing me to call your family home during holidays throughout my years in Ibadan. Thank you for adding to Mom's coaching by teaching me how to manage a home and care for children. You have been my second mother. I am grateful.

To my elder brother Edet, thank you for being a great parent to me, for your unceasing love, and for stopping at nothing to make me pursue what you knew was best for me. Thank you for giving generously of yourself and your resources to provide for me. You contributed significantly to the person that I am today. Thank you for always being there for me. You are the type of brother that only the very blessed are lucky enough to have.

To my brother Mfon, my immediate big brother, you were my protector and friend. Someone I could always count on. Thank you for moving Heaven and Earth to be present at my wedding at short notice. You were a brother that I knew I could always count on. Rest in peace.

To my younger brother Etim, you have always been my helper. In the early post-liberation of Oron, after schools reopened, you risked encounters with the unpredictable soldiers, time and again to bring me food and needed supplies. Now, you inconvenience yourself to accord me the privilege of calling your home, a place to stay whenever I visit Lagos. I cannot thank you enough.

My baby sister Imaobong (Coco), playing with you, and taking care of you were some of the reasons holidays were usually fun and a pleasure for me during my high school years. In later years, when I needed help, you traveled to Canada to help out with my children during your holidays. You have been the little sister I needed and wanted. Thank you.

To my husband, Chris, thank you for all the years of putting up with me. Your love has been my strength.

To my children, Imo, Nse, Ime, and Enobong; being your mother has been one of the greatest joys of my life. Thank you for teaching me how to be a mother.

To Ating, Atim, and Iquo, you have each been a source of blessings. Thank you.

Contents

1

The Dream

It was two o'clock in the afternoon on a smoldering hot day. The air was thick with moisture and heat, and the uncompromising scorching rays of the sun radiated down as if maliciously punishing the sons of man. Breeze, which could have moderated the discomfort, was ostentatiously absent, appearing reluctant to interfere with the sun's plan against mankind.

Under this uncompromising heat, I was walking the path from our house toward the street, a distance of about two hundred meters. I moved briskly, determined to accomplish my errand quickly and get back into the respite of the house. Suddenly, I sensed a shadow over me. My heart almost skipped a beat because I knew instinctively that the shadow meant stealth bombers in the sky. I made an abrupt turn and started to run towards the house. Looking up and over my shoulder, I could see there were at least four bombers on this raid.

Oh no, I thought, *one or two bombers usually inflict such horrendous damage, imagine what four can do? I must get out of their way as quickly as possible.*

Before I could complete the thought, I heard the feared whistling sound, the sound we had all become accustomed to; the sound that struck fear into every heart and sent prayers upward as people ran for their lives. It was the whistling sound of bombs pushing through the air as they hurdled toward the ground. I scrambled to determine their direction so I could deduce the best escape strategy. But it seemed already too late as I felt a scorching heat directly above my head.

Prior to this day, I had never had a close encounter with a bomb but had heard they were usually accompanied by searing heat. Therefore, I knew doom was near, almost at hand. My brain went into overdrive, trying to deduce how to survive this impending doom. My strategy of running back to the house for safety seemed already too late, as the fiery heat indicated the close proximity of the bomb and the inadequate time for any plan to succeed. Fear engulfed me. My heart pounded loudly as I tried to think of anything that could ensure my survival. But before I could act on any plan, everything went dark and silent.

For a few moments, I was in a state of shock. The silence was eerily peaceful. I enjoyed the peace and quiet for a moment. It was not that times of quietness were lacking in my life, but those times of quietness were unsettling because they were born out of purposelessness, fear, uncertainty, or frustration. That made it tedious and stressful. The quietness I was experiencing now was different. It was peaceful. The realization that this was unusual jolted me back to awareness.

Where am I? I thought. Then I remembered, *Oh, I have just been bombed.*

I was scared, and a series of bewildering thoughts bombarded my mind.

What happens to people after they are bombed?

They usually die, was the response.

Am I dead? Is that why it appears so peaceful, my mind wondered.

Are these thoughts part of the out-of-body experience I've heard of as people are dying? Or do dead people think?

Even though I did not like these thoughts, I could not unthink them. I was in a situation I'd never encountered before. I wasn't sure whether I was dead or alive.

Our existence since the onset of the war had become very mundane. During the day, we hid from soldiers as one never knew what they were after. For teenage girls like me, there was no need to wonder; an encounter with a soldier could be a death sentence as it could result in being captured, taken to their barracks, and used as sex slaves. Staying at home and indoors was no insurance against capture because some boys who got into trouble with soldiers could use information about girls' locations to bargain for their safety. So, there was always a sense of insecurity, no matter where we were and what we were doing. Things we could do to occupy the time were very limited. One could not go outside to play or go visit with friends as family members didn't want to be separated. Therefore, purposelessness and fear were the unrelenting plagues of everyday living.

There was little to do, except during the planting season when we helped plant the crops. We went to bed early at night and arose late in the morning once it was bright daylight—all in an effort to conserve kerosene when it was still available. When kerosene was no more, we had no choice but to rise with the light of the sun and end the day with its setting. Farm work was hard and tedious, and I had not participated in it since high school because I was at school during the planting season. My body ached from returning to such work after a three-year hiatus. However, the pain was still better than the purposeless existence that returned after the planting season was over and there was once more little to do. A sense of insecurity was always the predominant feeling.

It is difficult to comprehend at "normal" times how living without a purpose can be life-suffocating. Teenagers are known for loving to sleep in, however, how could one sleep well when all there was to look forward to was a long night that opened to a meaningless morning and a day possibly more dreadful than the one before? How could people, especially teenagers, live under such conditions day after day? This was our painful reality. That was why the feeling of peacefulness startled me, as many of us had long forgotten what real peace felt like. We had become accustomed to chaos, uncertainty, and fear.

How I longed for something to break the monotony and purposelessness, something daring and fun, something with excitement. What had just happened had a tiny bit of that: there was the adrenaline rush of trying to avoid the bomb, but that wasn't the kind of daring adventure I desired. These musings were interrupted and I was jolted back to reality when the earlier thoughts returned.

How do dead people know if they are dead? I asked myself again.

I didn't know anyone who had died and returned to tell what they'd experienced or what the moment of transition from life to death entailed.

If you are dead, probably nothing, unless there is something that dead people do.

Does that depend on where you go?

It appears peaceful here, so you probably are in heaven.

Great, thank God for that.

I thought about that for a split second and rejected it. I was not ready to be thankful for dying in my early teens. That was not how I had envisioned my life. I would feel cheated if I died now; there was so much more living in store for me. Even Heaven will have to wait. I may be happy to go there in my nineties but not now in my teens, I wanted to live. Even though life was restrained, purposeless, and frequently dangerous, the war would end someday, and life would return to "normal." I had to hold on until that happened.

I didn't know where these thoughts came from, yet they persisted. After a little while, they turned to my family.

Oh, my poor mother, I thought.

How she would hurt upon learning of my death. I hope her delicate heart can handle it. What if it can't? What if Mom collapses upon hearing of my demise? No, that can't be good. If Mom dies, who will take care of my little brother and my baby sister? Oh, God, please don't let Mom die. One death is enough, Lord. Please, please don't let her die too.

As my emotions turned to the possible consequences of my death on my family, I realized I was struggling to breathe, and there was debris in my mouth. That startled me, arresting the death thoughts. I drew a breath and could feel the debris not only in my mouth but all around me.

Could it be that I am still alive but just covered in debris?

This was my first encouraging thought. Hope began to rise in me. I took another breath. Dead people don't breathe, I was breathing, so I must be alive. Even though life was purposeless and filled with fear, living it was still worthwhile. I rejoiced at the realization that I was still alive.

It is intriguing that we do not often value what we have until it is nearly taken from us. At such times, ironically, we begin to appreciate what was previously unappreciated and even fight for it. I was grateful and thankful to be alive.

The next question that invaded my mind was, *How do I ensure I continue to stay alive?*

My brain went into action. I tried to open my eyes slightly but quickly realized that was not wise as the debris was pushing against my entire body, including my eyelids.

I must be buried deep in debris. If that is so, then I have to get out as quickly as possible before I suffocate, were my next thoughts.

I tried to move but was restrained by a heavy weight on my back. I stopped, lay still, and tried to think.

Even though I cannot move if I am to survive, I must create an air pocket so I continue to breathe.

I tried to move my right arm. It did not move.

That is not a good sign, I thought. *But I can still feel the arm, which must indicate that it is still attached to my body. That is good news, but I still need to get out of here as quickly as possible so that I don't suffocate. What else can I try?"*

Try to move your left arm, my mind instructed me.

I tried, and it moved just a little.

The debris pile over me on that side must be less, I reasoned.

I began to put more effort into creating an air pocket, spitting the debris out of my mouth and carefully moving my left arm as much as I could. With time and effort, my left arm was freed enough for me to very carefully use it to push some debris away from my face. After a small push, I would lay still and assess the situation because the last thing I wanted was to cause the debris above to collapse down on me. With time, I was able to clear enough debris away from my face and also create enough space to enable me push on my left elbow and slightly raise the left side of my upper torso.

Next, I focused on my lower body. I pulled and pushed very gently with my left leg as if I was treading water. I was surprised that the debris moved more easily this time. Now that my left side was less restricted, I turned my attention to my right side. I slowly and carefully threaded my left arm across my chest to my right side and pulled my upper right torso towards my left. There was a little movement. I repeated the procedure several times. Each success inspired the next. After many repetitions, my right hand was freed enough that I could pull it close to my side and use my elbows as levers on which to push up and raise my upper torso.

I wanted to be careful, as I was not sure of what surrounded me. I did not want to push too fast and have something fall and break my neck, back, or head. With these successes, I began to hope. Hope is an amazing thing. It gives a spark to life even at the worst of times. I re-evaluated my situation and cautiously concluded that the debris in which I was buried was perhaps not too extensive. I continued to wiggle, pull and push my body, and after what seemed like an eternity, I could see some light. I was energized and overjoyed. The push and pull continued until I pulled myself out of the debris completely and stood up.

I made it, I made it! The realization resounded in my heart.

I was drenched in sweat, which made the dirt and debris cling to my body, but this did not bother me, the greatest thing was that I was alive, and my body was intact. I had survived a direct bombing and still had all my body parts intact. How amazing was that!

I looked down at my clothes and was just about to start shaking some of the dust and clingy debris off when a new whistling sound rattled my heart. I looked up, and my jubilation turned to panic. The new whistling sounds above my head were announcing another series of bombs. I was flabbergasted, astonished, bewildered, and devastated.

Whoever heard of the same person being bombed twice in one day, and within a very short expanse of time? my astonished mind questioned.

Was this bombing raid targeted specifically at me? How do they know me? What did I do to become a target? How can I get away again this time? my mind asked.

My future flashed before my eyes. I could "see" my body parts in little bits and pieces thrown all over the place and mixed in with the dirt and debris.

What an ugly way to die. Would there be anything to bury? my devastated mind queried.

At first, I felt I did not have the energy, stamina, or time to fight this second bombing. I almost accepted what appeared to be the inevitable. Then something rose up in me. It was defiance, resilience, tenacity, and the desire to fight for my life. A new surge of energy engulfed me; I was determined not to die. I had survived the first bomb by a miracle, and I was not going to allow this second attempt to take me out. I was spared the first time for a reason, and I must be spared again.

What if you are not spared? What if you surviving the first bomb was a fluke?

I tried to shut out every other negative thought so I could focus on survival. Having been to the brink of death and returned the last time, I was not giving up. I wanted to live and have my plans, hopes, and dreams materialize. I wanted to continue in school, finish high school, attend university, acquire all the education that I needed, then get married, and have children. I wanted to care for my mom and dad when they were old. They had cared for me since birth, sacrificed to pay school fees, and given me most of what I needed. I had to repay them, reward them, and show them gratitude and appreciation for all they had done for me. This, therefore, was not the right time to die. I was determined not to die.

I refuse to die. I cannot die. I will not die, I screamed as loudly as possible in my thoughts—as if screaming it would inform the forces working against me of my resolve and instigate their retreat.

Even though a part of me kept repeating the above phrases, another, the pessimistic side chimed in: *Be realistic, Jane. How can you evade death again this time? The odds are against you. The bomb is almost practically on top of your head. You don't have the time to dodge it. It's too late; it's all over for you, girl. Say your prayers because this is it.*

In desperation, a deep gut-wrenching cry emanated from my mouth, heart, and soul, "God, please help me. Help me, please, I don't want to die. Please, please, help me."

I wasn't sure how He could help me that late in the process, as the bomb was almost on top of my head. The vaporizing heat was closer to my scalp this time than it had been the first time. It felt as if my hair was on fire. Was it possible that I could still be saved? If I were to be saved, it would have to be a miracle. I needed a miracle. A miracle is something that defies all explanations, right? Then one could still happen and I needed one this microsecond. A miracle was my only option, and I was not letting it go. If I did, my life would be over. I was determined not to let that happen.

When you're desperate, you don't rationalize. You just believe. I had to believe that a miracle was coming my way. I needed that miracle now. I had heard that God was a miracle worker. This was His opportunity to show that miracle-working ability on my behalf. I reasoned that He could cause the bomb to fail to explode, or provide a sudden huge wind gust to blow it off course so that it explodes elsewhere. Those were two possibilities through which the miracle could materialize. I hung onto them with whatever faith I had. I needed to stay alive.

Then something completely unanticipated and unexpected happened. As soon as I cried out to God, an audible voice spoke to me. It was very clear and distinct. I was not imagining it. The voice said, "Don't be afraid. I will be with you; I will help you and protect you. I will protect not only you but your entire family. Not one of you will be lost."

Don't ask me where the voice came from. I can't answer that, but I remember that the voice soothed my fears; it resounded in the deepest parts of my being. It was not a voice I heard only with my ears; it was a voice that reverberated from my ears to the deepest parts of my being. I couldn't tell the direction from which it came, yet it was as clear as a chiming clock on a sleepless night. I had never experienced something like that before, but somehow, I knew it was God.

2

Owing God

I awoke. My heart was pounding. My bedding was drenched in sweat. My entire body was shaking. I sat up, very relieved it had all been a dream. A horrific nightmare, but still a dream. I reached for my head and touched my hair to determine if it was intact or had been burned. The touch informed me that I still had hair. I ran my fingers through it and felt it was unsinged. I was then able to let out my held breath.

Bewildering thoughts raced through my brain at incredible speed. I'd never had that close an encounter with a bomb in real life, and neither did I know of anyone who had and lived to talk about it. They usually died. If they were lucky, they would be killed instantly with parts left to bury. If they were not so lucky, their body might be blown to pieces or they might endure devastating shrapnel wounds. They would suffer, sometimes for hours, with excruciating pain before they finally died. Those were not soothing thoughts, and I didn't want to entertain them. I didn't want to go back to sleep either, for fear that the nightmare could return. I just wanted to rejoice and celebrate the fact that I was still alive.

As I settled into this spirit of thanksgiving, a troubling thought occurred to me.

Don't people sometimes dream of things that will happen to them in the future? Could this be a warning that you will be incinerated by a bomb?

A flash of fear pierced through my heart. I tried to calm myself, reasoning that I had already had enough trauma for one night. I tried to focus on God's promise of protection. But try as I would, horrible imaginings continued to invade my mind. The thought of what the experience would have looked like, had it been real and not a dream, intrigued me. Would it have presented the same as in the dream or differently? Would my body have been shredded into tiny pieces and death been quick, or would my limbs have been torn off so that I suffered before death finally came? What if the bomb did not directly hit me, and I was just buried in deep debris and died a slow, torturous death by asphyxiation? My body began to tremble again. I knew I had to abandon this line of thought but had no idea how to make that happen.

I wanted to get up and do something to distract myself from the thoughts, but I didn't want to wake my little brother, who shared the room with me and was sleeping just a few feet away. Nor did I want to wake Mom and Dad, who had become light sleepers and would wake up at the slightest noise, especially if it came from our bedroom. They were always wanting to ensure that we were safe.

Then another thought occurred to me.

So, God spoke to you in the dream. Remember that whenever God spoke to or did something for people, He always made demands on them and wanted something in return. What demands do you think He is going to place on you? What if you don't like them? Now, you owe Him. Actually, this is the second time you owe God. Remember how He heard your cry and revived your Mom two years ago? How have you repaid Him? You are in trouble because you owe God big. What will you do if His demand entails things you do not like or want to do? Remember when you were eight years old and Mrs. Mado prophesied that God had a call on your life and was going to use you for His purpose? Maybe this is the beginning of the call. What are you going to do?"

I remember the two referenced incidents very well. I was playing outside with many of my friends on a beautiful moonlit night when Mrs. Mado came and invited us to her house. She gave us some snacks and started talking to us about God. Then she prophesied over me that God had a call on my life. What does an eight-year-old do with a prophecy? I had no idea what that meant, but I told Mom about it and continued on with my life.

Shortly after this prophecy, I had a dream in which Mrs. Mado and I were standing in a huge field in the middle of the afternoon on a very hot day. All of a sudden, big chunks of ice began to fall from the sky. In the tropics, when you live by the Atlantic Ocean, at only about four degrees above the equator, you only see ice when you look in the freezer or ice bucket. To suddenly witness balls of ice copiously falling from the sky on a very hot day was mesmerizing and frightening. What was happening? What did it mean? Mrs. Mado immediately declared, "This must be a very significant sign. I need to see what the Bible says about it."

With that, she ran into her house, and I was left alone as the dream continued.

I picked up some of the ice balls. They were cold but, for some reason, did not melt as quickly as ice would when taken out of the freezer on a hot day. I was still trying to comprehend this strange occurrence when my attention was drawn to the sky darkening in the middle of the afternoon. I was confused. How could these very strange things be happening? How can the sky turn dark in the middle of the day? I turned my gaze upwards; the day was turning dark, not because it was evening but because the sunlight was being eclipsed. At first, what was blocking the sun appeared to be a huge moving cloud. As it descended closer to Earth, it became clear that the cloud was composed of a crowd of people descending from the sky.

First, they appeared as a big cloud of dots. But as the descent continued, the dots grew bigger, and I could see the human form. I was transfixed as countless people emerged from the cloud onto the massive field. The end of the field was not visible, as the crowd covered it completely. In the midst of this mass of humanity was a smaller group. In its center was seated a person on a majestic and opulent throne. A comparatively smaller crowd formed a semi-circle behind Him and bowed down before him. The brilliance from the throne, and the one who sat there, was so blinding that it was difficult to look directly at Him.

After staring at this small group for a while, I turned my gaze back to the larger crowd. It extended beyond what my eyes could see. As I looked closer, I noticed that the larger crowd was moving toward the small one in the middle. However, they did not approach as a mob, rather, they formed a line that slowly moved toward the one who sat on the throne. As they approached Him, they were stopped by an invisible line, a divide. As each person reached this line, they turned either left or right. Those who turned to the left of him who sat on the throne fell on their faces and started weeping and wailing as if in terror. Those who turned to the right of the one who sat on the throne fell on their knees and started worshipping and praising Him.

There was no one directing this traffic, yet somehow, at the invisible line, people appeared to know where they belonged. I was very mesmerized as I watched this scene. The people who went left at the invisible line seemed horrified and screamed. Their reactions scared my childhood heart, and I was determined never to be in a position that would cause me to go left at that invisible line.

I wanted to know who the people were who went to the left, and what had they done. I definitely didn't want to go to the left, as I suspected that those were people with whom God was not pleased. I wanted to please God so that I would not go to that horrifying place. When I awoke from the dream, I prayed that God would help me please Him, and do things that would help me go to the side where people worshiped rather than wailed.

The other occurrence referenced, the miraculous healing of my mother, happened when I was in my second year of high school. My high school was, as were all other high schools, a boarding school. We spent about nine months of the year at school. The nine months were divided into three semesters of about three-month durations. We had two three-week holidays and a longer holiday at Christmastime. However, in the middle of every semester, we had a weekend break named "the half-term break." Students were allowed to go home on Friday, and return to school on Monday evening if their parents had requested that they come home.

Letters were usually sent to our parents informing them of the impending weekend off. They were asked to inform the school of where they wanted their daughter to spend the weekend. Since traveling at the time was arduous, the choices were either to return home (for those who lived within about a twenty-mile radius of the school) or stay on campus (for those who lived farther away). My parents lived within twenty miles of the school, so I always went home. I looked forward to half-term holidays as they provided me with the chance to see Mom and Dad and my younger siblings and restock my snack box.

Restocking the snack box was extremely important, as our food at the school was inadequate both in quality and quantity for growing teenage girls. Even though it was "illegal," we brought back as much nonperishable snack food as we could. However, the high temperature and humidity of the tropics caused spoilage of the food within four to six weeks. Therefore, the opportunity to restock at the six-week point during half-terms was perfect. All snacks were eaten in secret to avoid breaking the "illegal" rule of eating non-cafeteria-supplied food at the school. That was a rule nobody obeyed, as we may all have developed kwashiorkor and perhaps died of malnutrition or starvation if we did.

I always looked forward to going home. I expected Mom to be waiting by the door when I arrived. She would also have prepared my favorite meal. As the taxi drew closer to my hometown and our home, my heart leaped with joy, as the anticipation of a warm welcome danced in my mind. It would be so much fun to play with my baby sister. The taxi finally stopped in front of the house, and I stepped out.

Shock; the drapes in the house were not opened. That was most unusual as it was about noon. My heart began to pound. I knew something was very wrong. I ran to the front door and tried to turn the handle. It was locked. I flew to the side door, it was unlocked, I hurried inside. With a distressed voice, I called out "Maamma, Maamma."

No answer.

As I rushed towards Mom's bedroom, the baby came out. I picked her up and ran into the room. It was dark but I could see a person on the bed. I ran to the window and threw the drapes wide open and put the baby down. I could now see Mom on the bed. I ran to her and gently shook her, calling out, "Maamma, Maamma." There was no response. I tried hard to convince myself that she was only sleeping. My heart was racing. I bent toward her face to see if I could detect any breath.

My heart sank. What was I going to do? Those were no telephones in the rural community where we lived. How could I get help? Where was the maid? We always had a live-in maid who helped Mom. Where was she? Mom often gave the maid her time off when I was coming home so that I could learn housekeeping by doing it. When the maid was there, she often tried to help me, but Mom wanted me to do the work myself so I could master the tasks through several repetitions.

In our culture, a person's hometown is not necessarily where he or she lives, but where his or her ancestors' traditional land is. Even when people live in a particular area for several generations, if they cannot trace their lineage to the founders of that place, they couldn't claim that place as their homeland. My homeland is Oron. It is seventy square kilometers in size and has a population of 250,000 people. Long ago, homelands were usually founded by a man and his family. As the family grew and multiplied, some would move to different areas, and before long, the homeland would grow and become a cluster of several smaller related towns which together constitute the homeland. These smaller clusters I refer to as hometowns. My hometown is Oyubia. It is one of the thirty-six hometowns which together constitute Oron, my homeland.

Even though Oyubia was my hometown, I had never lived there for long periods. My Dad was a teacher. Schools provided on-campus accommodations for their teachers. Every now and then, teachers would be transferred to different schools located in different hometowns in the homeland. Our family always lived wherever Dad was stationed, but we visited our hometown, Oyubia during holidays. During my first year of high school, Dad was transferred to Oyubia, my hometown. He received permission to live in our house and not on campus. But I was at the boarding school, therefore didn't get to know many of the neighbors. Furthermore, each home was located on an acreage, and significantly separated from each other, therefore, it was not easy to meet and know the neighbors without a concerted effort. More importantly on this day, it was the middle of the afternoon. Adults are not usually home in the middle of the day. So, my options for getting help remained at zero.

Mom needed an ambulance to get her to the hospital. But getting an ambulance was complicated because someone had to physically go to the hospital and return with the ambulance and the driver. I'd never done that and did not know the procedure. The hospital was nine to ten miles away. Could I take a taxi there and bring back the ambulance? What would I do with the baby? My younger brother, Etim, had gone to school that morning without realizing that Mom was in danger. He was not going to be home until about 3 p.m. Dad was out of town for a conference and would not be back until Sunday night. Even if I could get the ambulance, how would I pay for it? I had no access to money and I knew payment preceded service at the hospital.

My bewildered heart sank. How does a thirteen-year-old manage a crisis of this magnitude? My legs began to wobble. I tried to steady myself by grabbing the end of the headboard. In the process, my hand knocked over the Bible that Mom often kept beside her on the night table. The Bible and my knees hit the floor simultaneously. The Bible flew open at Psalm 23. As I tried to steady myself, I caught sight of the Psalm and began to weep as I read it: *The Lord is my shepherd; I shall not want.*

I said to God, "This is your Word. Here you are saying that you are my shepherd, so I shall not want. If this woman dies, you know I shall be very much in want. You know it will be over for me as I may have to leave school to take care of my baby sister. Please, please help me. Let me see your power. Let me see today the miracles that you have performed for others. I have heard so much about your ability to turn things around. Please, please God, turn this around for me today. I know I may not be one of your favorite people, but please have mercy on me. Please, Lord, do not let me be in want today."

I went on and on and on as I wept and prayed. It is difficult to recall all that transpired that afternoon as I knelt beside that bed, wept, and prayed. My heart was broken. I was desperate and in despair. I knew Psalm 23 very well. Mom and Dad had made us memorize it. I had recited it many times, but it had always been just words. Somehow, on this day, it was different. Right there and then, those words became a lifeline for me, I held on tightly to them and was not letting go. It was all that I had.

Now, I know that the words of that Psalm became *rhema* words to me that day as I wept and repeated them back to God over and over and over again, pouring out my heart and soul to Him. Like Jacob of Genesis 32, I was not letting go of Him until He answered my prayer until He blessed me just as He'd blessed Jacob. All I could hear were my sobs.

Then suddenly, I heard another sound. It sounded like a breath. My heart almost jumped into my throat. I jumped up and looked at Mom. Her eyes were open, and I could see and hear her breathing. Was this real or was I hallucinating? I bent over closer to see her more clearly. Surely, she was breathing, her eyes were open. I hugged her tightly. I was afraid to let go as I looked into her eyes as tears continued to run down my cheeks. She reached her hand out to me. I clutched it and encased it in both of mine. She was alive, she was alive, my heart rejoiced.

I cannot say whether Mom was dead or just near death when I first arrived home that day. However, she did appear lifeless, and for the span of time (over an hour) that I cried and prayed, there were no signs of life. But my mother being so close to death is not the point, what is important is that God brought her back from wherever she was. He heard my cry for help. He saw my desperation and felt the anguish of my soul. Psalm 51: 17 reads: *The sacrifice you desire is a broken spirit. You will not reject a broken and repentant heart, O God.*

A broken and repentant heart was all I had that day. I think I must have confessed and repented of every possible sin that I thought I could possibly have committed as I begged God for Mom's life. I am so glad He took pity on me and saved Mom. She was not healed from her heart problems, but from that day onwards, her quality of life improved significantly. I do not recall her ever having another near-death episode after that day. Why she was not completely healed is a question I can't answer. God did not heal Apostle Paul completely either, even though he begged Him. God's ways are not ours. However, I was very grateful to God for hearing and answering my prayer that day and for the improvement in Mom's quality of life thereafter.

God answered my prayer that day, and from my belief system at the time, it meant I owed Him. He had saved Mom from death at my request; what was He going to demand of me in return?

Remembering the "Judgment Day" dream increased my anxiety and discomfort as I recalled the anguished cries of the ones who went to the left. I did not want to go there. But what did people have to do to go there? That's what I wanted to know. Also, what did Mrs. Mado's prophesy that God "had a call on my life" really mean?

I have heard of pastors who were said to have God's "call on their life." There were also some of the people I knew who spoke in tongues and prophesied. While I had nothing against these people or God, their lifestyle was not the one I wanted. If Mrs. Mado's prophesy was correct, would I be condemned to the left if I did not choose the lifestyle of the "called"? What were all the implications of having God's call on one's life? Was that even a real thing or was Mrs. Mado just making something up? I was just a child of eight, why would God have a call on my life?

I felt a tight discomfort in my throat. I believed God was going to ask me to be like those "very godly" people. I knew the Bible well enough to quickly recall and review the lives of those whom God "called." Many of them were neither popular nor comfortable. Even the ones who were regarded as godly men and women were usually somehow different. Many of them were not highly educated. Even at a young age, I knew my goal in life was not to be a preacher or have a healing ministry like "the godly people" had. My goal was to get as much education as possible and then settle in one of the big cities with a husband and children. I was not interested in continuing to live in the rural area where these godly people lived. My place was in a big city. I would definitely visit my hometown every now and then, but living there permanently was completely out of the question. How could I then accept the "call" to do the types of things that I perceived only the people who lived in the rural areas did? I was sure the people in the cities did not indulge in such practices. Therefore, the two groups appeared to me to be on parallel tracks. Was there any way the tracks could amicably intersect?

The godly women I knew also fasted a lot. They seemed to enjoy fasting. I could not imagine or understand how anyone could voluntarily give up eating for days. I have always loved and enjoyed good food and was flabbergasted that some people would voluntarily choose not to eat. I was in awe of them and never wanted to have anything to do with their fasting lifestyle if I could help it. One of these women was my mother, Maamma. Don't get me wrong, I loved and respected my mother very, very much. She was a great woman, my rock, almost the only person in the entire universe I trusted completely. I knew there was almost nothing she wouldn't do for me if her doing it was going to be beneficial to me. What I prayed for the most was that God would keep her alive until I finished school and got a good job so I could buy her and Dad beautiful things as a "Thank you" for all they had done for me. I loved my Dad very much too, but Mom was not just a parent, she was also my very close friend and confidant. As long as she was alive, all was well for me on planet Earth. However, a few things petrified me about her and I hoped not to inherit them from her. These were fasting, prophesy, and discernment gifts. They frightened me. It was okay for her to fast and pray for me, pray for my protection and success. I liked that. Knowing that she was praying for me always made me feel safe, secure, and protected. However, I never wanted to be the one doing the fasting and praying, at least not at that time.

I wanted the war to end so we could return to school. The war had turned everything upside down. There hadn't been any school for almost a year. I liked school and was very good at it. I loved to learn. I loved math and literature in general and Shakespeare in particular. I loved the continuous challenges of working hard to be the one at the top of my class. School was challenging and vibrant; it was full of new things to learn, new goals to set, and hard work to accomplish them. Some people did not like the challenges, but I did. It made life exciting, and this was the type of excitement I enjoyed. I wanted this time of fear and boredom to end. My competitive nature needed challenges to thrive. School provided those challenges, and I wanted to return to them.

The value of a good education was drilled into each one of us in the family very early in life. Mom and Dad often said a good education was the tree on which many good things hung. I wanted not just a good education but a great education. I knew Mom and Dad were committed to paying school fees. They often told us that where any one of us children ended up on the education ladder was entirely dependent on the child, as they were willing and prepared to pay any and all school fees that would enable us to climb the education ladder as high as we desired. How could a girl with such options not want to reach for the sun, especially in a patriarchal society? If this dream and the thought that now assailed me were to materialize, how could I reconcile fasting and reading people's minds with a great education?

The fear of what these dreams might mean was fanned by my perception of God. I envisioned Him then as a mean old man, sitting somewhere with a huge stick in His hand, just watching and waiting to hit anyone who would dare to get out of line. I also perceived Him as a killjoy, someone whose sole purpose was to keep fun as far away as the East is from the West, especially from teenagers. I was petrified of Him, yet also drawn to Him because I'd heard He had the power to save anyone He wanted. Moreover, everyone said He was the only one keeping Mom breathing. I wanted to love Him and be on His good side so He would continue to keep her alive. My dilemma now was how I could please Him and still have the type of lifestyle I desired. Was it possible to be well-educated, have a good life, and still be on God's good side? At the time, and from what I had heard, the two were not compatible. That was my dilemma. Who could teach me how to successfully maneuver the tightrope before me?

I knew a lot about the Bible. We read from it every evening at home during evening prayers. School also began every day with devotions where we read from the Bible, sang from the Methodist Hymn Book, and prayed before classes. In both elementary and high schools, Scripture was not an optional subject. The Methodist Church was the predominant mainline church in our area, so almost all schools were Methodist schools, and God was front and center at school. So, I was very familiar with the Bible and many of its characters.

Many of the sermons I heard focused on God's anger and fury—not so much on His mercy, grace, and love. There were many sermons about God's power against people who did not obey Him. People like Jonah, Ahab, Saul, and the various other kings in the Old Testament who were overthrown because of unrighteousness. Even when the preaching was from the New Testament, the focus was often more on Christ's frustrations with the Pharisees and other religious people than on His display of love and compassion. It is possible that messages about God's mercy and grace were preached occasionally, but as often happens, the human brain, untrained and unregulated tends to grasp tighter and focus more on the negatives. All these fostered the impression in me that God was a killjoy old man. This made me very fearful of Him.

Looking back now, I can see how distorted my perception of God was. Now, I know He is loving and kind, but I never "knew" that side of Him then. Hence my fearfulness of Him. Could it be that I never "heard" His love sermons because my preconceived ideas about Him closed my mind to them? Have you ever felt that way about God too? How do we find out about His true nature? How do we get to know the true nature of someone we cannot see and only depend on other people's opinions? Human beings are imperfect, no matter how godly we appear, we all make mistakes, often understand in part, and sometimes mistake our own conceptualization of things as God's. Therefore, our image of what God is like could be clouded by the medium through which we perceive Him.

What was the purpose of the nightmare that set all these thoughts in motion? Was God speaking to me purposefully as an answer to my cry for help? Or was it just a random nightmare? Deuteronomy 18: 21–22 says: *But you may wonder, "How will we know whether or not a prophecy is from the Lord?" If the prophet speaks in the Lord's name, but his prediction does not happen or come true, you will know that the Lord did not give that message. That prophet has spoken without my authority and need not be feared.*

In this situation, would the promise of protection for me and my family during the war come true? If we were safe and survived the war, would that be a coincidence just like other people who were impacted by the war and yet emerged unscathed? Or would there be some situations that would indicate supernatural intervention? Also, was my fear that God would demand atrocious things of me—the insinuation that His call on my life would be anti-education, anti-fun, and anti-prosperity—representative of God's nature? Do I give up my education to please God or do I pursue it? Would God kill my mother to punish me? So many dreadful and confounding questions emanated from one nightmare. Time often sheds light on things we do not understand at the time of their occurrence. What will time reveal about my fears?

Our opinions and how we perceive and interpret events are very important. Let's make this a joint expedition, a joint venture, and explore together. I will recount and present what happened to me and my family during the war and a little beyond. I will let you draw your own conclusions concerning whether any of it had anything to do with the dream, the voice, and the promise. We are now all part of the cast, the crew, part of the detective team working hard to carefully find and extract pieces of evidence and weigh them, decipher the truth, and come to an evidence-based conclusion. Are you ready?

3

The Context

"Kids, get up. Mom needs help."

Those were words I was very familiar with, they were words that filled my heart with anxiety. They always meant that Mom was very ill and could die. Upon hearing these words, we all sprang into action. Each person knew exactly what to do, as we were well-trained in our tasks.

When I was about four or five, my task was to keep the spoon inserted into Mom's mouth in place. There was always a clean spoon in the bedroom just for that purpose. When Dad called, I had to get the spoon quickly. Dad would use it to depress Mom's tongue, and it was my task to sit beside her and keep the spoon in place. When I was older, I learned that we placed the spoon into Mom's mouth and held it down to ensure that her tongue did not fall back into her throat and block her airway. My brother Mfon's task was to heat up water and fill water bottles to place around Mom's feet to keep them warm. We also tucked blankets around her to keep her warm and placed pillows under her legs to keep them elevated to help her diastolic blood return to the heart.

As long as I can remember, Mom had heart valve problems. One of the consequences of this was that her heart was unable to pump oxygenated blood efficiently to all parts of her body. This had many repercussions, the worst of them being continuous fatigue, shortness of breath, and chest pain. Therefore, anything, even a cold, that further impair her heart function could be deadly. No one knew exactly how and when the damage occurred, but doctors suspected that it was caused by a bout of rheumatic fever early in her adulthood. It preceded my birth. There was no effective treatment for mitral valve problems then. Efficient management of her health, especially when her heart was in crisis was what was needed to keep her alive. That's why it was so important for each one of us to know what to do and do it as perfectly as possible when Mom's heart was in crisis.

Early Childhood Memories and Experiences

As I was growing up, people always said that Mom still being alive was a miracle, as doctors had given up on her even before I was conceived. I learned more details about Mom's health and the circumstance surrounding my birth by asking questions about things and situations that were peculiar to me in the family

In the Nigerian tradition, baby girls have their ears pierced quite early in life, often before their first birthday. By the time they start school, they are all wearing beautiful earrings. However, unlike most of the girls, I was not wearing earrings. I told Mom I wanted earrings. They looked so pretty. Why did I not have some? Mom told me that I could not wear earrings because my ears were not pierced. I asked why they were not pierced.

The answer informed me about the circumstance surrounding my birth. Mom had been particularly ill, and her heart was very weak when she was expecting me. Indeed, the doctor didn't think her heart was strong enough to cater for both of us through the nine months of pregnancy. To make matters worse, the area where we lived at the time, even though it had a hospital, did not have a resident physician. Mom needed to be under the care of a physician, but the doctor who attended to patients at our hospital lived and worked primarily in another town, quite a long way off. He only visited and spent scheduled times at our hospital.

This placed people who had conditions that required continuous physician care in a very precarious situation. They could either receive whatever help the nurses could provide and go home to await the doctor's next scheduled visit to our hospital or travel to the hospital where he was resident. This was not an easy option, as travel was very difficult due to bad roads. Moreover, hospitals had no feeding program or cafeteria at that time. Sick people always had to have a healthy family member with them to cater to their nutritional needs. Therefore, receiving treatment at a distant town was beset with problems. This was not an option for Mom as she had my older siblings to care for. She disliked turning the care of her children over to anyone for any significant period of time. Furthermore, how would she manage the feeding problem if she were to move to the town where the doctor was resident for the duration of the pregnancy?

It was clear to the professionals that Mom's heart was quite weak and they predicted four possible outcomes for Mom and me, based on their knowledge of the state of Mom's heart:

1. The baby (me) could spontaneously abort because pregnancy puts extra strain on the heart. If Mom's heart was not strong enough to handle the extra stress of providing needed nourishment for the baby, then the baby could spontaneously abort.
2. The baby (me) could die in utero if Mom's heart was not able to supply it with the nutrients it needed to thrive.
3. Both of us could die during the pregnancy, again if the heart could not cope with the stress and strain.
4. We could both be very lucky, and Mom could carry me to term and I would be born safe and healthy.

What does one do when only one of four possible outcomes is a desirable one? There was not much anyone could do. Mom had always overcome the odds. Orphaned at age four, she was accustomed to surviving situations and conditions that would have sunk others. She was sure we'd both make it. She handed the situation over to God, and He sent her help in the form of an English midwife who befriended her. This midwife visited Mom often at home, to monitor her condition and provide whatever help she could. She monitored and recorded the baby's heart rate as well to be readily aware of any problems.

Mom and Dad, though worried, never lost hope. They believed that the God who'd given them the life growing inside Mom was able to preserve both mother and child. The pregnancy progressed normally even though Mom was still very ill and weak. At about the eighth month, when Mom went for a checkup, the doctor was in the hospital. After examining Mom and finding that her heart was very stressed, and I was mature and strong enough to be born, he suggested that labor be induced and I be delivered while he was still at the hospital just in case his intervention was needed. Mom and Dad consented, and labor was induced. Mom was sedated during the labor and birth to reduce the stress on her heart. I was born after eight months of gestation, a little premature but gorgeous, healthy, and strong. I was a miraculous gift. In Jeremiah 29:11–14(a) we read: *"For I know the plans I have for you," says the Lord. "They are plans for good and not for disaster, to give you a future and a hope. In those days when you pray, I will listen. If you look for me wholeheartedly, you will find me. I will be found by you," says the Lord. "I will end your captivity and restore your fortunes."*

Sometimes, it's difficult to be hopeful when things look bleak— when the wisest professionals give you only one chance out of four of being alive. It's difficult to be hopeful unless you're willing to trust God; abandon yourself to Him; and put all your hope, trust, and fate in His hands. You have to be willing to accept whatever He chooses for you and trust it's the best—even when it doesn't come in the package you had anticipated or hoped for. If God chooses it for you, then it will be in line with His will and plan for you. You just need to trust Him. The fact that I'm alive and writing this book indicates that the Lord's will and plan for Mom and me were not for us to perish even though the odds were very much against us.

How do all these relate to ear piercing? After my birth, Mom was still very ill and weak and could not adequately care for me the way she normally cared for her babies. She told me I was the baby everyone helped care for because she had neither the strength nor the energy. She also said I was very colicky and cried a lot, and when I cried, I continuously flailed my hands and feet around. She was concerned that if my ears were pierced, during a crying episode, my fingers could get caught in the thread that kept the pierced hole open until it healed. If that happened, the ear could be deformed. Furthermore, ear piercing carried a risk of infection, as it was usually done with a big needle and stacked layers of thread. The wound had to be kept clean and disinfected appropriately. Mom said she just didn't have the energy to provide all that care. When she thought about all these possibilities and combined them with the trauma of the pregnancy and premature birth, she couldn't bring herself to inflict one more pain on me in the form of ear piercing.

Thus, my ears were not pierced as a baby. As I grew older and discovered that I couldn't wear earrings without my ears being pierced, I wanted them pierced. But when I saw the size of the needle used for the piercing, I decided to wait. By the time I was seven or eight, my desire for earrings superseded my fear of the needle, I told Mom I was ready, and my ears were pierced. I still recall having to apply liquid antiseptic on the thread several times a day and gently pull it back and forth to keep the wound from becoming infected.

I heard the story of my birth in its entirety again in my teen years. I am the only child in the family with an English name. As I grew into my teen years, I was curious about how that came to be. I asked Mom. She told me the whole story again about her ill health, the pregnancy, and the English midwife who befriended her and helped her tremendously. Because of the way she graciously helped Mom, when I was born a girl, Mom and Dad decided to name me after her: Jane, God's gracious gift.

God had a plan for my life and had begun to pursue me long before I was born. Mom had been ill with the heart problem for a long time, and she had a few babies during that time. But she was never as ill and weak as when she was expecting me. Even though I was given only one in four odds of ever seeing the light of day, when God stepped in, those odds became meaningless. Only God's odds counted, and His odds for me were 100 percent positive.

Part of the reason I'm writing this book is to tell people everywhere how awesome God is and how He can obliterate even the worst predictions. He loved me even before a single one of my days came into being. I want to tell anyone and everyone about the amazing things the Lord has done for me. I was a love gift to Mom and Dad. My healthy birth was just the beginning of the many miracles God would perform in my life. He loved me and had a plan for my life before I was conceived. As is stated in Psalm 139:16: *You saw me before I was born. Every day of my life was recorded in your book. Every moment was laid out before a single day had passed.*

Cultivating the Attitude of Gratitude

In the song "Goodness of God" by Jenn Johnson, the songwriter affirms her love for God. She indicates that God's mercy, goodness, and faithfulness never failed her and are available to her from the moment she wakes up until she returns to sleep. She loves His voice; iterates how He has been there for her through every trial and difficulty. Therefore, she will sing and proclaim His goodness with every breath, because God's goodness runs after her every day. I agreed with the songwriter that God's goodness does run after us; it certainly has been running after me. I can testify to His goodness. Even during those days when I thought He was a killjoy tyrant, He never stopped loving me and pursuing me. Have some unexplainable things happened to you? Do you sometimes wonder if they are all just random chance occurrences, or could there be an unseen hand directing them?

Just like many, I took almost everything for granted and complained about slight inconveniences until I met a very beautiful, active, fun-loving young lady who had a lot of amazing dreams for her life. She was just about to turn thirty when she had an accident that left her paralyzed from the neck down. She was no longer able to move her hands and feet. She needed someone to help her with everything. But she refused to give up, refused to wallow in self-pity. Rather, she worked hard for two years just to re-learn how to maneuver one of her hands to her face to wipe her tears—something most of us do automatically in microseconds without even the slightest thought.

What would she not give to be able to wipe her tears without extreme thought, pain, and energy? How she longs to recover the ability to feed herself, brush her teeth, and comb her hair. Simple things she never gave a thought to before the accident are now Herculean tasks she trains hard just to regain the ability to perform. Yet, she remains positive, has drawn closer to God, and has become a more grateful and thankful person, who sees our automatic actions as privileges. I never saw them as privileges until I met her. Do you see your abilities as privileges and gifts to be thankful for?

Another friend has progressively lost her independence to advancing multiple sclerosis. The sense of independence, something we all cherish as adults is progressively being stolen from her by this incapacitating illness. She is no longer able to stand up or get in or out of bed, use the bathroom, or get dressed by herself; yet she beams with joy and gratitude. She looks beyond what she can no longer do and is thankful for what she can still do. Her attitude challenges me and causes me to think twice before complaining about trivial matters. It places things in perspective for me. I had to repent for taking my life and the ability to walk anywhere I want and speak for granted. Can you get out of bed, get dressed, and use the bathroom by yourself? Do you give thanks for these abilities?

As I ponder the human tendency to easily forget the good things that happen to us, and the good that people do for us, but remember clearly the wrongs that we encounter, I wonder how God must feel about human beings. When good things happen, we readily take credit for them. However, when bad things happen, we immediately ask, "Where was God?" "How can God allow this to happen?" Who of us would like to be God, the person who receives no credit for good happening, but is blamed for every bad one?

No wonder the Bible says that we've all sinned and fallen short of God's demands. According to His justice, we should be eternally punished. But He sent Christ to take our punishment so our sins can be forgiven if we believe in Him. We may not even think we are sinners as it is easy to look good in our own eyes. But deep down we know that we sometimes succumb to temptations despite our best efforts. God knew we would never overcome sin by ourselves and would have to pay the penalty that justice demands. He loves us so much that He chose to pay for our redemption by sending His faultless son, Jesus Christ, to die in our place. Because He was faultless, death could not hold Him. Therefore, Jesus Christ had to rise from the dead so that anyone *"who believes in Him would have eternal life"* (John 3:16).

4

Beyond the Methodist Church

My Dad had three inanimate loves—teaching literacy and numeracy, preaching the Word on Sundays, and farming. Teaching was his main occupation. Being a lay minister of the Methodist Church was his second love, and then there was farming. During his time, the Methodist Training Academy trained students to be either teachers or ministers. People usually trained for just one, but Dad trained for both.

Though he loved teaching, he was aware that many of the small-town churches were too small to sustain a resident minister. Receiving the dual training of teacher and minister enabled him to help. On weekdays he taught school, but on Sundays, he was a volunteer minister. I can still recall Mom and Dad working together on Saturdays on sermons Dad would deliver on a Sunday. Then, on Sunday evenings, Dad would tell us how the sermon was received. He was very loved and appreciated by the churches he served. They lovingly called him "Titia Jamesi." Titia was the vernacular for "Teacher." Dad's first name was James, but to differentiate him from other "James" they called him "Jamesi." So, he was the one and only "Titia Jamesi."

The Methodist church was the church of my fathers. My grandfather, Chief Amana Esio, the clan head, was a renowned carpenter. The quality of his work was so good that, when he created a piece of furniture, it was perceived as *utim* which means "indestructible." After a while, the nickname was applied not only to the furniture he made but also to him personally. People just referred to him as "Utim."

Grandpa's Dad was one of the prominent chiefs who welcomed the pioneer Methodist missionaries to our area. He persuaded other chiefs of the area to extend hospitality to them. He converted to Christianity. Methodism then became the family "religion." Grandpa, just like his father, embraced Christianity and participated in building the Methodist Church in our hometown, Oyubia. His carpenter shop was charged with producing the pews and all the other woodwork (doors, windows, tables, chairs, the altar, offering bowls, etc.) for the church.

When the Missionaries first arrived, my people were very distrusting of White people, because they knew of, and had heard about those who had come earlier purportedly as traders and missionaries, but who ended up using their gun power to threaten, kill, steal, and kidnap our people and ship them to the West as slaves. Even though the present bunch came exclusively as missionaries, people were still suspicious and not willing to give them an ear.

However, the Elders and Chiefs observed the new bunch carefully and noticed they seemed genuine. After verifying they had no guns, they thought it prudent to give them an audience and hear about the God they espoused. After several encounters, my Ancestors believed in the Gospel and converted to Christianity. The missionaries wanted to establish a church and a school and were apportioned land by the chiefs for that purpose.

A school was started in my hometown during Grandpa's time. He chose to send just one of his sons to the school at first. The town watched the school very carefully and closely to ensure the children were not abducted. Grandpa also talked with his son regularly to garner what was transpiring in the classrooms. When it was apparent the school and even the church were not "fronts" for something sinister, more parents sent more of their sons to school. In the beginning, parents were willing to send only their sons to school, daughters were kept home. My grandpa sent his five sons to school and gave them biblical names in addition to their traditional names. My dad was his fourth son.

Dad's oldest brother Andrew was also a minister of the Methodist Church and an evangelist. Therefore, when Dad decided to be certified as a teacher and a preacher, he was partially following in his elder brother's footsteps. Even though the preaching was volunteer, it was almost a full-time job. Dad preached somewhere on most Sundays. The only times he didn't preach regularly was when Mom's health was very poor, and he was occupied with directing the care of her and the children.

Searching for Answers, Finding Hope

My family was—and still is—very entrenched in Methodism. It is "the family religion." The Methodist Church was the predominant church in our area at the time. It believed in salvation by grace and the other important tenets of Christianity. However, miracles, divine healing and spiritual gifts were not encouraged. They were regarded as vestiges of the past. Hospitals and modern medicine were supposed to replace divine healing, and higher education supplant spiritual gifts. This was sufficient for those who had no need for spiritual healing. But for people like my parents who did, those who had illnesses that hospitals could not remedy, where were they supposed to turn? Where could they find help?

As Dad and Mom studied the Bible, they felt more and more convinced that miracles should still be possible and occurring. Why would some attributes of God be upheld and celebrated while others are ignored and denied without proof? Was the absence of miracles God's fault or a result of human failure? As they studied and prayed, the eyes of their understanding began to open more. The Bible says: *Jesus Christ is the same yesterday, today, and forever* (Hebrews 13:8).

If that is true, why should divine healing not be possible? Why should miracles not still happen? Was my being born healthy when the professionals had thought the chances of that happening were slim, a miracle? The more my parents studied the Bible, the more they realized that the church was missing some important aspects of the Gospel. Eventually, Mom and Dad abandoned some tenets of the church to come into a new and vibrant relationship with God.

Maybe God had looked a few decades into the future and seen Dad as the person in charge of evangelism and church planting later on in his life. Maybe He didn't want him planting "dead" churches with meaningless rituals that lacked the power and presence of God. He did not want my eldest brother Edet, who took over from Dad, to plant dead churches either. Could it be that He used Mom's illness to draw our entire family into experiencing and spreading renewal?

Love and Zeal for Evangelism

Dad's love of serving God was on open display when, after retiring from teaching, he became the senior society steward of Oyubia Methodist Church and deputy chairman of the Church Council. As the senior steward, he was responsible for maintaining and upgrading the church's infrastructure. He put all his resources into that assignment. As the headquarter of Oyubia Circuit of Methodist churches, the senior steward is also responsible for planting and growing the local churches in the circuit. Dad headed the evangelical campaign to establish and grow those local churches.

My family has continued to be very involved in the Methodist Church. A few years after Dad passed away, my brother, Edet, even though an engineer, became the lay president of the Diocese of Oyubia. During his tenure, he continued to establish Schools of Evangelism and Discipleship to propagate the Gospel just like Dad. He was also Chairman of the church investment company, the investment adviser to Methodist Church Nigeria, Pro-chancellor and a board member of Wesley University in Ondo, and Lay preacher at Methodist Church of the Trinity at the Headquarters of Methodist Church of Nigeria.

I am mentioning all these not to brag, but to give God the glory and to explore the importance of the timing of my family coming into renewal. God orchestrated things such that the Methodist Church in our area came into renewal at the right time.

Was God making sure the churches that would be planted by my family would be alive and presenting the full Gospel? I see parallels between how God brought my family into renewal and the story of Cornelius, the centurion in Acts 10. Cornelius had the zeal to serve God but lacked the appropriate knowledge, so God sent Peter to provide him with what he needed to be a true and effective witness for Christ. This seems to be what God did with my family, using Mom's illness.

What would have been the outcome if my family's efforts only went into offering people religion? We know that if religion could save, there would have been no need for Christ to come. God desires us not to focus on keeping rules and regulations but on forming a vibrant loving relationship with Him and seeking after His presence. Religion, man's attempt to satisfy God's standard of righteousness by keeping rules can be life-suffocating, while trusting the finished work of Christ on the cross and having a relationship with God is life-generating and life-sustaining.

The Mount Zion Church

It's intriguing that God often uses adverse circumstances to bring about His purposes. When people have a thorn in their flesh, they will wrestle with anyone who can remove the thorn, alleviate the pain and bring resolution. For my parents, the only option left for Mom's life was God. As they continued to wrestle with God about Mom's situation, Dad was transferred to a town where a family was also at the crossroad of desperation. Their only child had a disease for which there was no cure. Physicians gave them the same news they had given Mom and Dad: "There is nothing anyone can do for you anymore."

They were told to prepare themselves for their only child's death. They were advised to make her as comfortable as they could for the time she had left. Their church was not of much help either as they believed the physicians. So, the parents prayed and began to search the scriptures. Eventually, they reasoned that, if the Bible was the truth, then divine healing should still be available and receivable. They began to fast and pray, clinging to God with all their strength. Their child received divine healing and lived. They started a church denomination in our area named The Mount Zion Church.

This denomination was different from the mainline denominations (Methodist, Lutheran, Catholic, etc.). It did not have fancy buildings, and its pastors did not attend Biblical Academies to learn how to preach and earn diplomas to hang on the wall thereafter. Rather they understudied and worked under the supervision of established pastors until they were deemed ready to manage a church of their own. However, this church was growing exponentially as people in desperate situations found Jesus and hope. Miracles were commonplace there, as were the gifts of the Spirit. This was new to many who were acquainted only with the mainline churches' doctrines. Some mainline church adherents mocked the Mount Zion Church; however, they could not deny the miracles and other strange occurrences that happened there. For example, a man who had never been to school, but desperately desired to read and study the Bible suddenly gained the ability to read. People were flabbergasted. They could not explain how that could happen. If what they witnessed was not from God, then who was it from? How could they explain such an unusual occurrence?

Show and Tell

Even though Dad believed that miracles should still happen, and God had the power to do whatever He chose, he was still somewhat skeptical about some prophetic gifts like the word of wisdom and the word of knowledge. These were puzzling to him, even though Mom exhibited them. He could not comprehend how someone could know what had transpired elsewhere without being there or being informed about it. He thought some of those were made-up stories, and like Thomas of old, would not believe it unless he actually witnessed one himself.

One evening before Mom and I went to an evening prayer meeting, the topic of word of wisdom and knowledge arose. Dad joined the conversation. I can't remember exactly what we were talking about, but it involved how the woman in whose house the prayer meeting was being held was very proficient in these gifts. Dad asked for details.

We gave him some examples. My dad was a very funny man. He didn't believe us, so he started dramatizing what we were saying. It was hilarious, and we all had rib-hurting laughter. We invited him to come along to the prayer meeting, saying that perhaps the gift could be in operation that night, and he could see for himself. He agreed.

We arrived a little late. However, as soon as we sat down, the woman started laughing hilariously, just as we had laughed at home. She then stood right in front of Dad and continued to laugh. Then she began to say some of the things Dad had said at home. Dad was flabbergasted and in shock. He said, if a significant period of time had elapsed between when we had the discussion at home and the onset of the prayer meeting, it would have been impossible for anyone to convince him that someone from our household had not told the woman what had transpired at our home. But we'd all left the house together shortly after the hilarious laughter and come directly to the prayer meeting. Therefore, the chance of someone having had the opportunity to talk to the woman before our arrival was precluded.

5

My Mom, Maamma

My Mom, Maamma was still a very ill woman. I was in constant dread of her dying. I did not want to be motherless. I encountered a young boy who was motherless when I was about nine years old. I only knew him for a short time. I had no idea what had happened to his mother, but he always looked very sad and seemed uncared for. His stepmother often yelled at him and his Dad physically abused him. His siblings who were the natural children of his stepmother were not treated the same way. What I witnessed and his countenance convinced me that being motherless was the absolute worst and most horrible thing that can ever happen to any child. I prayed hard for my Mom, and I tried extra hard to be on God's good side so He wouldn't let her die.

Mom, Maamma, had been motherless herself. She was orphaned as a child of four and endured great suffering due to her parentless state. Even though her maternal grandparents pleaded and asked to raise her and her sister, Mom's paternal family refused, because according to culture and tradition, the child belonged to the paternal family. Mom and her sister were separated and given to different paternal relatives to raise. Mom was very familiar with the disadvantages of being parentless. She had come to terms with not experiencing the soothing voice of a mother to whom she could run as a child or consult as an adult. She'd learned to live without knowing the security that comes from the protection, comfort, and provision of a father. She was well versed in being a second thought to the family charged with raising her. These experiences caused her to long for God even before she knew Him. She didn't want her children to suffer the same fate.

My mom was my hero. She was a persistent and tireless advocate for girls' rights. She believed both boys and girls should have equal opportunities and privileges, especially when it pertained to education. Being an advocate for girls' rights in a patriarchal society was neither popular nor easy, but Mom was determined and fearless. She worked hard to convince families that investing in girls' education was as wise and beneficial to the family and society as the same investment in boys. She made sure her daughters had exactly the same opportunities and privileges that her sons had and that her sons were as well-versed in housework (cooking, cleaning, laundry, and childcare) as her daughters. The pervasive view then was that the man's job was to bring home the "bacon." Running the home, caring for the kids, and even managing some of the work on the farm were all viewed as a woman's job.

Mom was not receptive to such fairytales. She perceived that knowing how to prepare meals, keep your environment and clothes clean, and take care of children were all part of the basics of human living. She often said, "You don't know what the world of the future may look like. It may not always be easy to find help. If you don't have the basic skills you need to survive, you may find yourself in trouble. Furthermore, anytime you depend exclusively on someone to provide your basic essential services, you become a slave to that person. Is that what you want?"

This was not something that was generally practiced in our patriarchal society of the time. Friends made fun of my brothers for learning and participating in cooking, cleaning, and childcare. All those chores were considered "women's work," but Mom made her sons do them because she considered them "human work." This ideology is changing at a very fast pace, as many intelligent men, who want to remain married, are now participating in house chores more and more, especially when both spouses' incomes are needed for the family to meet all its needs. Furthermore, it is becoming very difficult to find reliable domestic help and the woman cannot be expected to work at the office all day and come home to do all the home chores.

An Astute and Very Successful Businesswoman

Mom was a very astute businesswoman. Due to her health issues, she was unable to engage in strenuous tasks. She found a very convenient business model that didn't aggravate her condition. She was a wholesale merchant who bought merchandise wholesale from big city merchants and then subdivided them into smaller packages for sale to retail merchants. The wholesale merchants arrived early in the morning at the market. Mom would buy from them and then begin the task of subdividing and repackaging them according to the orders of her retail merchants who retrieved their orders later in the morning or in the early afternoon. By the end of the day, Mom would have bought and sold a significant amount of goods without having to do too much strenuous work. These transactions usually took place one day a week.

There were no supermarkets then as there are today. However, there were several markets and market days. Indeed, every day except Sundays had a market sometime during the day. Those were small neighborhood markets that operated either in the morning or evening. But one market—Oruko Market—was particularly huge and important. It took place from dawn to dusk every eighth day, except when that day fell on a Sunday, and was held in a market space that accommodated several thousand people. This was the market where Mom carried out her transactions every week.

Depending on where Dad was stationed, Mom also sold local goods wholesale to the big city merchants from whom she bought manufactured goods. She had this network of merchants from whom she bought and to whom she sold. She built such great relationships with both her suppliers and her retail merchants that they were very loyal to her. It was a convenient alliance, which provided stability for her business even during times when she was too ill to be present at the market. As long as someone was there to stand in for her, pay the city merchants, and subdivide the goods for retail merchants, the network worked splendidly.

I loved to accompany Mom to the Oruko market whenever it fell on a Saturday or during holidays when I was in elementary school. I was usually a big help to her in watching the merchandise if she had to go to a different section of the market. Therefore, she often rewarded me with a gift at the end of the day. It was usually something small but a thing that I cherished.

The thing I liked most about accompanying Mom to Oruko market was what happened in the middle of the day after the retail merchants had retrieved their goods. Mom and I would often go to a good restaurant that only operated on market days to serve the many people who spent all day there. Mom would ask me to pick what we should eat. The portions were usually huge and one serving would feed both of us. I was often the only child in the restaurant, something that made me feel very special.

My Homeland

My homeland, Oron, is in the southeastern tip of Nigeria. It has the Atlantic Ocean at its southern border. The estuary to the Cross River and the Cross River itself, form the Eastern border. The Ibibio people live to the North of us. My homeland and its people have been in existence as far back as 2370 BC. Being surrounded by rivers and the ocean, the land is very fertile. Being four degrees above the equator, it is always warm and humid, with about twelve hours of daylight and darkness each day. It's a place where practically everything, including beautiful wildflowers, grows in abundance. The main industries then were farming and fishing. Today, there is much more diversification, as oil and gas have been discovered. Manufacturing and other coastal businesses now complement fishing and farming.

I was born when Dad was teaching at a town Ebughu, on the shores of the Atlantic Ocean. This was the fishing capital of the homeland with an abundance of fishermen and fishing boats. Many fishermen had alliances with local merchants who could buy all their catch wholesale. Mom was one such merchant. She had many boats that only sold to her. This was a symbiotic relationship. The land merchants prepared the supplies the fishermen needed for their time out at sea, so when the fishermen docked, they didn't have to worry about going to town just to get supplies. Their "partners" would have their supplies all ready for them.

Mom had a huge building exclusively for smoking and drying fish. She had employees who brought in the right type of wood. The foremen and Mom managed the operations to ensure the right amount of heat for the right size of fish and the right level of dryness. When her boats came in, Mom would sell some of the fish fresh to retail merchants, but the majority of it was either smoked or dried. This was before the era of mass refrigeration in our area. The only way to preserve fish on a large scale was either to smoke or dry them. Most of Mom's smoked and dried fish were sold to the city merchants, from whom she bought manufactured goods.

Because of her health condition, Mom wasn't able to move merchandise around. She had a stall. Her customers (those who bought from her and those from whom she bought) knew where her stall was. Mom hired men to deliver her merchandise to the stall early, already packaged and marked for the different merchants who would deliver their goods to her and retrieve what they were purchasing from her. She also had staff who came later to help her reapportion some merchandise to appropriate sizes for retail merchants. Even though the type of goods she sold depended on where Dad was stationed, some things (candy, bath soap, laundry soap, sugar, packaged oatmeal, canned milk, canned fish, and different types of malt, salt, and a variety of biscuits) were staples.

By the time I was about ten years old, Mom's health was significantly poorer. Moreover, Dad had been transferred to a town quite far away from the big Oruko market. The distance, combined with the very bad road and poor health, made it difficult for Mom to continue with the business on the scale she previously had. She changed her business from wholesale to retail and was supplied by merchants who were able to deliver to our home. It was amazing how loyal some of her allies were and the extent to which they would go to help her. Her retail store was attached to the house, and she just had to open the doors and sit. People came and bought what they needed, and if she was too ill to sit out there, helpers would serve customers.

Retailing was a much smaller enterprise, so Mom diversified by investing in livestock. In our area at the time, commercial livestock farming consisted mainly of goats, sheep, and chickens. Goats were traditionally a big part of celebrations, and because of their popularity, goat management was a thriving industry. Farmers managed goats for others and were paid with some of the litter—a good incentive for the caretakers to look after the livestock well, as the more the livestock prospered, the more they prospered. Mom had a few farmers managing goats for her. However, after the near-death episode mentioned earlier, her health improved significantly and Mom returned to the wholesale business.

The Love of Farming

Both my parents loved farming. We grew most of what we ate. There was one special type of yam, *mkpuk*, that Dad liked to grow in addition to all the others. Very few people grew this yam because it was very labor-intensive, expensive, and demanded much attention. It was difficult to find it to purchase, as the people who grew it didn't sell it. Because of the labor involved, people only grew small quantities of mkpuk for home consumption.

Dad did not do most of the work by himself. He hired people to clear and prepare the land and dig the huge holes in which seedlings were planted. Since the tuber produced would sometimes be eighteen to twenty-four inches long and four to eight inches in diameter, the hole in which the seedling was planted had to be huge. Dad would mix in the fertilizer and position the seeding himself, as any mistake that damaged the shoot could render the piece ungrowable, then helpers would cover the plant under his watchful eyes. After the shoots emerged, they had to be staked with sturdy branches cut specifically for that purpose. The foliage of a mkpuk plant during its growing season could resemble that of 10-15 large philodendron plants with each vine being up to 30 feet long. These had to be folded tightly and carefully around a very sturdy stake. The width of the folded foliage was often indicative of the size of the tuber growing underground.

We grew a huge variety of produce in our gardens. Mkpuk was the king of yams. Sinking your teeth into cooked mkpuk was paradise. Everything about growing it was about three to four times as demanding and expensive as growing any other type of yam because very few people grew it. Commodities that are rare and labor-intensive tend to be expensive. I understand people have almost completely stopped growing it because of the labor cost and the fact that the planting, unlike some other yams, cannot be easily mechanized. One reason my parents loved growing their own food was because it enabled them to know exactly the conditions under which the produce was grown and were sure they were feeding their children the best food available.

Strange Rituals

After some years, Dad was transferred away from Oruko, the huge market town to Okuko. Due to Mom's health, and the very bad roads which made traveling herculean tasks, Mom found it stressful to travel to the market early enough to meet with the city merchants. Therefore, she could not continue with her wholesale business. Mom and Dad then decided that Mom should move to Oyubia to oversee the repair of our home there. Okuko was about seven miles from Oyubia. We spent weekends at Oyubia with Mom and returned to Okuko on Sunday nights. Mom had a very reliable live-in maid. There was a vibrant Mount Zion Church at Oyubia and very close to our house. Mom became an active member and leader in that church. In less than a year, the repairs were completed and Mom moved back to Okuko with us.

Mom liked to fast. Whenever she sensed a "call to a fast," she would make arrangements for our meals and other needs before she started the fast.

These were water fasts. The call to a fast sometimes came through dreams. She often started fasting and praying without knowing how long the fast was going to last. She only stopped when she "sensed the breakthrough." Such a practice scared me to death.

Mount Zion Church practiced fasting, tithing, and honoring the Lord with "first fruits." As already mentioned, my parents and most of the people in the community grew most of what they ate. Excess produce was sold for additional income. My parents farmed a significant portion of land each year. We often had an abundant harvest. However, whenever the crops were harvested, Mom had a ritual we had to go through before we ate anything.

As I got older and came across Deuteronomy 26:1–11, I began to understand her strange rituals. The passage says: *When you enter the land the Lord your God is giving you as a special possession and you have conquered it and settled there, put some of the first produce from each crop you harvest into a basket and bring it to the designated place of worship— the place the Lord your God chooses for his name to be honored ... Afterward you may go and celebrate because of all the good things the Lord your God has given to you and your household. Remember to include the Levites and the foreigners living among you in the celebration.*

Accordingly, we did not eat any produce, until the first fruits had been "presented to the Lord." Even after the presentation, if there was some produce of exceptional quality, some of it was set aside for the Lord. All the things to be "set aside for or to be presented to the Lord" were taken to church and placed on a certain part of the Altar, designated for that purpose. After the service, they became the property of the Pastor.

Mom's gift of prophesy and word of knowledge was problematic for me. It made her appear weird. One never knew when she was going to receive a revelation on something, so it was just best not to do anything questionable when she was around. Her spiritual gifts struck fear into my heart. Her relationship with God was strong. I also wanted a relationship with God, not a strong one, and not because I loved Him but mostly because I wanted to avoid His punishment. Because I perceived God to be vindictive and uncaring, I imagined that He could inflict the harshest punishment on me if I offended Him. That most dreaded punishment to me was allowing Mom to die. Since everyone said He was the only one who kept her alive, my childhood heart believed that He could withdraw that protection anytime and cause her to die if I offended Him. Therefore, I wanted to please God. I wanted to have a relationship with God that was cordial enough for Him to hear my prayers and not punish me when I sinned but not cordial enough for Him to ask me to do anything for Him, especially weird things like fasting. In a nutshell, I wanted a God whom I directed, instructed, and controlled rather than one who directed and instructed me. Does that sound familiar?

It's amazing how vivid and strong childhood fears can be. Why did I hold so strongly to the view that God was a vindictive tyrant? How can we reconcile that view with that of King David, whose view of God says: *The Lord is merciful and compassionate, slow to get angry and filled with unfailing love* (Psalm 145:8)

Whose view was more accurate, more representative of God's character? King David certainly understood God better than I did. But God in his mercy and grace understood all my childhood confusion and did not give up on me. Rather, He pursued me with even greater, unrelenting fervor. He sought every opportunity to show me how much He loved and cared for me. His call on humanity is often not burdensome. Jesus declared this in Mathew 11:29–30: *Take my yoke upon you. Let me teach you, because I am humble and gentle at heart, and you will find rest for your souls. For my yoke is easy to bear, and the burden I give you is light.*

Sometimes, the things we are most afraid of yielding to God, often become the very thing He uses to bless us tremendously when we finally yield them to Him. The ones that come to my mind are the fear of fasting and tithing. It's difficult not to be scared of these when you look at it with a rational mind. Going without food is not easy. We are conditioned to eat. As soon as a child is born, everything it can access goes into the mouth. It's the same thing with tithing. We want to keep our money, but God tells us tithing is how we can prosper. Doesn't that seem upside down?

Many people are afraid of doing some of the things that God says will bring us tremendous blessings and growth in our spiritual walk. I love the way science operates. In it, when you are not sure of something, you put it to the test to see if what you think is true will happen. Maybe we should do the same with things God asks us to do. I do not mean just doing it once and then making a conclusion. In science, the experiment has to be replicated many times until you're sure the conditions are so well controlled that your results are not due to or influenced by confounding factors. When you have a high confidence level in your results, you can then proclaim it without any doubts.

Malachi 3:10 says: *"Bring all the tithes into the storehouse so there will be enough food in my Temple. If you do," says the Lord of Heaven's Armies, "I will open the windows of heaven for you. I will pour out a blessing so great you won't have enough room to take it in! Try it! Put me to the test!"*

Having enough is not just limited to earthly goods. There's a tremendous joy that comes from giving and helping others in need. Sometimes we think of blessings just in terms of money. While having money is always good and we should be thankful, it is not the be-all that leads to happiness. There are many blessings money cannot buy. Wealth doesn't guarantee happiness. Some very rich people could be very unhappy. Having good health and true friends and a trustworthy family are some of the blessings that money cannot buy.

Modern science tells us that intermittent fasting is healthy and good for us. Many non-religious people fast regularly. Was God trying to give us joy and good health when He asked us to fast every now and then? There was a time I believed that if I fasted for more than a day, I would certainly die. Then, I was amazingly surprised when I did that and death did not ensue. On the contrary, my health improved. You may say, "How can that be?" I said the same until I tried it. But there's a catch. You also have to pray too. Is that a deal breaker? Praying is just talking to God. I'm sure you have some questions and other things you would like to ask Him.

I recall how God blessed Mom's business extravagantly. Even though she was sometimes not well enough to show up at the market or didn't have the energy to advertise her merchandise, God made a way for her. People knew where her stall was, and they would walk past other stalls selling similar goods to buy from her. Could it be that her business flourished because she loved God and, out of that love, tithed and gave generously to those in need?

6

The War Begins

Experiencing war, any war, is not something people easily forget. Some wars are fought with words. These may leave no physical scars, but their emotional toll can be more devastating than the physical ones. However, a war fought with guns, bullets, and bombs is in a class by itself, as bombs and artillery have a language all their own. Such wars are particularly devastating for the ones caught between the warring factions, where the line between friend and fiend is blurred. Such wars leave both deep physical and emotional scars.

The war zone is not a place for the living. Even the dead would abhor it if they could speak, for it grants neither group dignity nor respect. In it, the idea of normalcy, of law and order, is but a painful tantalizing fantasy, the reminiscence of a time long gone. Longing for any semblance of predictability and of what were once signs of civilization becomes nothing but an exercise in futility. Reality entails learning to be comfortable with the uncomfortable and friends with mediocrity because the gun and the person holding it are the law. He alone is the sole arbiter of who is worthy of life and who is condemned to death.

Trust in the war zone is a commodity in very short supply, and dignity becomes a rare product hard to find. This is particularly salient when the army perceives civilians as possible adversaries, and civilians reciprocate the characterization. The predominance of such belligerent portrayals and lack of trust on both sides makes living difficult. The struggle for survival takes precedence over all else and produces the propensity for humanity to display itself at its most depraved state; it also elicits the tendency for humanity to present itself at its most heroic, compassionate, and godly best.

The war zone was the place where the true nature of people became clear when they found themselves between a rock and a hard place. There, one could witness heroic acts of kindness and selflessness, and also recoil from hideous acts of sheer brutality. Fear was always preeminent, and prolonged exposure in the zone played havoc on the mind in terms of Post Traumatic Stress Disorder. Change happened at a dizzying speed. One moment your house could be standing, and the next it could be replaced by a huge crater in the ground. The only predictability, was unpredictability, the only certainty, uncertainty. The war zone was where I found myself as a young teen during the Nigerian Civil War.

High School

At that time, and in the area where I grew up, going to high school was a defining moment for a girl. Boys were expected to attend high school if their families could afford the fees, but things were different for girls, as some families deemed elementary education sufficient for girls. They reasoned that a girl would eventually get married, and then have a man to take care of and provide for, her and the children. Thankfully, there were families, including mine, who did not share this archaic notion of girls. Such families believed that both boys and girls should have equal opportunities at creating the future they desired for themselves by granting them equitable opportunities for education.

Schools were mostly church-owned and operated. The Methodist Church was the dominant church in my area, so most schools were

Methodist schools. High schools were boarding schools, separate for boys and girls, and never in close proximity. There was only one small, poorly equipped high school for girls in my area compared to two large and better-equipped ones for boys. Every prospective student had to compete with over a hundred other girls for the few available spaces.

The application process before the entrance examination was the first step for our high school entry. Out of more than a hundred students who would write the exam, about sixty would be invited for personal interviews. The results of your elementary school examinations, particularly the final exam (taken by every student in the province on the same day and graded by teachers in different parts of the province to eliminate favoritism), were also significant leveraging factors in the selection of the thirty girls for the first year. Girls selected for high school were deemed to have the "potential" to make something of themselves. However, getting in was just the beginning of an arduous process. Like the present-day MasterChef, each girl had to continuously prove that she deserved to continue to be there.

High school fees were relatively high. There were fees for tuition, room and board, books, and other supplies. Students had to pay for uniforms and there were different uniforms for different activities. All these made attending high school relatively expensive when compared to the average income of the populace. Students who had the good fortune of having families who were able to afford the fees worked hard to achieve good grades and, thereby, maintain their place in the school. Students were also very aware of the sacrifice their parents were making to send them to school and wanted to show appreciation by working hard to secure good grades.

The high school I attended provided additional incentives for students to work hard. Every week, tests on different subjects were written and grades awarded. At the end of each week, these were tallied and a descending list of student names with their marks, from the highest to the lowest for each class was produced. During Saturday morning assembly, the names of the top three students and the bottom three students for each class were read aloud and then the list was posted on the bulletin board for the rest of the week. Every student wanted to be among the top performers or at least be in the middle. Nobody wanted to be among the bottom three. In my class, there were three of us who consistently had our names as the top three. My desire and ambition were not to be among the top three but to be at the top of the three every week.

Things Fall Apart

Getting good grades and other mundane things that girls confined to a prison-like setting do were our uttermost pursuits at high school. Then one day, everything changed. The civil war began. Not ever having encountered war or anything remotely similar, we were nonchalant about it and just focused on our school work. The actual fighting was far away in the northern and western borders of the breakaway region which were very far away from my homeland where the school was. Therefore, it didn't seem to affect our day-to-day activities in any significant way. A majority of girls in the school were supportive of the east seceding from Nigeria. However, some students thought it would be better for the country to remain intact if the politicians could find ways of resolving their differences amicably. Thus, we had these interesting and sometimes heated discussions and debates about the war.

About a month after the war's onset, a van full of soldiers arrived at our school. They held a meeting with our principal, and after they left, she called a hasty assembly. Calling an assembly in the middle of the week was unprecedented and strange; since everything in our school was regimented. Nothing ever changed or deviated an inch from the norm. You could walk through each day blindfolded because every activity had its time, place, and procedure, and the matron's bell announced the transitions.

Our principal and many of our staff were British. Our school was the second girls' high school our principal, Miss Skipsey, had founded in Eastern Nigeria. She was a middle-aged woman, who was brilliant and exceptionally strict. She never gave an inch on any issue. We loved, respected, but also dreaded her. She could advocate fearlessly for the school to the church and the local government on issues she deemed important. We also knew she cared deeply for each student's success. However, one never wanted to be in her bad books or be caught doing anything forbidden.

The school controlled every aspect of our lives. We were told when to go to sleep, when to get up, shower, eat, do chores, go to class, study, take a nap, and so on. Every time of the day had its scheduled task. Our outgoing letters were read before being mailed, and incoming mail was read before being passed on to us. We were almost never allowed out of the enclave except for very few reasons such as illness that the Matron could not remedy. If we needed essential supplies such as bath soap, toothpaste, toothbrushes, and laundry detergents, we placed orders for them once a week. The day watchman determined what we could purchase and how much we should pay for them. He created a list of what he deemed essentials, and if an item was not on it, we could not buy it. Even our money was logged with the school, and whenever we needed some, we had to explain how much we needed and why we needed it.

We never had outings except for holidays that our parents had pre-approved. The only non-holiday time we ever left the school was on Easter Sunday mornings. We were allowed out to the nearby town for about an hour to sing Easter songs and rejoice that Christ has risen. We stayed tightly together as a group under the watchful eyes of the prefects. The only deviation was stopping and gathering wildflowers along the roadside to decorate the chapel for the Easter service.

Therefore, when the principal called this hasty assembly on a weekday, we all knew something ominous was about to ensue. She stood at the entrance of the hall as we filed in—very unusual of her. She was standing there, like a mother trying to protect her children from the evil that was about to unfold. Even though her demeanor deepened our concern, we never imagined how our lives would change from that day forward.

Our principal, who always appeared confident and in control, exhibited none of that iron-like character for which she was so famous that day. She informed us that the government had requested that everyone be sent home for a few days while soldiers explored and fortified the area around the school. We were advised to take only a weekend bag, as we were only going to be away for a few days. We were, however, instructed to pack up all our belongings and put them in storage, so soldiers could stay in our dorms during the fortification period. She said she'd send letters to inform us of when to return as soon as she received the clearance. Even though we were usually happy to leave the "prison" for home, this time there was a certain sense of foreboding that wasn't easy to describe.

Purposelessness - the Enemy of the Soul

The first few days at home were heavenly. The war was a distant event somewhere far away. We listened to the news about it, and the adults discussed it in hushed voices. But not too long thereafter, a shift in what was perceived as "normal" began, and increased at an ever-accelerating pace.

First, all high schools were closed. The reason given was that they were all located near the coast and could be easily attacked from the sea. However, when all elementary schools were also ordered closed, including those not near the coast, people began to suspect ulterior motives. As schools were emptied of students, those located at strategic locations became filled with soldiers. Military drills replaced academic ones. The sounds of students learning and laughing were replaced by the noise of gunfire. Those who lived near the schools felt harassed by the new tenants and, if they could, quickly moved away.

The next shock was when civil servants had their employment terminated. There was no more work to be done and no money to pay salaries. Everything was now focused on the war effort. Within a short period of time, one industry after the other and one government service after the other shut down. There was almost nothing left. These were just the beginning of sorrows.

Things deepened, and the big blow came when a drastic limit was placed on the amount of money people could withdraw from their bank accounts. The amount allowed was hardly enough to feed a family for a week, but people were supposed to use that for at least two weeks. This was made particularly distressing because there were shortages of everyday essentials, and if one could find them, the prices were prohibitive. Soap, milk, flour, gasoline, kerosene, and anything not locally produced were in short supply. However, the most difficult items to live without were salt and kerosene. With the power plant closed, there was no electricity. People had to find kerosene lamps. So, when kerosene shortages ensued, it was a plunge into darkness.

Mom's health had improved significantly before the war started, and she had returned to her wholesale business. When the supply of goods started to be unpredictable, she decided to convert most of her money into a stockpile of essential nonperishable goods. She didn't think keeping money in the bank was safe any longer and advised those who still did to withdraw as much of it as they could when that was still possible. She had the premonition that if things continued the way they were, it might become difficult to access money from the bank. Some people didn't think keeping money at home was safe. They were also skeptical that banks could ever prevent people from accessing their money.

There are some things that are regarded as norms in every society. Work is one of them. We had never experienced or imagined a society where no one went to work. How could there be such a society? Even in ancient days, people went hunting and fishing and gathered fruits and roots for food and building materials for shelter for their families. That was work for them. But in the twentieth century, how could there be a community where there was no employment? How would members of such a community survive? These were not just philosophical questions; they were our reality.

We have no idea what a blessing work of any kind, no matter how mundane is until the ability to work is taken away; until we wake up day after day and remember that we have nowhere to go, nothing to do, no means of earning a penny, and no way of maintaining a lifestyle once taken for granted. When that happens, it's as if a part of who we are is ripped away from us. It's then that we may have trouble articulating who we are and what makes us human. It's then that we begin to truly appreciate the enormous positive mental health impact of employment for adults and school for students.

When things started happening in unexpected ways and the unimaginable became the norm, our minds became confused, and a state of continuous agitation ensued as our brain tried to decide where it should fit these new realities into its schema. When the unimaginable proliferated and new levels of the unthinkable began occurring, people became confused and bewildered and prayed that every new unimaginable occurrence would be the last. However, those prayers seemed never to have left the earth, they seemed to lack the power to penetrate heaven's gates, as things continued to go from bad to worse and from worse to abominable.

By this time, people wondered what "worst" would look like and what it would constitute. They didn't have to wonder for long, as the worst occurred when federal Nigeria changed its currency in an effort to strangle the secessionist regime by rendering the country's previous currency worthless. Federal Nigeria made plans to change its currency and had everything ready for a smooth exchange and transition for its citizens before making the announcement, giving foreign countries a relatively short period of time to exchange what they had for the new currency.

The secessionist regime was caught off guard by this sudden change, but they were very resourceful. They quickly sought out friendly and sympathetic countries who could exchange the currency for them. They ordered everyone in the region to deposit their soon-to-be useless currency in banks so they could be exchanged for the new currency. Many people suspected they might not get their money back, but they had no other options. After a certain date, the old currency became useless, and no one could buy or sell with it. Furthermore, it was made very clear that being caught with the old Nigerian currency after that certain date would be considered an act of treason. Therefore, what reason could not accomplish, fear did. Most people took whatever little money they had to the bank.

The period between depositing the old currency in the bank and the new currency becoming available was stressful. There just was no currency. How do people buy and sell without currency? Some resorted to a credit system, where people bought on credit with the hope of paying for the goods once currency became available again. It was a difficult situation for both merchants and customers. Some merchants accepted the credit system, while others decided to trade by barter. After what seemed like an eternity, the long-awaited new currency arrived. But alas, it was not the new Nigerian currency; rather, it was a currency hastily manufactured by the secessionist's regime that had no value outside the enclave and that was in very short supply because, like everything else, the raw materials for producing it were in short supply.

People lined up for several hours at banks just to access a little money. At first, people were allowed to withdraw reasonable quantities to compensate for the exchange time when no currency was available. But soon thereafter, the amount available for people to withdraw became less and less. Lining up at the bank for hours and sometimes almost all day became a weekly affair, as money rationing ensued and people were only allowed one small withdrawal per week. As the amount each family was allowed became less and less, despair grew.

Suddenly one morning, to everyone's anguish, the bank doors were left wide open, but everything inside was gone. All the bank records and whatever else of value had disappeared. Even the locks were too valuable to be left behind. The bare walls were the only things left. The prevailing story was that soldiers arrived with commands from the government for managers to open the vaults, and everything in them, including the records, was taken away. How does one process such information? How does one process a state where you are unemployed, have no hope of regaining employment, and what little savings you had have just been taken away? It is unusual to see grown men weep, but that was exactly what ensued as people saw their situation downgrade from desperate to hopeless.

New Ways to Buy and Sell

It was official. Trade by barter was the way to buy and sell. Those who still had some money, even the secessionist currency, were kings. They could trade easily. Merchants who had sold on credit during the currency exchange period found themselves in a dilemma; their customers did not have the currency to pay off their debt. The merchant either had to accept whatever form of payment the customer had or count the debt as a loss. Many were very good-natured about it.

The dilemma still remained: How would people feed their families when they had no money and no means of getting some? Thus began an exodus from the cities to the homelands. Fortunately, my homeland is rich in fertile agricultural land, and even those who were city dwellers and unfamiliar with growing their own food learned how to do so quickly. There were many crops one could grow quickly and others that, even when mature, could remain in the field for a year or two, and people harvested just what they needed as they needed. People grew whatever they could to feed their families.

The advantage of being back in one's own ancestral homeland was that relatives were ready and willing to provide some land for their former city-dwelling relatives to cultivate and help them learn gardening techniques. The newcomers quickly learned how to grow basic food items. Luckily, a significant portion of our diet consists of vegetables, fruits, and complex carbohydrates, many of which grow quickly. Relatives and neighbors helped out until what was grown was mature. It was not long before most families had vegetables, spices, and fruits they could live on and exchange for other items they needed.

The more difficult trade to make was for protein or something exotic like soap, shampoo, salt, or goods not manufactured locally. Some quickly learned how to hunt game, fish, or find people in the coastal areas who were willing to trade for fish. However, making any trade wasn't easy, as the trader had to find another person/family who not only needed what they had but also had what they needed. That was the complexity of "trading" and just one aspect of the complicated system people had to become accustomed to. On the whole, many people just gave away the excess of what they had. And as that happened more frequently, many had enough, and there were few who lacked survival essentials.

Life As We Knew It Ceased to Exist

By this time, all schools had been closed for several months. Hospitals in the area had also been closed, as there was no electricity, no money to buy medications and no medications to be bought. Nurses and doctors no longer had the essentials needed to practice their trade. Furthermore, hospitals were unsafe as they were frequent targets of bombing raids. Almost all professionals were unemployed. This unemployment was acerbated by the problem of lack of housing. In the Nigerian tradition, employers provided accommodation for their employees, therefore when people's employment ceased, so did their right to the accommodation.

As bad as these outcomes of the war were, the most devastating effect was the breakdown of trust between people of different tribes who had lived and worked side by side happily for decades. Now, they were suspicious of each other. People felt unsafe except when in their own hometown and among their own relatives. At first, men sent their wives and children to their hometowns, while they tried to find sporadic work, such as off-loading military equipment. Early in the conflict, payments were made for such sporadic work with currency, but as the war progressed and the government had less money, the form of payment changed to whatever goods the soldiers had. Even this stopped when goods became scarce. Soldiers then just commandeered people to do whatever they needed to be done.

With no way of earning money, the men returned home to their ancestral homeland and started planting edible crops. The most pitiful sight was that of highly skilled professionals who had lived and raised their families in large cities. When they returned to their hometowns, they had no money, no home, and no means of making a living. Those who'd kept in touch with and helped their poor relatives over the years were much better off, as the relatives took care of them and helped them settle readily. The most helpless were those who, in the good times, had forgotten their relatives in the rural homeland. They had no leverage and were completely dependent on the kindness and generosity of those relatives they'd neglected and looked down on during the good times.

My parents, who never missed a teachable moment, used such opportunities to reiterate to us the importance of being kind and humble and helping those in need. They impressed upon us the importance of never forgetting our roots, where we come from, and who our relatives are. They stressed the importance of lending a helping hand to people whenever possible and treating every human being with dignity and respect no matter what their prevailing situation may appear to be. They pointed out the importance of building relationships and treasuring those relationships wherever we find ourselves. They did not have to belabor the point, as we could see clearly how the people who had maintained their relationships with their relatives and hometown fared when compared to those who had looked down on their rural and less affluent relatives during their time of opulence.

7

Smuggled and Captured

The scarcity of everything was bewildering. It was particularly distressing for those accustomed to city life, and who never experienced rural living. Being suddenly thrust into rural life with no familiar amenities was demoralizing and daunting. Children who were only familiar with electric lights had to learn to use kerosene lamps (when kerosene could still be found). When kerosene ceased to be available, they had to learn how to make and operate homemade candles and torches. Life, for many, was nothing but misery.

As bad as everything was, by far the biggest enemy was the loss of purpose. There was nothing to do. We often don't appreciate how having something to do, something to look forward to, no matter how mundane, accords meaning to life. When one becomes deprived of everything but fear, life becomes mediocre and loses meaning.

Even stepping outside was dangerous. Bombs were dropping from the skies in ever-increasing numbers, and there were no bomb shelters. If boys were outside, they could be captured and forced into the army, and girls taken as sex slaves by soldiers. Children could not play outside or visit with friends or other family members, as families were afraid of being apart, just in case there should be a bombing raid or the family had to flee in a hurry.

What does a teenager do in bed for ten to twelve hours every night? How does he or she maintain sanity with nothing to look forward to the next day? Staying in bed for ten to twelve hours a night for a few days may be enjoyable. A few weeks or even a month could be manageable. But one year? How does a teenager cope when all that was familiar is no more and the only thing to look forward to is limbo and fear?

Even those who didn't like school longed for "the good old days" when school offered, at minimum, something to do, somewhere to go, sports to play, and opportunities to interact with others and have fun. For those who liked school and who had dreams of how they wanted their lives to unfold, the present existence was torturous. The war was suffocating all hopes and dreams. Life lost its meaning. Finding a reason to exist for another day was a daily exercise.

Splitting the Family

The home ceased to be a relative respite when the bombing raids from federal Nigeria intensified. Bombs rained down from the skies like flakes of snow on a wintry day. Homes were no longer safe, as a house and all its contents were incinerated if a bomb fell on it. There did not seem to be any pattern to the bombing raids. Homes appeared to be randomly targeted. There was also danger outside, as the secessionist soldiers were distrustful of civilians, especially leaders. Therefore, staying in one's home was a risky venture from all sides. My hometown was particularly targeted because many of the people there supported a Western Federal party before the war.

My paternal grandmother, now in her mid-nineties, had lived in a suite attached to our home ever since Dad was an adult. That was the tradition. The oldest son took care of his widowed mother, and she lived with his family for the rest of her life unless she remarried. My grandma was unwilling to leave her home for any reason, especially because she had mobility and vision issues by now. Her suite had been remodeled so that everything she needed was in close proximity and within easy reach for her.

Dad was concerned about my safety. He felt I would be safer if Mom, my younger brother Etim, my baby sister Imaobong, and I moved to the next town, Okosi, where he last taught and we still had accommodation. This little town was less prominent than my hometown, and our home there was farther away from the main street and less recognizable. Dad and my second brother, Mfon, had to stay in our hometown to care for Grandma, as she argued that she was better off dead in a familiar environment than become a nuisance to herself and others in an unfamiliar one. Her care provider, a young lady, had been summoned home by her family, as they deemed continuing to stay in our home with Grandma too dangerous.

When the war started, Mfon had been at a point where life as he wanted it was just about to unfold. He'd always wanted to be an engineer and just before the war started, he had been awarded an Academic Excellence Scholarship by Shell to study engineering in a university in London. At that time in Nigeria, the elementary and high schools' calendar year started in January and ended in December, while the universities' year was from September to June. Therefore, when students finished high school in December if they were going to university, they had to wait until September to start classes. High school graduates, therefore, sought employment for the intermediary eight months between finishing high school and starting university.

Mfon did not have to search for employment, as Shell offered him a job while awaiting his departure to London. He was posted to Port Harcourt, a town that was the center of Shell's operations in Nigeria. When the war started, the Shell operations where Mfon was employed shut down, as it was located in the area occupied by the breakaway regime. Everyone was sent home. This area, which contained most of the nation's wealth, was targeted and quickly captured by Federal troops. But by then, Mfon had returned to our hometown, deep inside the breakaway region. Thus, he was trapped in the enclave, cut off from Shell and his dream of studying engineering in London.

As the days transitioned into weeks and weeks into months, Mfon grew more and more desperate. He was to have left for London toward the end of July. But August had passed, as had also September, with him having no way to get out of the war zone. By October, he decided that waiting for the war to end before pursuing his dreams was not good enough. He needed to do something. He investigated and found some fishermen who were smuggling people in small fishing boats across the Atlantic Ocean to the Federal territory.

Imagine sailing in the Atlantic Ocean in a small fishing boat. My parents investigated and found that most of the journeys were not successful, as the people faced dangers from the sea, the secessionist army, and the Nigerian army.

Many who attempted this perilous journey drowned, as little fishing boats were no match for the high winds and waves of the Atlantic Ocean. During attempted crossings, if they were caught by secessionist soldiers, they were branded spies and/or traitors and shot. So, the journey always started in the dead of moonless nights when the waters were calm and it was difficult for the soldiers to spot the boats. There was also peril from the Nigerian soldiers, who sometimes couldn't ascertain whether those who came over were friends or foes. Thus, the chances of making the journey successfully was, at its best, very slim.

However, the desperation of those, like Mfon, who wanted to escape and the money that the smugglers made kept the business alive and well. Furthermore, the fishermen were familiar with the rough seas. Most had been fishing the ocean all their lives and were good swimmers. So, if the boat capsized, they were more likely to survive. It was their passengers who were most at risk. However, every "escaper" believed they would be one of the few to beat the odds and successfully cross to the other side.

My parents were very concerned about Mfon's determination to take his chances with these smugglers. Mom and Dad tried to dissuade him but to no avail. He was fed up with the situation and argued that anything was better than just existing. He was determined to take his chances no matter what. Mom turned to her trusted weapon—prayer, and fasting. After that, my parents went looking for and found the smugglers, enquired of them about their next journey, and paid a deposit. They were told when to bring Mfon for the sailing.

All this was done with the uttermost discretion so as not to arouse suspicion because, by this time, many of the seaports and coastal regions were patrolled by the Federal Nigerian Navy to ensure the secessionist army could not smuggle anything into their enclave by sea. Indeed, many seaports had already been captured. My homeland's seaport was one of the very few left under the secessionists' control. So, both armies were invested in controlling the few remaining seaports. They were vigilant in watching the sea.

Mom and Dad took Mfon to the smugglers one night, and after paying and committing him to the Lord, they left so they could get home before daybreak. They had no idea when the sailing was going to take place, as that all depended on the calmness of the sea and the right amount of moonlessness. I still recall the days following my parents' return from delivering Mfon to the smugglers. Dad came over and spent most of the day with us. He returned to feed Grandma in the evening. It was as if there was a death in the family. Mom and Dad hardly spoke but fasted and prayed. We didn't know exactly when the crossing was taking place. Life was very tense.

As days passed, and it was obvious that the crossing would at least have been attempted, we longed to learn something, to know if Mfon had crossed successfully or drowned. Anything was better than the state of suspense we were in. I was very close to my brother Mfon and found the time extremely stressful. Mom and Dad said all we had was God, and He was sufficient. For my own sake and sanity, I had to believe them.

After many excruciating weeks, when my parents felt it probable that Mfon would have sailed and the smugglers returned, they went searching for them to inquire about how Mfon had fared. We learned then that he'd nearly perished because, on the first attempted crossing, they'd encountered rough seas, and the fishing boat had almost capsized.

But God had intervened, and they were able to make it back to shore before daybreak.

After a few days, the second attempt was successful. They said he'd arrived safely at the nearest Federal Nigerian seaport. That was all they were supposed to do. Whatever happened to the person thereafter was not their concern. We had no way of verifying even their part of the story but just had to trust God.

After our area was liberated by the federal forces several months later, and we could contact the outside world once again, we confirmed that Mfon had indeed arrived safely at the Federal seaport and was able to make his way to Shell. He also contacted our elder siblings: our brother Edet (the oldest son) and our sister Adiaha (the firstborn of the family). They were both studying in London at this time. All three worked together to help Mfon get to London and his university. He was several months late in starting his course but was able to catch up easily. It all ended well. God is faithful.

Captured

Mfon's departure increased my loneliness and isolation. Even though we had lived in different houses, we still came together every now and then, told stories, and talked about the books we'd read from our home library. Though our living in different homes increased my safety, it also created some risks, as every week or so, someone had to take food supplies to Dad and Grandma.

Mfon often came for the supplies for their sustenance. After, he "escaped," sometimes Dad came for the supplies. But at other times, I had to make the journey. It wasn't considered very high risk, as the journey could be made mostly within the network of back-alley paths that had been created to keep people from walking on the streets and being exposed to soldiers. The problem arose when the path didn't pass directly by one's destination or when the destination was on the opposite side of the street, thus necessitating exposure while crossing the street.

This was the conundrum I faced every time I had to take supplies to Dad and exchange the books I'd finished reading for new ones at our home library. I needed to cross the street to the alley path on the opposite side and then walk a block to our house. I had crossed successfully several times, but one-day disaster struck. Usually, when I came to where I needed to cross the street to the other side, I would stop and listen for the sound of a car engine (by this time, soldiers were the only ones who drove cars). This day, when I stopped and listened, all was silent. I started to cross and out of nowhere, a car with four soldiers appeared and blocked my way.

Two soldiers jumped out of the car and grabbed me. They took me to the car, where the one sitting in the back seat identified himself as the commander. He told me he wanted me to come with them. I told him I couldn't because I had a sick mother at home and a very old grandmother, both of whom needed my care. I showed him the supplies I had with me for my grandma. He said those were not big issues. He would take me to deliver the supplies to my grandma, and he would take me home to visit Mom to ensure she was all right at appropriate intervals, but I needed to go with him that day. I tried every argument, but nothing seemed to deter him. In fact, he was becoming irritated by what he called "my stalling tactics." I was so scared that I felt disoriented. I could not think. Then I remembered that Mom often prayed silently whenever she was in a tight spot. I started praying inaudibly.

The soldiers forced me into the car between the commander and one of his bodyguards. They drove me to our house and two bodyguards accompanied me to deliver the supplies to Grandma. I was relieved that Dad was not home when we got to the house, as he would have tried everything to stop the soldiers from taking me with them. I'm not sure what they might have done to him. However, it was important for me to let someone know what had happened; else it would appear I'd vanished into thin air. I tried to tell Grandma that the soldiers had captured me. She appeared mesmerized, and I wasn't sure if she understood what I was saying. Within a few minutes, my time was up, and as a lamb led to slaughter, I was dragged away to the waiting car.

As they drove away, the commander started a conversation, but I did not hear a word as my head was in tumult. I was scared out of my mind. All the stories I'd heard of girls who had been captured and abused by soldiers flooded my mind. I was petrified. All the hopes and dreams I had for my life began to scurry through my brain as if saying a last and final goodbye, as it appeared my life was coming to an untimely end. I was oblivious to whatever was happening around me in the car. I couldn't believe this was actually happening to me. I wished it was a dream like the one I had about the bombing. But no, it wasn't. This was happening in real time and in real life. I was finished.

Then I heard some words that jolted me back to reality. I thought I heard him mention the name of my high school, Mary Hanney. I turned and faced him and asked him to please repeat what he had just said. He said he was the commander of the unit that was stationed at Mary Hanney Secondary School. That was the name of my high school. Those words brought some coherence back to my brain. The thought of retrieving my books, clothes, and other belongings from the school danced across my brain like the Sugar Plum Fairy in *The Nutcracker*. I engaged him in a conversation about the school. He seemed pleased that I was now more interested in a conversation.

I asked about the state of the school and what had happened to it. He told me the school was intact. His soldiers occupied the dorms, but the storage where our belongings had been packed was untouched. I told him that the students had left all their belongings there when the school closed because we'd been told we were going to be away for just a few days. Just like all the others, I'd left almost all my belongings there. I asked if it would be possible for me to retrieve them. He said, "Yes."

Then the conversation turned personal. I asked if he had any siblings. Yes, he did. Any sisters? Yes, there were. In fact, there was one just about my age, he said. I didn't know why I asked those questions. It must have been God who made me ask them because the information I uncovered through them later became very useful.

Astonishing Grace and Favor

We arrived at the school. He invited me to go with him to his quarters. I asked if I could see and get my stuff first. He agreed. He sent some of the soldiers to go with me to the storage room. Everything was intact, each in its place just as we had left them. I pointed out my suitcases and cartons of books. The soldiers carried them all to the commander's quarters. I asked him if the stuff could be placed in the trunk of the car instead of his quarters so the soldiers didn't have to come back to do that later. He agreed and it was done.

We went inside. He asked his attendant to bring some coffee. He poured me a cup. I told him I didn't drink coffee. He asked why I wouldn't drink coffee, as everyone loved coffee. I told him I didn't drink it because I'd had a very bad reaction to it previously. He didn't believe me. He said there was nobody who couldn't drink coffee and that I'd been stalling for long enough. In a loud voice, he screamed, "Drink it."

I immediately took a big gulp.

Within minutes, sweat was pouring from my brows. My face was practically turning red, my body began to shake, and I appeared quite ill. He thought I was pretending. He asked me to sit down, as he continued to talk and watch me. I began to moan.

At some point, when I keeled over and was having difficulty breathing, he realized I was indeed ill. Some of the young people who had become soldiers during that war were actually students; many were university students. I have a suspicion that this young man may have been a medical student. When he saw the signs of what appeared to be an anaphylactic reaction, he became alarmed, especially as I had told him I'd had a previous bad reaction to coffee. But he wasn't about to let me go that easily. As time elapsed, my condition deteriorated. I started to throw up, and my breathing difficulty became more pronounced.

I believed I was dying. I began to weep. Disturbing thoughts assailed me. Dying in my early teens was bad enough, but dying at the soldiers' barracks would add insult to injury. What would people think about my being at the barracks? Would they assume I'd gone there willingly? Would my parents know the truth? Would anyone actually know where I was? What would the soldiers do with my body? Would they have the decency to return it to my parents so that I could have a burial? Or would they just dump it somewhere? The ocean was nearby, so they could just dump it in the ocean. No need to even dig a grave. These thoughts increased my agony. I decided to confront him with them between sobs, haltering breaths and whizzes.

I said to him, "I told you I didn't drink coffee because I react very badly to it, but you did not believe me and you made me drink it. Now I am dying. You told me you have a little sister about my age. How would you feel if someone did this to her? I am just like her, beginning to explore my teenage years, and now you are cutting that short for me. How would your mother feel if someone did this to your little sister? What will happen to my sick mother? Who will take care of her? What are you going to do with my body? Please can you return it to my family? At least they can bury it." I began to wail as I tried to face my untimely demise. My body continued to shake. The commander was very quiet and was becoming very uncomfortable.

I pressed on with more pleadings and self-pity. "How would you feel if someone did not allow your little sister the decency to die at home? Can you please give me that tiny dignity of dying at home in the arms of my mother? Can you at least do that for me now and take me to her?"

That question seemed to strike a chord. He quickly called his bodyguard and told them he had to take me home. They helped me into the car that all my stuff had already been loaded into, and I was on my way home. I was still very ill and moaning all through the journey which took less than twenty minutes but seemed like two hours.

Finally, we arrived at the street where I, Mom, and my younger siblings lived. I pointed out the house. The car stopped, and the soldiers helped me into the house where I immediately collapsed onto the couch. Mom was astonished to see me in such a poor state as I had been perfectly healthy when I'd left the house several hours earlier. She was also flabbergasted about why I was surrounded by soldiers. She ran to my side. The soldiers off-loaded my suitcases and cartons of books into the house and then they drove away.

Mom had become anxious when it had started to get dark and I had not returned. My trips to the other house usually took about three hours. This time I was gone for more than five. She sat beside me, put her arms around me, and watched me without saying a word. I continued to weep. My body was still shaking. As Mom continued to watch me in silence, my body gradually stopped shaking. My stomach, which had been churning like a washing machine, was now becoming calm and returning to normal. The illness that had assailed me with such vehemence and speed seemed to be dying down. Even though I was still weeping, these were now tears of relief, joy, and gratitude to God. However, I was a little confused and did not understand what was happening. Less than an hour ago, I'd felt very ill and believed I was dying. How could I be feeling almost okay now without any remediation or medical intervention?

A Joy that Comes My Way Through Pain

After a while, I regained enough composure to speak. I recounted to Mom everything that had transpired that afternoon. She was astonished but not surprised. She had felt the urge to pray for me but had no idea what for. We both cried together. It all seemed like a dream, a very bad nightmare.

To ensure that I was not dreaming or going insane, I tried to recount the events of that afternoon again to myself. Several hours prior, I was the captured slave of soldiers and I felt my life was over. Then, I was going to my high school. There, I retrieved all the things I had left there when schools closed. Following that, I was struck with a mysterious illness and believed I was dying. The soldiers must have believed the same too as they took me home with all the belongings I'd left at school. All these happened without a hair on my head being touched. Did it really happen or was I imagining it? This was an impossible miracle. Who ever heard of such a thing? Mom held me close for a long time. It was as if she was afraid that, if she let go of me, I would disappear. She kept praising God for His miraculous intervention.

Some people reading this book may think I feigned the illness. That would be untrue. It would be impossible to feign an illness so convincingly that the soldiers would believe it. I was truly very ill and had no control over my symptoms, either when they appeared or when they resolved. I was just as astonished as anyone else at how quickly the illness came and the speed with which it resolved after I returned home and the danger was past. This shows the extent to which God will go to protect and save people when He chooses to do so.

As I reflected on this, the lyrics of the song "Reckless Love" by Cory Asbury came to my mind. The lyrics tell a story of how God's love surrounded him even in his infancy. How prophetic was that for me? God's love, protection, and goodness have been over me from the day I was conceived. God used the coffee as a vehicle to deliver me that day. The amazing thing is that I didn't even know Him as I should then. My parents did, but I didn't. I was just religious and full of fear of Him. I did not deserve it, and I couldn't earn it, but still, He gave Himself away. He would stop at nothing to help me.

I think God orchestrated the whole capture episode to enable me to retrieve my belongings from the school. He knew how important those belongings, especially the books, were going be to me after our area was liberated. That I did not know or love Him then was no barrier. How could God love one little girl so completely and unconditionally? I am in awe. I am so thankful that He chose to love me and draw me to Himself.

I often still wonder why I react badly to coffee. I have not met another person who has a deadly reaction to this much-loved beverage. I first tasted coffee in high school. We were tea drinkers in my family. I discovered the utility of coffee in high school during year-end exams when students were tested on what they learned over the entire year. Many students drank coffee to help them stay awake and study for the exams. I joined my classmates drinking coffee as I studied for my first end-of-year exam. I can't recall exactly what happened, but I suspect it must have been very bad as I gave the rest of my big jar of coffee away after a few sips of the first cup. I had to devise another way of staying alert to study adequately which was healthier for me.

I still do not quite understand what my relationship with coffee is. Even at present, if I'm in a room where coffee is being brewed, I begin to experience heartburn, nausea, and heart palpitations within a few minutes. If I don't leave the room, I could become quite ill. Even drinking tea with hot water from a flask that was used previously to serve coffee causes me heartburn and heart palpitations. Therefore, I avoid coffee like a plague.

I am grateful that God used my reaction to coffee to save my life. Whenever I think about coffee, I am reminded of the Scripture that says: *And we know that God causes everything to work together for the good of those who love God and are called according to his purpose for them"*(Romans 8:28). Having something that is life-threatening is supposed to be bad. But as this scripture says, God can cause it to be for good. He caused it to work for my good, and the illness which it instigated disappeared as suddenly as it appeared as soon as I was safe. Do you have something in your life that appears negative? Despair not, for you never know how God can use it for His glory and your good.

From the day of my capture and release, and for the rest of the war, my ears were always tuned to the sound of car engines even when I was asleep. I never really completely slept well from that day until our liberation. I was always afraid the soldiers may come back for me and if I was not able to hear them coming to escape in time, then I would be back in jeopardy.

We didn't have another place we could move to, so I had to hatch a plan that would help me escape if they ever returned. I surveyed our backyard and found an area near the fence that had several shrubs behind which I could hide. I also reasoned that hiding behind them may not be sufficient, and that I may need to exit the yard, depending on the circumstance. With Mom's help, I opened up a part of the fence behind the shrubs but then replaced it such that it could be quickly and easily opened and replaced such that it wouldn't be obvious that someone may have left the yard.

The Soldiers Return

Maybe God wanted to affirm to me that my capture and release was very real. One evening just as dusk was falling, I heard the sound of a car engine. I didn't wait to find out whether it was on the main road or if it had come into the school premises where we lived. Something in my heart told me to run. I did. I ran out the back door to my hiding place and watched from there. Yes, the car carried the soldiers, and they had come back for me. They suspected I could run out of the back door, so before they turned into the school premises, they stopped and let out a soldier to enter our premises through the side gate and watch the back door in case I attempted to escape through that route.

But thanks be to God, He had already alerted me to run. I had already left the house and was hiding behind the shrubs. They knocked on the front door. When nobody answered, they tried to kick it in. Then Mom opened the door. The soldiers said they had come to see how I was doing. Mom did not say a word. They asked where I was. She still did not say a word. They realized they were not going to get a response from her, so they began to search the house room by room. Mom just watched them. When they did not find me, they left. I think these soldiers were a much more respectful bunch. Some others, especially those who were high on something, may have done something hurtful to Mom or my younger siblings. These did not. Praise be to God.

In my hiding place behind the shrubs, my body trembled as I watched the soldier at the back door. After he and the rest of them left, I was too scared to go back into the house. Mom had to come and persuade me. I was reluctant to go back into the house, but she reassured me that they were gone and unlikely to return that night. For the rest of the time that the war continued in our area, I rarely ever relaxed or slept well. I would doze off and sleep lightly, waking up at every little noise. Some nights, I didn't even doze. I was always afraid of missing the sound of the car engine or hearing it when it was too late to escape. Any unexpected knock at the door made me jump up and exit the house by the back door and hide before the door was opened. I was traumatized and became hypervigilant.

I believe God has a huge purpose for my life, and I know He'll accomplish it to the minutest detail. He caused Mom and I to defy the odds of not surviving the pregnancy for a reason. That was just one incident, and anyone could say it was no big deal as an incident can happen in anyone's life. This unusual deliverance from the soldiers was another one. Would this be the last or will there be a string of unusual incidences? If there are, could we dismiss them all as coincidences? Or could we examine them closely to determine if there is some supernatural involvement?

8

Miraculously Sheltered

The war intensified about three months after I recovered my belongings from the school. The bombing raids that had previously occurred two to three times a day were now almost continuous, and the targets, indiscriminate. Furthermore, the secessionist soldiers were becoming more irritable, more aggressive, more distrusting, and there were many more of them. An increased number of troops seemed to arrive in our area every day. All these made homes too dangerous during the day. People started leaving their homes to hide in the bush. Therefore, early in the morning, there would be an exodus of people from their homes to nearby farmlands and a return at dusk. This became our routine for several weeks.

During this time, there were rumors that Federal troops were planning to launch an attack on our coast. From time to time, sounds of heavy artillery coming from the ocean could be heard. There were rumors that our area was the next target for the Federal troops. It made strategic war sense. The other two big seaports that had been part of the breakaway region had already been captured. Our seaport was the only significant one left, and if it was captured, the breakaway area would be completely landlocked. However, as long as the sounds of heavy artillery were distant, we carried on as "usual" as possible with the life we had become accustomed to.

The conflict accelerated. The situation became dire when those who lived near the waterfront started moving inland in a hurry because of a great influx of soldiers to the coastal area. The sound of heavy artillery was becoming more frequent, and it was not only coming from far in the ocean but also from the secessionist soldiers who had mounted more big guns at strategic locations along the shoreline. Also, fishermen who still dared go out fishing reported the presence of a huge ship sitting far out in the ocean. It was so far out that people couldn't really see it from the shore. These were signs of an impending battle and some people, especially those who had relatives further inland, decided to flee their oceanfront properties. Others who worried about what could happen to their property chose to remain—men sent their families inland while they remained in their homes for as long as they could, to protect the property.

These stories, the great influx of soldiers to the coastal areas, and their increased irritability were indications that things could soon be changing, that we could soon be experiencing the war as we had not yet experienced it. Everyone was very apprehensive and families who had not yet made escape and survival plans quickly put one in place. People were very nervous, but because we had never experienced war and had no idea what being at the waterfront would entail, we could not imagine what awaited us and the potential risks that would ensue.

My hometown was about twelve to fifteen miles from the waterfront. That would not normally be considered a long distance, but because the roads were bad due to a lack of repairs since the onset of the war and craters from bombs traveling anywhere was extremely arduous. Therefore, even the soldiers could not move fast, so the people who lived many miles inland were not immediately impacted. Things were tense, but we had become accustomed to tenseness. As long as the battle continued to be restricted to the sea and the coastal areas, and there were no Federal troops on shore, we knew we were not yet at the war front. There were rumors that some Federal soldiers who were either from our homeland or those who could speak our language had already come ashore, and mixed in with the civilian population to spy out the land. That seemed to explain the increased suspicion and irritability of the secessionist soldiers. If that were true, it would be difficult to tell who was a civilian and who was a spy.

Adding to our misery were the air raids, which were continuous from dawn to dusk. Those fishermen who had seen the huge ship sitting offshore said they seemed to have planes on them. If that was true, the bombers then didn't have to travel far to carry out their heinous acts. That could explain why they were able to arrive so early in the morning and continue their attacks all day. The planes appeared to be dropping bombs indiscriminately. No home was safe. What could we do and where could we go? How could we survive what was happening? We were sure it was going to get worse, much worse, before it got better. The question on everyone's mind was how to survive until the "better" arrived. This was not something to leave to chance. Families firmed up their strategic escape and survival plans and tried as much as possible to stay together so that if they had to flee, they would flee as a unit.

The most sought-after places to flee were remote villages with non-vehicle-accessible roads. One such place was a tiny logging village of about forty people, five miles from where we lived. It had no paved roads and was completely surrounded by water. Its only link to the outside world was a bridge made of two very long tree trunks placed across the river. This was a place where only loggers and those who wanted to escape from civilization for a short while went. There were probably only about a dozen cottages there. The lumber cut from this area was usually floated downstream on the river to where it was loaded onto trucks for transportation to the mills.

Most people chose this town as the perfect hiding place. It was nicknamed "The Village of Refuge," a place where people could run to and feel safe whenever the fighting came ashore. Since it had no roads, it was unlikely that soldiers would want to go there, as they normally needed vehicles to transport themselves, their equipment, and supplies. Furthermore, this place was in the opposite direction to civilization. No one who was not associated with the logging industry would want to go there. Fortunately, my parents were friends with someone who owned a cottage there. He offered us a room in his cottage. We packed a suitcase with a few vital necessities that could be spared and took them there in advance.

My family was still divided and living in two towns. Dad was staying with and taking care of his mom. We could not leave her by herself. Mom, my younger brother Etim, my baby sister Imaobong, and I were still staying about four miles away at the next town.

The Hiding Place: The Village of Refuge

The group that included Mom continued the practice of leaving for the farmland at dawn and returning at dusk. One particular area with big trees and soft grass was a great area to be, as the trees shielded us from the skies, and the soft grass provided cushioning to help with the all-day sitting and laying down. One afternoon, as we did whatever could help us pass the long monotonous hours while trying very hard to keep away the bugs things suddenly changed. We heard a continuous sound of heavy artillery coming from the coastal area. The sounds were getting louder. Some of the people from our town who had not joined the morning exodus for the bush suddenly came running, carrying whatever they could. They brought news that Federal troops had indeed come ashore, and there was heavy fighting. They also circulated rumors that some people who lived closer to the shoreline had been caught in the crossfire and lost their lives. Even as people from the first group were still speaking, more people from the town came rushing by. The exodus from town had begun. People and families were running, carrying whatever they could, and heading to wherever they thought was safe. Everyone was in a panic.

We knew it was time to head to the village of refuge. However, the question on our minds was, "Should we head straight there, or was it safe to get to our home first and retrieve the few essentials we'd packed for this moment?" We had identified the essentials, made packages of them every morning, and assigned each person which package they were responsible for before we left for the farmlands. This was so that, whenever we had to flee, each person would know exactly what to pick up and where it could be picked up.

Mom thought it too risky to try to get to the house. So, we headed straight to the village of refuge. Our concern then turned to Dad and Grandma. What would they do? It was not safe for them to remain in the house, but would Grandma agree to leave the house? Her mobility was very poor at this time. If she agreed to move, where would they go? How would she be transported? If they chose to stay in town, was it safe? Would they be okay?

We arrived at the village of refuge and checked into the cottage of our friend. We were still very anxious about Dad's safety. After the first wave of escapees from town, things seemed to level off. By evening, the people who came later said things were quieter and back to "normal," as the secessionist army had repelled the Federal attack, and Federal troops were back offshore. However, families still trickled into the village, as nobody wanted to be caught in the crossfire. By morning the population of the village had grown to several hundred people. People occupied whatever space they could find. We were part of the lucky few who had a roof over their heads.

We stayed in the village for another day, and when all still appeared quiet, some people cautiously returned to town to retrieve some essentials. They all returned safely. This seemed to give some credibility to the story that Federal troops had been successfully repelled.

Death Is Defeated

By the afternoon, many people had made the trip back to town and returned safely. I asked Mom if I could go with the next group to bring back some supplies. She didn't think it was a good idea, but I persisted. I reminded her of the importance of the things we needed to retrieve and also cited the many groups who had made the journey and returned safely. She reluctantly agreed that I could go.

As mentioned earlier, my Mom had heart problems, which sometimes made her very frail. Even though we had taken a few things to the village of refuge, they did not include her medication, as she had little of it left. We had not been able to refill her prescriptions since the hostilities began, so Mom had rationed what she had and only took a pill when she was feeling particularly bad. This was a very high-stress period. With the war at our doorstep and us not knowing what was happening with Dad, Mom was stressed. Her heart was beginning to act up. I wanted to get the medication, more pillows, blankets, and hot water bottles—our tools for managing the situation whenever her heart was in distress. Already, her ankles were beginning to swell, and we didn't have enough pillows to elevate them. Since we stayed out in the hot sun all day long during our time of leaving our homes in the morning and returning at dusk, it was not a good idea to have the pills with us. So, it was important that I go back to town and retrieve these essentials.

I set out with a group of ten adults. I took my younger brother Etim with me. We followed a bush path that ran all the way from the village of refuge to the school compound where we lived. School compounds were usually in the form of a U. The main street of the town would be at the mouth of the U and the soccer field in between the two parallel sides. The classrooms and bathrooms for the school were on one of the parallel sides, and to the middle of the curved part of the bottom of the U. Teacher's houses were on the other parallel side, with the principal's residence being the house closest to the students' section at the curved section. There was a path at the bottom of the U between the students' section and the principal's residence. This path just happened to be one that easily joined up with the road that led to the village of refuge. So, when people exited the path, they would be right in the open space between the classrooms and residences with the soccer field in front of them. They could then walk along the road in front of teachers' houses or the classrooms to the street from where they could enter the various other paths that had been created during the war.

When we arrived at the end of the bush path by the school, the leader made us pause and listen for any sounds or indications of soldiers' presence. There was dead silence, so he assumed it was safe to quickly emerge and take whichever path one needed to get to where they needed to go. My father's house was about three houses away from this space. As the group started to get out in the open, something within made me stop. Since the day I was captured, I had developed a mighty phobia for open spaces, even if it was just for a split second. I was reluctant to get out in that open space. I pulled my brother back and told him we should go back and walk along the fences, even though there was no path. We waded through the grass along the fence until we arrived at our backyard. We opened my makeshift escape fence gate and entered the house through the back door.

After taking all we needed and as much as we could carry, we went back out through the fence and made our way back to the village. As we approached the village, we could hear wailing. My heart quickened as it always did whenever there was unexpected sorrow. My first thought was, *Please God, let it not be Mom who has passed away.* We walked faster. As we emerged into the village, some people stared at us as if perplexed. Some screamed. Some ran towards us, while others ran away from us. I was anxious to know what was going on, especially as I did not see Mom. We walked down to our cottage and found Mom. She was alive. I could breathe.

She hugged us and held us close. It was then that we learned that all the adults in the group with whom we had gone back to town were dead. When they'd emerged from the bush path onto the soccer field, soldiers captured then shot them all. The next group that went to town found their bodies, and the assumption was that everyone from the group was dead. That explained why some people screamed and some ran from us when they saw us; they thought they were seeing ghosts.

Etim and I, the only children in the group, were the only ones who returned. How was that possible? How could a child decide on a strategy that the adults didn't consider, thus saving herself and her brother? How did God orchestrate this? If I had not been captured, would I have developed the phobia for exposed spaces that was instrumental in my decision not to follow the adults into the open space of the school?

Was there more to the capture than just the retrieval of my books and other belongings? I believe it was all part of the plan—the plan that was embedded in the promise. The promise from the dream in the first chapter, and part of the plan for my life.

When I reflect on this incident, my heart still flutters. We were snatched from the jaws of death. I now know and believe that it was God who whispered that change in strategy into my heart. He is a promise-keeping God. Despite the fact that I didn't really know Him then and was scared to death of Him, He forgave me and kept His own part of the bargain. He overlooked my erroneous image of Him, and instead of displaying the characteristics of the sadistic old man I imagined Him to be, He displayed loving kindness, and forgiveness because that is His nature. How could I have been so wrong about Him?

Life in the Village of Refuge

For the next several days, nobody left the village. The population had now grown to several hundred people. There were very few houses in the place, and most of them were small and rough. After all, they were cottages for loggers. People put up blankets, bedsheets, branches, sticks, or whatever they could access to make some enclosure for themselves and their families on the ground. These were sufficient when it wasn't raining.

But when it rained, life was miserable, especially at night. People needed shelter, especially the very young, the sick, and the old. This was when a piece of dirt or wood floor inside a cottage became more valuable than gold. Who would have thought a piece of dirt floor could be so precious? It was during this time that we learned to sleep sitting up. We packed ourselves like sardines to accommodate as many people as possible under the roof and away from the wetness and the cold outside. This situation brought out the best in people, as all collaborated to provide room, warmth, and shelter for those who needed them most. Some of us teenagers didn't mind giving up our spaces under a roof for the elderly, the ill, and mothers with babies. Sometimes we had to take turns staying outside so it wasn't always the same people staying out in the cold and rain all night. I was accustomed to not sleeping anyway, so it wasn't a huge adjustment for me. Amazingly, none of us became ill. God is incredible.

The days were spent foraging for food. We had to quickly learn which wild fruits, roots, vegetables, and herbs were edible and which were not. We would go out in groups to search for those fruits, roots, vegetables, and herbs, bring them back, and let those adults who knew best determine what we could eat and what was not edible. Whatever was gathered was communal property.

There were some women who cooked and some who looked after the children. The men built shelters and kept an eye out over the village day and night to ensure the village was safe. Collaboration and watching out for each other were the order of the day. Some of the men fished, and some gathered wood for cooking and for keeping warm. There was something everyone could contribute to make life just a little bit better for all. Thankfully, we were in the village for only about two weeks. Then we were able to return to our homes.

Our Family Home Spared

After the outing that ended in death, no one ventured outside the village. People were just too scared of ending up like the group we'd gone to town with. For more than a week, nobody left the village. Then some people came from town to inform us that we had been liberated by Federal troops and that our area was now completely and firmly under Federal control. However, the memory of the previous outing that had ended in death, except for Etim and me, was still fresh in people's minds. Therefore, nobody was in a hurry to venture out just yet.

The next day, a few more people came from town and relayed the same story, the liberation of the area was complete. A few of the men decided to go and witness it for themselves before coming back for their families. By that evening, they were back and confirmed that the war front had moved beyond our towns, and it was safe to return home if one still had a home to return to, as retreating soldiers had burned many houses. Upon hearing this, my heart sank. I thought: *Surely our two homes must have been burnt. Why wouldn't they be? What are the chances that my father's house could have been spared? After all, he was one of the leaders, a chief in the community, and a supporter of a Federal party before the war. Furthermore, when I was captured, the soldier had taken me to both homes. So, they knew where our homes were located. Also, they had taken me back home without hurting me in any way. That must not have been pleasing to them. They would definitely take their revenge now by torching both houses and burning theam to the ground.*

Our biggest prayer was that Dad and Grandma would not be in the house when they set it on fire.

We were one of the last people to leave the village. Mom wanted to make sure it was completely safe before we left. Besides, we didn't know if we still had a home to return to. Nobody was able to tell us if any of our homes were still standing. That was not the most important thing on our minds though, the most important thing was that Mom and the three of us kids were safe. If Dad and Grandma were also safe, then we would be all right. It would be difficult not to have a home, but we could always rebuild.

However, when we finally made it home, our house at the school was still intact. The only worry now was Dad, Grandma, and our home in the hometown. Before long, Dad came by. He reported that many homes on the main streets of our hometown were set on fire by retreating soldiers. However, they stopped torching the homes at the block of homes just before ours. Dad and Grandma had locked the doors and hidden in the house. If the burning hadn't stopped where it did, if our home had been torched, they probably would have perished. Were all my family members' safety, and our homes not being torched just another coincidence, good luck, or part of the promise?

We were home. We were safe. As far as our area was concerned, the active war was over. An area about eighty miles from my hometown was now the war front. This area experienced more protracted fighting because it was the boundary separating the minority groups of the East and Igboland, where the majority of people of the East who felt most threatened by Federal Nigeria lived. Indeed, the massacre of the Igbo people in Northern Nigeria was one of the precursors of the war.

Therefore, this boundary was highly fortified. While almost all non-Igbo areas were captured by Federal troupes within a year, it took an additional two years for them to make life miserable enough for the secessionist regime to surrender. The war in Igboland was long, protracted, and ugly. Many innocent, young, and brilliant people perished.

There were many orphaned, displaced, or "lost" children at this protracted war boundary who were brought to our area for safety. We sheltered one little six-year-old girl for a while. She was so traumatized she screamed from nightmares most nights. Even during the day, she was always seeing things not visible to others. We didn't know anything about PTSD then, and even if we did, we would have been unable to help her. After a few months, just as she was beginning to show tiny signs of progress in recovery, the military police (who acted as social services) then came for her. The war front had finally moved beyond her hometown, and they wanted to reunite her with her parents or relatives.

We never saw her again but often wondered what had happened to her. That war was so brutal; many children were orphaned and some were lost for a while before being reunited with relatives if their parents were no more. It was also then that we realized how lucky we were that the war front had moved quickly past our area. Even though there were many deaths, as some people were caught in the crossfire between the two armies, the number of casualties in our area was relatively low. We all began to think of how and where we could start rebuilding our lives.

In our family, the most important task for us was to find out the whereabouts of my brother Mfon. Had he indeed arrived safely in Federal territory and was alive and well? To really have peace, we needed to find the answer to this question. It was not easy to contact people anywhere as telephones were not yet operational again and mail was extremely slow. Besides, we didn't know whom to contact, except for my two older siblings who were in London. They were also anxious to contact us to find out if we were all alive and safe. They knew people in the Federal territory who could more easily contact us and relay the message back to them. When the friend contacted us, he relayed the message that Mfon had indeed arrived safely in Federal territory and had left for London and started his university education. When we got this news, we were overjoyed. We thought the war had ended for us, and being a true lover of Shakespeare, I exclaimed, "All is well that ends well." Later experiences proved my jubilation at this point to be premature. The war still had more surprises and heartaches for us, but God made them testimony-building experiences.

Why Don't Most People Encounter God?

When school reopened, I recounted the story of my capture and release without any harm to a few of my new classmates. None of them believed it. In fact, some called me an outright liar. They were adamant that it was impossible for a girl to have been captured by soldiers, taken to their residence, and then released unscathed. I know they did not quite comprehend the *amazing grace of God*. There were many other girls who were captured and who did not experience the same grace. I'm sure it was not because of anything I did but all because of God's great love and compassion. He had a plan for my life, and when the catastrophe that could have derailed that plan occurred, He stepped in and rescued me. All praise and glory to Him.

When I reflect on this incident and God's great intervention, I am reminded of the passage in Romans that says that God demonstrates His love for us in that, even while we were still sinners, Christ died for us (Romans 5:8). My relationship with God at the time of the war was not right, but because I was raised by godly parents, I knew about God. Indeed, I had *assumed* I knew Him, but I now realize that I had mostly *known of* God but did not actually *know* God. There is a huge difference between the two.

When you *know of* someone, that knowledge is often mostly garnered from others and hearsay, which could be tainted by the opinions, biases, and prejudices of the source of the information. However, when you truly *know* someone, such knowledge is usually based on personal encounters with the person and first-hand knowledge of the person. The more time you spend with the person, the closer the relationship becomes, and the more your knowledge and perception of the person are likely to be a truer representation of the person.

One may wonder how people, human beings, can have personal encounters with an invisible God. There are many references in the Bible of God inviting us to come to Him. We probably fail to accomplish this task because we want to get to Him through our own path and not the one He has prescribed. Some of us want a god that we can command and boss around rather than one that we need to listen to, worship, and obey. I think that could be the roadblock that keeps us from having personal encounters with Him and really getting to *know* Him.

As a biochemist, when I worked at the lab, I could assay enzymes and other substances and get accurate results by following the prescribed procedures of the people who created and perfected the procedures. A change in color or the movement of the needle of the assay machine told me volumes. However, someone who didn't understand the science behind the process would not understand how and why that movement of the needle and the intensity of the color change indicated what I said it did. If I tried to do the assay my way and did not follow the prescribed procedure and protocol of the creators, I would not get the expected results. I could then say the procedure was not true. But would that be true? Would that make it so? Most instruments that are not used according to the manufacturers' prescription are not likely to produce the prescribed results. Is it wise not to follow prescribed procedures but expect to get the right results? That could be why many of us fail to get personal encounters with God. We want to get to Him in our own prescribed way and not His.

I also relied on my parent's faith. Because they made us memorize scripture, go to church, participate in helping people in need, and be "good kids," I thought I knew God. I am very grateful that God later revealed to me that He does not have grandchildren; He only has children. The faith of our parents will only take us so far. Each one of us must come to a point in our lives when we make our own conscious and deliberate choice about what we want to do with Christ. Anyone reading this book who does not yet have a relationship with God should stop now and genuinely invite Him into his/her heart. It is simple yet profound. We all need to invite Jesus Christ into our hearts to be our Lord and Savior. We may do so by saying those words in as simple a form as possible, but if it's from the depth of our heart and soul and we truly mean it, He will answer and come into our hearts. It's a decision I have never regretted, and I'm sure no one will ever regret it.

Is the Worst Really Over?

Up to this point, I've recounted the story of how the war began, its impact on us, and how my family and I miraculously escaped disaster and even death. We were now back at our homes, and the war front had moved past our area. We were no longer in imminent danger from bombs, but the threat from soldiers did not change, as the Federal soldiers were as bad, if not worse than the secessionist ones. However, I was beginning to sleep during the night again as the threat of the return of the soldiers who'd captured me, returning for me was over. Schools reopened. Could one then say that the worst was over? For many families in our area, that was true. All they needed to do was start to rebuild their lives. However, for my family, the war still had traumas and heartache in store.

9

Covered and Protected

The liberation of our region came as a huge relief to everyone. Hope began to rise, and there was a feeling that we could breathe again. Even though conditions were not ideal and the Federal soldiers were as terrifying and disrespectful as the secessionist ones, there was comfort in the realization that the worst was probably behind us. There was still no law and order, no money, and no employment. One of the first things people wanted though, was for the children to return to school. We had already missed a whole year of school. So, even those who did not like school were eager to return to classes, as it provided something to do, somewhere to go and a break from the excruciating tedium to which we'd become accustomed.

Some aid began to trickle in and with it some of the once familiar everyday items. I can still recall the first time I held a bottle of shampoo in my hands again. Oh, the delicious fragrance of bath soap, the refreshing aroma of shampoo, and the pleasure of using antiperspirant again. Having these items back was like paradise. At first, they came only in tiny little gift bags, donated by some charitable organization—

just small quantities. They seemed so precious that I used them very sparingly, knowing that, when they were finished, I may not have access to them again for a while.

Also milk, oh wonderful milk, which had become extinct when Mom's stockpile was gone, was back again. How nice it was to taste tea again with milk and some biscuits to enjoy it with. Even though we had cows, we didn't milk them. I'm not sure why. Our milk came from the north either canned or powdered. Even though Mom had a stockpile of goods such as sugar, biscuits, soap, candy, canned milk, and salt, most were sold out about halfway through the war. When some of these resurfaced after our liberation, we were like those who dreamed. Oh, the rare pleasure and joy of savoring candy again. Things we had taken for granted before the war and craved during the year-long apocalypse were back. How nice it was to savor their presence and enjoy their company again. For a teenager who had to forgo these "pleasures" for an entire year, their return was simply paradise.

God is so amazing, He had caused Mom to buy and stockpile some of these items, then sell them when the prices were astronomical. Selling them provided us with money to live on, pay for Mfon's escape, and my expenses to return to school. God had foreseen these future expenses down the road and provided the funds through this stockpile of goods more than a year in advance. Salt was also back. What a pleasure it was to taste food cooked with adequate salt again. It was amazing how salt became the biggest source of income for the family. On what turned out to be the true last day of the huge Oruko market that was held once every eight days, the market was bombed. There was chaos, dead bodies, and body parts torn apart by the bombs everywhere. People were in shock and just ran for their lives. The regular order of things was broken. Because of the chaos, some of the wholesalers from the big cities could not locate some of their customers to whom to deliver their goods. Everyone just wanted to get away from the market as quickly as possible.

The city merchants were in a conundrum about what to do with the merchandise they couldn't sell. They certainly could not transport them back, so they tried to offload them at ridiculously low prices to anyone who would buy them. Mom had already purchased her normal quota, but some merchants begged her to buy more. To help them, she did even though she didn't know what she was going to do with all the stockpiles of salt, sugar, and laundry soap. Therefore, we had a huge amount of salt and sugar added to the vast stockpile of essentials that Mom had already purchased. These items, especially salt, turned out to be a gold mine for us. About a month or so after this, the prices of these items began to rise rapidly. I later understood that salt is an ingredient needed to make gunpowder. Therefore, the army was stockpiling what was available, and the Federal Army worked hard to prevent the secessionist government from importing any salt. Within a few months of the war's onset, whatever salt was available was selling at unimaginable prices.

Mom gave a lot of the salt away, especially to the poor families who could not pay for it. Even though we had salt for the family's use until our area was liberated, we were not allowed to use it as liberally as before the war. Mom and Dad said we had to share in what everyone was going through even though we had the salt. Besides, we had no idea when the war was going to end. So, Mom said it was prudent for us to use sparingly those things we could not replenish and give some away to those who needed them as food without any salt at all was difficult to consume. Therefore, we had become accustomed to bland food, as the rationing of salt became the order of the day, especially during the last six pre-liberation months.

Then, there was the return of kerosene—and the joy of being able to buy kerosene and light kerosene lamps again. It wasn't electricity, but it was much better than homemade candles. It was like springtime; things that had appeared dead and gone forever were returning, coming back into our lives. How amazing, how wonderful. As a young teen, these were the immediate joys that liberation brought. I'm sure the adults had a completely different perspective.

Schools Reopen

Within a few months of the liberation of our area, schools reopened. For elementary school students, there were no major issues. However, the girls in high schools had a problem. There was only one girls' high school in the whole of my homeland, and it did not offer any science subjects. This was problematic for high school girls who had attended schools that taught science before the war. They had nowhere to go. Even when the other girls' high school sixty miles away that offered science subjects reopened, many female students from my homeland could not attend it, as traveling was still very dangerous. The Federal soldiers were not more respectful of girls than the secessionist ones. In fact, they were worse when it came to commandeering girls.

The school system in Nigeria was similar to the British. The Elementary schools were day schools. They went from ABC (kindergarten equivalent) to Standard Six (seven years in all). At the end of Standard Six, all the students in the same province wrote the same exam on the same day and time. During the Standard Six year, those aspiring to attend high school would apply to the different high schools, then take an entrance exam, and if they did well enough be invited for an interview. Success at the interview gave them a spot at the high school and their parents had to pay a required deposit during the allotted period to hold their place in the school.

High school was a five-year program. The same cohorts went from Class One to Class Five. Every high school was a boarding school. The final high school year was very tasking as students had to take the O Level Exam, an examination written by all English-speaking West African Countries (Gambia, Sierra Leone, Liberia, Ghana & Nigeria), on the same day and at the same time. The two-year syllabus was set for the final exam, a few years in advance. So, students were tested on what they had learned according to the syllabus over the previous two years. The examination lasted several days. Students were examined on eight subjects; their six best scores constituted their Aggregate scores. A score of A was awarded Aggregate 1; B, 2; C 3; D 4. The best possible score was Aggregate Six.

If one did well at the O Levels and were intending to attend university, then they applied to attend a high school that offered A Level. This was an intensive two-year program where students focused on and gained in-depth knowledge of three subjects that were prerequisites to whatever career path they intended to pursue at university. Not all high schools offered A Levels.

The high school in my homeland offered only O Levels. Again, girls were in danger from all sides and still needed to limit their exposure anywhere they could encounter soldiers. That was indeed a Herculean task, as there were soldiers everywhere. There were checkpoints mounted by soldiers about every two miles on almost every roadway. So, traveling even a few miles meant encountering many groups of soldiers at checkpoints.

The lone girls' high school in my homeland was located in a secluded area near the coast. Getting to the school, especially for those from towns "far away" like mine, meant passing through several checkpoints. Many girls tried to limit the number of checkpoints they encountered by making detours through small back-alley roads where possible. Even then, these provided no guarantee of safety. Furthermore, gas for the public and public transportation was still very difficult to access. Therefore, the available form of transportation was either by foot or bicycle, making elaborate detours more onerous.

School in an Unfamiliar Format

High schools before the war were all boarding schools. When school reopened, we were not immediately allowed to move back into our school residence. The school had been overrun by soldiers from both sides. The secessionist soldiers had resided there, and when Federal troops took over, they probably viewed everything with suspicion. So, boxes and suitcases were ransacked and contents dumped out.

The campus was overgrown, as the lawn had not been maintained for more than a year. There was debris everywhere. The place needed to be cleaned up and unused ammunition left behind safely disposed of before students could be allowed to move back in. The security gates were broken down so it wasn't safe for girls to return to residence. Exacerbating the situation was the fact that there seemed to be no one in charge. Schools were, at that time, established, owned, and run by churches. The churches had been negatively impacted by the war as nobody had money to pay Pastors or maintain the church. After liberation, messages sent from head offices in Federal territories took a long time to arrive. So, there was nobody immediately able to arrange for the grass to be cut. Even if people could volunteer to cut the grass, it could not be done until the soldiers had inspected the area and disposed of all abandoned ammunition.

The school we returned to after liberation was very different from the one we'd left at the beginning of the war. I was in my fourth year in high school when the war broke out. High school classes were comprised of the same cohort of students from the first year (class 1) to the last (class 5), and since we spent over nine out of the twelve months of the year at school, our schoolmates and classmates were almost like sisters.

Going back to school after liberation was clouded with sadness. Out of the thirty girls in my class, only four of us, who were local, returned. The other twenty-six, who were from other parts of the country, didn't return. The four of us often talked about them, wondering where they were, how they were faring, and what may have happened to them. We hoped and prayed they were alive and safe.

When we first returned to school, it was a day school. Being that my hometown was about twelve miles from the school, I had to find somewhere closer to school to stay. Fortunately for me, one of the senior girls who had completed her O Levels and was now doing her A Levels in the boys' high school invited me and one of her classmates from my hometown to stay with her and her family. She lived about three miles from my high school. They were very gracious to us. Even though the house wasn't big, and all three of us shared a room, we were comfortable. Best of all, there were no checkpoints between the school and this house. We were safe from harassment and having to strategize every time we left the house on how to avoid encountering soldiers. Hallelujah!

It took several months for us to settle into a routine. The church paid for the grass to be cut and for the exterior premises to be cleaned up. However, the interior, the dorms, and the classrooms were not cleaned up. We had to clean those up ourselves. Our beloved principal, Miss Skipsey, was no longer there. We learned later that she and the other British teachers had returned to Britain soon after the students left and before it became impossible for people to leave the secessionist enclave. We were thankful they were safe. The local teachers returned but not the British ones, therefore, the school needed to hire new teachers, and enough of them before learning could return.

Attending school was a very different situation now. We had a new principal and several new teachers. The school in its original pre-war format had a huge kitchen, two chefs, and several attendants who prepared all our meals. Now there was no such thing. The kitchen had been ransacked, and the big pots, pans, stoves, and other kitchen utensils needed to prepare meals for 150 teenage girls were gone. Everyone was responsible for preparing her own meals. Every student had to buy her own pots, pans, plates, and food and determine how to cook it.

There was no electricity, but fortunately, kerosene had returned. However, small portable kerosene cookers were very, very difficult to find. I think only one student in the entire school was able to secure one. The rest of us had to resort to firewood and locally-produced iron tripods to cook our meals. We had to devise ways to store the food in the hot climate without it going bad. We had to cook just enough for the day every day, as there was no way to preserve the food. Planning and preparing meals under these circumstances was difficult in a culture where the diet is significantly plant-based. We had to purchase foods that were not easily perishable, as it was difficult to go to the market during the week, especially for those of us preparing for our O Level exams.

The school was in a remote area, three miles from the market. Therefore, school was no longer just about numeracy and literacy; meal planning, cooking, and preservation became part of learning. There were no nearby restaurants or grocery stores that we could run to during the week to pick up supplies. To get anything, we had to walk those three miles to town to buy food and then carry it back to the campus.

Life was busy and strange and in a format that made innovation and the ability to adjust continually as conditions changed prerequisites for success. Most of us didn't mind the difficulties, we were just very happy to be back at school, even in a format that was very difficult. It's amazing how adversity changes people and their perspectives, how going through a period of hopelessness and fear changed people's outlook on life. Even though things were very difficult now when we remembered the purposelessness and hopelessness of the war year, we were happy to endure whatever we needed to endure, as long as, in the end, it provided hope and a desirable future.

An Unexpected Visitor

Within a short period of time, we'd settled into this new format of education. The first year of returning to school was a short one as we had to still maintain the January to December school year and many months had already gone by. The Christmas holiday was very short as we needed to return to school early in an effort to make up for all the time we had lost during the war. The new year marked the beginning of my final year of high school. All the girls in our area who had attended different high schools pre-war were all now in the one school, the only girls' high school in our area. We had almost all the teachers we needed. Those of us who were in our final year of O-Level exams were very busy trying to catch up with the syllabus. Then one afternoon, I was summoned to the principal's office in the middle of classes. That was most unusual and not normally a positive thing. As I walked to the office, I tried to think of what I might have done wrong. Had I broken any rules? There were hardly any rules anymore and no real consequences for breaking any that existed. So, what was this all about? Why was I being made to miss part of my lecture? I tried to convince myself that the reason for my summons was positive.

When I arrived at the office, the principal smiled at me. That was a good sign. When one is summoned out of class to the principal's office in the middle of the day, a smile is rarely what is encountered. But before she could speak, I noticed a very distinguished young man in an impeccable suit sitting across the table from her. As I looked toward him, he stood up and started walking toward me. He called my name and spoke a few words to me in our native tongue. For a moment, my heart almost skipped a beat as I realized that he was my eldest brother Edet, who had completed his Ph.D. in engineering in London during the war. I was not aware he'd returned to Nigeria. I was about six years old when I last saw him. Now, eleven years later, he was standing in front of me. How on earth did I recognize someone I'd last seen in eleven years? Even before he left for London, I had seen him very infrequently because he went to a high school that was very far away and outside our area. He probably started high school when I was just a baby. Moreover, his A-Level years were spent in Lagos, and he did not come home during those last two years in Nigeria before departing for London.

My memory of him in person was very faint, and the picture of him that hung in a prominent place in our living room was that of a young high school student. The man in front of me now looked nothing like the one in that picture. He was a distinguished-looking grown man with a beard in an impeccable three-piece suit, the likes of which I'd not seen. The saying that "blood is thicker than water" must be true at many levels. There are just some things we may never fully understand. I think the power of blood connections or kinship is one of them. That's the only way I can explain my recognizing my brother Edet that day.

He asked the principal if he could take me out of school for a few days, and she said, "Yes." I quickly packed a small bag, informed some of my friends I was going home for a few days, and off we went. It was a huge honor and a cause for celebration for my family. The firstborn son of the family had successfully completed his Ph.D. in engineering in Britain and returned to his homeland. My hometown was one of those to which the saying, "It takes a village to raise a child," practically applied. Everyone was happy, and Edet's return was cause for a big celebration. The whole town celebrated with us. After a few days at home getting reacquainted with my big brother, I returned to school, and he returned to his employment with Shell in Western Nigeria.

God's Secret Agent

Biology was the only science subject that my high school offered. It also didn't offer advanced subjects such as Additional Math. However, in my fourth year, the year the war started, one of our teachers (a very brilliant math teacher who wanted to attend university to study math, physics or engineering but did not yet have the funds), obtained permission from the principal to teach Additional Math to a select group of students in my class. Additional math comprised of advanced levels of geometry, algebra, calculus, and trigonometry. Six students from my class were selected for this pilot program, I was one of them. He told us we'd be helping each other because teaching the subject would keep it fresh in his mind for university, and we would benefit from learning a subject we could find useful in the future. His words turned out to be prophetic for me.

I loved math. To me, it was the easiest subject in the universe. It is logical and consistent and the principles do not change. Unlike other subjects for which one had to read and study unlimited pages of content, for math, one only needed to understand the guiding principles, the conditions under which those principles applied, and how they were applied. I loved the simplicity of it. My brain effortlessly grasps principles that are logical, straightforward, and consistent. Besides, I loved the challenge of solving math problems. If I did not get the solution readily, finding out why was always rewarding.

As "the chosen six" (our nickname), we loved our unique privilege. During the evening prep class, we would gather, practice the principles, solve problems, and encourage each other. We enjoyed this unique privilege for about six months before the war sent us all home, and my beloved group of six disbanded forever. After the school reopened in my area, I was the only one of the six who returned. Fortunately, the math teacher also returned. He convinced the new principal that a subject for just one student in the entire school was worthwhile. It took him a little longer to convince me of the same. We tried to interest the other girls in my class just for moral support, but most of them hated even basic math and only learned it because it was a required subject. After that, I resigned myself to my one-student class.

Continuing with this class was problematic for me because we were required to write exams on a maximum of eight subjects, and their final aggregate was based on the best six scores. This presented a dilemma for me. Since my school offered a limited number of courses, I had just enough courses including geography. Geography was my least-liked subject. I couldn't understand why I was required to learn about the terrain, produce, average temperatures, snowfall, and rainfall in Canada, the United States, and Europe. I had never seen snow, of what benefit was such knowledge to me? I did not live in any of those countries, neither was I planning to do so. At that time, I had no desire or interest in living outside Nigeria. If I had to learn those facts about Nigeria, it may have made sense, as I would have been learning about statistics that impacted me.

My brain doesn't grasp discrete and disjointed statistics easily. So, I did not expect an A in geography. That left me with just seven subjects. If additional math replaced one of them (I was not expecting an A in it either because of the circumstance) then I had only the required six subjects. If I didn't do well in one of them, I would fail to attain the aggregate that I desired and was working extremely hard towards. I considered letting additional math displace a subject I was sure of doing well in, a huge risk.

Even though I loved additional math and was sure I could earn a passing grade, I wasn't sure what that grade would be. As the only student, I had no one to challenge me, no one with whom I could study and practice, and no one from whom I could seek help when I encountered problems. Even though my teacher was always happy to help, I could not access him often because male teachers did not live on campus nor was there a teachers' room for them to congregate when they were not teaching. Only female teachers had such a room. I always tried to access my math teacher just after he had finished his last class or when he had spare time in between classes and I was also free during that time. He was very kind to let me know his schedule. However, if I had a class when he finished his classes, he would be gone before I could seek his help.

The war had taken more than a year of school from us, and even after school resumed, months elapsed before we were back at school. We had about twenty months to learn a twenty-four-month syllabus and under very difficult circumstances. We had to plan meals, walk three miles each way to buy groceries, and then find ways to cook and preserve the food, as we had no electricity, no fridges, and no stoves. There were so many obstacles already. Therefore, substituting a subject I was not sure of performing well for one I was likely to, was too big a risk. It was not an ego thing; I was just being realistic. Being admitted into A Levels, my choice of university, and my future career all depended on the O-Level exam scores. Therefore, my future access to and pursuit of higher education hung on the grades from this exam. I wasn't willing to risk my future for any reason. I shared my concerns with my math teacher. He had an answer. He always had an answer and a solution for every obstacle we encountered in the pursuit of this additional math class.

Undaunted by my anxieties, my teacher found a provision that allowed students to take more than the eight allowable subjects if the additional subject was a pilot and under special circumstances. He convinced the principal to make the necessary application and seek permission from the examination council for the class to be registered as a pilot under special circumstances for our school. The permission was granted, and I became one of the very few students who wrote the West African School Leaving Exams on nine subjects instead of eight.

I visited my high school recently, several decades after I graduated from it, and I was told additional math was still not offered at the school. So, I remain the one and only student who has ever studied additional math at Mary Hanney Secondary School.

I also have another distinction. I am the only student to date who graduated from that high school with all arts subjects and then went on to study science at A Levels and university and successfully completed them with distinction within the normal allotted time period. I think all these happened because God, in His great mercy, who knows the future before it happens, was making a way for my future success by getting me to study additional math. It was in the year following the O Levels that I realized that this man, my math teacher, was God's secret agent and gift to me. God had sent him to prepare and equip me for what otherwise would have been an insurmountable challenge of learning chemistry and physics for the first time at A Levels, and in a class with students who'd all studied the subjects at O Levels and excelled in them. More will be said about this in the next chapter.

Disaster Looms

I was my math teacher's favorite student. Very few of the students liked regular math, but they had to take it because it was a mandatory subject. Every time we met, be it in the classroom or in the corridor, this teacher always had a smile and an encouraging word for me. Therefore, I was quite troubled one fateful day when I turned a sharp corner and came face-to-face with him, and he had no smile for me. What troubled me more than the lack of his usual smile or encouraging word was the fact that it appeared he wanted to avoid me. When I turned the sharp corner and met him face-to-face, he avoided making eye contact, seeming to want to turn and flee.

This was not the reaction I'd ever experienced from him, so my mind raced to find possible explanations. Since I had a very ill mother, whenever someone behaved unusually toward me, my first prevailing thought was usually that something has happened to Mom. I froze, staring at him. Then with a huge effort (I had a lump in my throat), I asked, "What's wrong?"

He turned his face away and looked down. I could see tears in his eyes.

My heart began to race and my legs started to wobble as my brain tried to discern what my teacher's behavior signified. I knew it could not be good news. I grasped a nearby pillar. As tears involuntarily began to roll down my face. I said, "Please just tell me, has my mom passed away?"

He continued to look away. I could not stand the suspense. I wanted to grab his hand and force him to tell me what it was. But I knew if I were to let go of the pillar, I would crumble to the ground. Even though he tried to hide his face, I could see more tears rolling down his face. With great effort, he finally spoke. "Have you heard from home?" he asked.

By this time, all strength had left my body. I didn't have enough energy to speak, so I just shook my head.

"Something terrible has happened," he continued.

I was trying very hard to keep breathing. It appeared my windpipes were tightening up, and I could hardly get air into my lungs.

"Your brother who just came back from Britain is dead."

I crumbled to the ground. My mind could not process that information. Mom had been very ill even before I was born. Even though I dreaded it, I somehow expected she would die sooner or later. My prayers had always been that it would be later, as much later as possible. But my brother who just came back from Britain? The one who had just completed several years of study and earned a Ph.D. in engineering, dead? The first son of the family, our pride and joy, dead? The one I had just met again only a few months ago, dead? It could not be.

Teachers and students gathered around me, trying to pick me up from the ground. They tried to help me stand, but my legs had forgotten how to do that. I could not stand. They tried to help me sit, but I could not do that either. I just kept crumbling to the ground. I didn't have the strength to cry or speak. I hardly had the energy to breathe. The principal was alerted, and several girls carried me to my room and lay me on my bed. The principal sat beside my bed for a while, something not witnessed before.

It is amazing that time appears to be at a standstill in times of intense crisis. I have no recollection of how much time elapsed from the time I encountered my math teacher to the time I could speak again.

Those details are lost in my consciousness. But I remember telling the principal I needed to go home. She agreed, and I left the school.

I have no memory of that journey. I have no idea how I got home. I cannot recall whether someone went with me. Someone must have because I don't think I was capable of making the journey by myself. All those details are lost in my memory. But I recall getting to the front door of our house and crumbling to the ground. Maybe the person who went with me knocked or the noise of my groaning alerted Dad that someone was at the door. He opened the door to find me crumbled on the ground. With tears streaming down his face, he helped me inside. Mom and Dad had hoped to keep the news from me until they knew more details of what had happened. But the news had spread like wildfire.

I am not sure how long it was after Dad helped me into the house before I saw Mom. She was partially seated in a chair in the parlor and holding onto the raised arm of the chair. It was obvious Mom and Dad had not slept in days. The room was dark, as the drapes were only partially drawn, therefore, it took a while for my eyes to adjust. I crawled to Mom and held unto her legs. She stretched out her hand and pulled me closer to her. There was absolute silence for a while, then she said, "Don't believe it. He is not dead."

I still didn't have enough energy to speak. I just stared at her.

She continued. "A few weeks ago, I had a dream. In that dream, I saw a big, prestigious cow. It looked healthy and full of life. All of a sudden, it was shot, and it fell to the ground. The shooting appeared to be random, and the cow appeared dead. I was disturbed that such a healthy cow should be shot and destroyed so meaninglessly. I looked more closely. It was then that I saw that it was still breathing, though sporadically. I felt the desire to pray and speak life into it. As I prayed for it, I noticed its breathing became more regular, and I sensed that it was going to live. I awoke.

"I felt that it was very significant and that it was not just a random dream but a revelation. Even though I was not sure or clear about what the revelation was or how it was related to me, I felt a strong desire to fast and pray. I went into a fast for several days until I felt it was accomplished. When the news came that Edet was shot and that he was dead, the Holy Spirit said to me, "That is the dream you had. You spoke life into him and prayed for him. Therefore, he is not dead but alive." So, I know he is alive. My problem is how I am going to get to him. Nobody seems to know where he is, but I am going to go and find him."

Slowly, I could feel some life coming back into me. If there was one person in the universe I knew I could rely on, it was Mom. If there was one person who "saw in the Spirit" from time to time, it was Mom. I knew the Lord revealed things to her sometimes. Was she right this time? I sincerely hoped so. But how was she going to find him? Nobody could tell us exactly where he was. The only information we had was that he was driving home from work one day and soldiers driving by shot him dead. If he was dead, where was his body? Nobody had answers.

Mom was ready to go find her son, but with the war still raging beyond our area, the only way to get to the West was by air, and there were no commercial flights. Flights were only for government officials, soldiers, bank executives who were trying to get banks reestablished, and contract merchants charged with ensuring that needed supplies were available for soldiers at the war front. We were not affiliated with any of these groups.

Furthermore, the nearest airport was at Calabar, a town across the river from us. The only way to get there was by ferry. It was not easy to get on that ferry since the priority was for it to take supplies to the Federal soldiers at the war front. After all the army supplies were loaded, if there was still room, the spots could be occupied by civilians. Being one of those civilians to board the ferry was an onerous task. There were no pre-purchase of tickets and no fixed number of tickets, as army supplies always had priority. People waited until all the military equipment and resources were loaded on. Then, if there was still room, an announcement would go out, and there would be a mad scramble of a hundred people or so, all vying for very few tickets. What ensued was usually a mad stampede to be one of the few to grab one of those precious tickets. Mom was not strong due to her heart condition, so ordinarily, chances that she could be one of those to get a ticket were slim. But somehow, God made a way. She got a ticket, got on the ferry, and was on her way.

Continuing Divine Interventions

Traveling at that time, even for the most seasoned and strong, was grueling. There were military checkpoints about every two miles and at every junction. If the soldiers didn't like your face or there were any issues, they could just shoot you. They had all the power and the weapons with which to demonstrate that power. How could this frail woman make such a hazardous journey alone?

Nigeria is a country with hundreds of languages. If one traveled about sixty to a hundred miles in any direction, he/she encountered people who spoke either a completely different language or a variant of a main language. Besides, the accents and intonations of the people from different areas of the country were very different, making it more challenging for people from different parts of the country to understand each other easily. That made it difficult to travel, especially outside the big cities, where people didn't speak English fluently. How would Mom understand the speeches of the people in the interior of the mid-west where she was going to start searching for Edet? The information we had was that he'd been shot on a rural road near an oil field. As the overall presiding engineer, he often visited the field to ensure everything was operating as it should. We were not sure if he was still in the area or if he had been flown to one of the big hospitals in a different area.

The oil field was located in Midwestern Nigeria. Edet's base was Lagos, in the West. There was no direct air link between Calabar and the Midwest then. So, one had to fly from Calabar to Lagos and then make the difficult and dangerous journey by road to the mid-west. What about the cultural barriers? The cultures of the people in the West and the Midwest were different from ours in the East. How was she going to interact with people whom she could not easily communicate with? How would she find out where Edet was? How was this woman going to navigate all these issues?

The flight from Calabar to Lagos was the easy part. From Lagos, she needed to find out where Edet was before making any travel plans. How would she find lodging in an area where hotels weren't at every corner like they are now? Would the money she had be sufficient? Remember that very, very few people had been able to earn money in about eighteen months. Dad had returned to teaching when schools reopened, but teachers were not being paid yet. Even though some people from our area lived in Lagos, Mom didn't know their addresses or how to contact them. All these were issues of great concern to everyone but Mom. She believed God would guide her and lead her to where her son was. I wished I could go with her, but I had to return to school.

Dad tried to dissuade her from going, but Mom was not the type of person one could dissuade from anything she'd set her mind on. She kept saying that God would guide her and lead her to her son. A part of me believed she would be all right, but the other part of me was petrified about all the other predicaments that could befall her. We could not afford to lose her as well. That would be too much. We did the only thing we knew—pray. Within a few days, Mom started her journey to Midwestern Nigeria to find her son. I returned to school.

As the first step, Mom had to find a way to get on the ferry and make her way to Calabar. She did. Calabar had been liberated about eight months earlier than our area, so life for citizens there was more normalized than ours. Living in Calabar was my older sister Adiaha's brother-in-law. He was the Chief Justice of the state. We had not met the family yet, because my sister met and married her husband in London just before the war began and they were still in London. However, in the Nigerian tradition, in-laws are family. So, Mom's first task was to find the Chief Justice, introduce herself, and seek his help in getting a flight to Lagos. She also needed his assistance in finding information on Edet's whereabouts.

As the Chief Justice, he had connections with chief justices of other states and was well-placed to be able to find information on my brother's whereabouts. The information gathered indicated my brother Edet had been shot and taken to a small-town hospital near the oil wells he'd gone to inspect, but he was not deemed to have survived. All accounts were that he was dead. The question still remained, if he is dead, where is his body? No one could answer that question. It was surprising because Shell was deemed one of the best employers in the country. They always took care of their own. Why then did they not know what had happened to one of their prominent employees? It was incomprehensible that no one seemed to know where he was or what had happened to him after he was shot.

Mom was undaunted by these problems and refused to believe her son was dead. On the contrary, she believed he was very much alive. All she needed to do was get to him. She got on a flight to Lagos and then began the perilous journey of several days by road through hundreds of miles to the small town where Edet was supposed to have been shot. Somehow, she made her way there and was able to communicate with people enough to find out which hospital Edet was at. That, in and of itself, was a huge miracle.

Back at School But Not Really

It is astounding how you can be physically present somewhere but mentally and emotionally absent. That was my predicament when I returned to school. My mind was fully preoccupied with what was going on in my family. Where was Mom? Was she safe? Was her heart holding up? What if she became as ill as she sometimes is and has difficulty breathing? What will happen to her? Who will elevate her legs and fill hot water bottles to keep her warm? If she was alive and strong, what did she find? I tried to convince my mind that I needed to be present in class, as it was important for me to do well in my O Level exams, but my mind seemed to have a different plan. I struggled. I kept asking any teachers if they had heard anything. The answer was always "no." I wondered whether they were telling me the truth or just trying not to be the bad news bearers.

At the time, the telephone was nonexistent at our school. Money was not being spent on infrastructure but on the war. There was no way to contact Dad or for Dad to contact me unless he physically came to the school. This was a twelve-mile journey, but it might as well have been a two-hundred-mile one because it took almost all day to make it to the school and back due to the several checkpoints and having to travel by bicycle, the only mode of transportation. Furthermore, the chance of encountering a trigger-happy soldier in a bad mood made the trip a dangerous one; and the very, very bad roads made it an onerous task. So, I tried to manage the best I could.

Alone, But Alone with God

My brother Edet was alive, but just barely. He had been in the hospital for more than a month. There were no relatives but a few friends whose lives he had touched, who visited and prayed for him. This small town was not his base but a place near the Shell offshore oil production platform he was in charge of. Normally, Shell would fly their employees who needed intensive medical attention to a bigger hospital for the best treatment possible. However, the prevailing rumor was that he was dead, so no such action was taken. Even then, Shell should have asked for his body but did not. That was God's intervention because if they had tried to move him from that location in the condition that he was in, he may have died or been paralyzed.

Because the doctors believed he would not survive, no heroic attempts to save him were made. They tried to lessen his pain but didn't do much else. When they left the hospital each night, they expected him to die during the night. But to their surprise and astonishment, each morning they returned and found him still alive. Edet was determined to live. However, as those days of incredible suffering and excruciating pain persisted, he began to despair. He went in and out of coma often.

Then one day, when he opened his eyes, there was a woman sitting beside his bed. Thinking he was hallucinating, he tried hard to focus. Behold, it was Mom. She was holding his hand. As tears drenched both their cheeks, she tightened her grip on his hand. When my brother Edet saw Mom, he became more determined than ever to live. Mom stayed at his bedside day and night. She only left when absolutely necessary and for as short periods of time as possible. She talked to him, encouraged him, and prayed for him and with him. He made a significant and miraculous turnaround toward recovery. When the doctors saw this and listened to Mom's unceasing pleadings, they started treating him more aggressively, though they still didn't believe he would survive.

He made astonishing progress day after day. Before long, he was stable enough for Shell to fly him to the best hospital in the country. There, he went through almost a year of aggressive rehabilitation. He had to learn to stand and then to walk. At first, he walked with the help of a walker and then a cane. After more rehabilitation, he walked without a cane but with a limp. Today, he does not have a limp when walks. He is a living super miracle.

Later, we heard the true story of what happened that fateful day. My brother Edet was driving back from visiting the oil platform when a truckload of soldiers spotted him. Because he grew a beard, one of them shouted, "Look, Ojuku." Immediately, several soldiers jumped out of the truck and pulled him over. They dragged him out of the car and began shooting at him. It happened very quickly and unexpectedly. After the first few bullets (all of which miraculously missed all his vital organs but shattered the bones of his legs and hip in many places) hit him, he fell to the ground. In the process, his wallet fell out. One of the soldiers picked it up and gave it to their Unit Commander who was sitting in the car watching. As the commander looked through the wallet, he encountered my brother's military pass which was signed by a friend of this commander. He realized that my brother was not Ojuku and that he had actually met him (my brother) a few days earlier at a club, and that my brother had bought him and his friends drinks. He immediately jumped out of the car just as one of his soldiers was about to incinerate my brother with a grenade. He shouted to his soldiers to hold their fire. He took a look at my brother and recognized him. He then told his soldiers, "This is Dr. Amana, not Ojuku."

It also happened that one of my brother's friends was passing by soon thereafter. When he saw what had happened to Edet, he stopped and worked with the soldiers to help arrange for him to be taken to the hospital where the bleeding could be stopped. If my brother Edet had not been taken to the hospital when he was, he may have bled to death. Even then, it was difficult to believe that someone who had suffered that many gunshots and lost so much blood could survive. Amid this incredible tragedy, God still made a way to facilitate Edet's survival.

Ojuku was the leader of the secessionist region. How could anyone with any brain cells think Ojuku, the head of state of the secessionist region, would be driving a car alone, in Federal Nigerian territory, hundreds of miles from the secessionist region, in broad daylight? The tragedy was that soldiers could do anything to anyone at any time with impunity as they rarely faced consequences for misconduct. The soldiers who shot my brother were not even near the war front. Imagine then what we faced with those near the war front in the east. That was why it was extremely important to avoid all soldier encounters as one could never predict what could transpire at any encounter.

Nobody who saw or heard the story of the shooting could believe that someone so critically injured could survive. It was a miracle—God's supernatural intervention. Was this part of the fulfillment of the dream's promise? Hebrews 6:16–19 says: *God also bound Himself with an oath, so that those who received the promise could be perfectly sure that He would never change His mind. So, God has given both His promise and His oath, these two things are unchangeable because it is impossible for God to lie. Therefore, we who have fled to Him for refuge can have great confidence as we hold to the hope that lies before us. This hope is a strong and trustworthy anchor for our souls. It leads us through the curtain into God's inner sanctuary."*

If God had not intervened, by the end of that war, only two out of the six children in our family would have remained. All my brothers and I would have died. Only my oldest and youngest sisters, one in London and the other a baby would still have been alive. But the Lord had a different plan for us. Psalm 33:17–21 says: *Don't count on your warhorse to give you victory—for all its strength, it cannot save you. But the Lord watches over those who fear Him, those who rely on His unfailing love. He rescues them from death and keeps them alive in times of famine. We put our hope in the Lord. He is our help and our shield. In Him, our hearts rejoice for we trust in His holy name.*

Who is your help and shield?

10

Determination Overrides Impossibilities

My brother Edet's recovery was as miraculous as his survival. Once he was out of the hospital and into intensive rehabilitation at the best hospital in the nation, he continued to make astounding progress. When he could walk again, Shell reassigned him to Lagos, where he began less intensive rehabilitation but continued to make astonishing progress.

Meanwhile, I was finishing my O Levels in the war zone where education was very difficult. The near impossibility task of finding the required textbooks to buy highlighted the great significance of God's provision in enabling me to retrieve my books through the military capture. Although we had to cater our own meals and there were many other difficulties, we were grateful we had survived the war and were able to get back to school. Where there is a will, there is a way. I was determined not just to do well at the O Levels exams, but to excel. Accomplishing my dreams depended on it.

O Levels were the building block for a person's future. A great performance in the exams opened many doors for further studies and employment, while mediocre performance could make accessing higher education difficult. The stakes were very high for those of us who had university ambitions. At the time, university vacancies in the country were less than a third of what was needed if everyone who desired to and had the funds to attend university were admitted, so I worked extremely hard at my studies so I could be in that favored third.

Finally, it was time to write the O Level exams. This was the culmination of five years of hard work and several hundred pounds in school fees. The junior students not taking the O Levels were sent home. I was lucky that one of the junior girls from my hometown asked if she could stay for the duration of the exams and help with my meals so I could focus and concentrate on last-minute studying for the exams. I was flabbergasted. That was kindness in the extreme. God had always made provisions for me. This was another great one.

After the O Level exams, my brother Edet asked me to move to Western Nigeria, I was happy and excited to leave the war zone. Attending school in the war zone had been extremely difficult, therefore my brother's invitation to relocate to the West for my A Levels was very exciting. I looked forward to my focus at school being hard work for good grades again without concerns about how I can fit food purchase and preparation into the timeframe. Furthermore, the West had big lively towns and life that hadn't been impoverished by the war. I would be sailing on a ship to Lagos and then traveling by road inland. I had never sailed on a ship before. I was excited and looking forward to this new adventure.

By this time, merchant ships were arriving regularly at Calabar, transporting military supplies for the Federal troops fighting the war. After they off-loaded the supplies, they'd previously sailed an empty ship back to Lagos. Then, someone had a brilliant idea: Why not transport passengers who want to leave the war zone on the return journey to Lagos? The only problem was that these were cargo ships, they had neither the license nor amenities for passengers. There were only a couple of bathrooms outside the crews' living quarters There were no kitchens or bedrooms—just open deck. But desperate times elicit desperate actions. People desperate to get out of the war zone were willing to do whatever it took to accomplish their goals. I was one of those desperate people. However, getting a ticket for the standing room on the ship was an onerous task.

Since this was not a legal business, as cargo ships aren't permitted to carry passengers, there were no places to buy tickets. The ship crew knew that people would be willing to pay whatever they requested just to get on the ship. The lure of the immense amount of money the crew stood to make overrode any moral thoughts to resist the temptation to indulge in the business. The ship crew had no equipment to make official tickets, therefore, when prospective passengers paid money to someone for passage, they received something scribbled on a piece of paper with the ship's picture on it. Their greatest concern was always whether what they had was authentic and would enable them to board the ship.

Many were duped. I didn't know how to get a ticket. But then I met someone who knew someone, who knew another person, who was friends with one of the ship's crew members. Through this person, I managed to get a ticket. My helper advised me to show up at the wharf very early before the crew was tasked with getting the ship ready for people to board, so his crew member friend could help me load my luggage and store it in a safe place before general boarding ensued. Since nobody kept track of ticket sales, there were usually more people than the ship could contain, therefore, getting onboard very early was vital.

I packed two large suitcases with everything I imagined I would need to start my new life in the West. This was a major move. I was leaving my childhood setting and entering the big league. I had visited Lagos briefly before, and I knew it was a huge, mesmerizing city, and very densely populated. The girl who grew up in the war-torn section of the country was now moving away from all that chaos to the big city to begin a new life. I was thankful. I was grateful. I was excited.

I arrived early at the wharf on the departure day. My helper was already there at the predetermined spot. When I saw the crowd that had already gathered, I was thankful that this man was there to help me. He was worth every penny I'd paid him. It would have been very difficult for me to carry my two huge suitcases and carry-ons into the ship without his help. God always knows my needs before I encounter them, prepares a resolution for my problems before they arise, and sends help when it is needed. He is good to me. Providing me with this young man was another way of Him looking after me.

My helper and his crew friend carried my luggage, and I walked through the crowd into the ship like a princess. The crew member said he would store my luggage in the best and safest location. He also showed me the best place to stay on the ship. I thanked him for all his help and picked the spot he suggested. Knowing this crew member was a huge blessing.

I was safely on the ship and at my spot before the chaos of general boarding ensued. My helper had advised me to bring a mat and blankets to sit on, some canned food, crackers, and bottles of water for the journey. These were in my carry-on bag. I kept this bag close to me. Even though I was born and raised by the Atlantic coast, I had never been out at sea. My helper had informed me about seasickness, but I had no idea what that was like. It didn't take long for me to find out once the ship started moving.

After the long chaotic general boarding and just as dusk fell, the long blast of the ship's horn announced its readiness to depart. The journey began with the evening breeze caressing our faces. Joy welled up in my heart. It was really happening. I was leaving behind the war-devastated area with its ever-abundant military checkpoints, the fear of being captured by soldiers, the studying with tiny kerosine lamps, having to prepare my meals with firewood and improvised stoves, and the general lack of almost everything—all the hardship, suffering, and fear were going to be behind me as I start a new life in the West.

As that ship began to sail, involuntary tears of gratitude and relief ran down my cheeks. I felt so loved and blessed. Many of my friends and classmates were remaining in the war zone, continuing to endure uncomfortable conditions, but I was leaving all that behind and sailing into a bright and potentially fulfilling future. I was grateful and appreciative of the God who made all these possible. If He had not intervened, if my brother Edet had died, none of these would have been possible. Had He watched over me and my family as He promised?

My musings and my attitude of gratitude were rudely interrupted. As we exited the estuary within which Calabar is situated and made our way into the open Atlantic Ocean, the wind was no longer warm; it was chilly and biting, and became even chillier as the night progressed and as we moved farther away from land.

Nigeria is a warm country with three distinct climate zones. There is a tropical monsoon climate in the South (near the Equator, my area); a tropical savannah climate in the central regions; and the Sahelian hot and semi-arid climate in the northern part of the country. While there could be significant daily temperature variations in the northern part, the South only experiences significant variations between seasons. However, during harmattan (November - December) when the prevailing winds are predominantly from the North the temperature variations between the day and the night could be significant. Anyhow, the lowest reported temperature for the South is 24 degrees, and the reported high is 37 degrees Celsius, otherwise, the regular normal temperature ranges between 30 and 36 degrees Celsius.

The great thing about harmattan is that the lowest temperatures occur during the night when one is comfortably snuggled in bed under blankets. The temperature begins to rise in the morning as the sun's beautiful rays warm up the air. My sailing to Lagos took place in December. Until that day, I don't think I had experienced harmattan without a blanket or sweater, therefore had never felt the full impact of the harmattan cold. Here in the open ocean without a barrier between me and the cold wind, it didn't take long before my teeth and everybody else's teeth began to chatter. We were all shivering. The splashing of the waves against the sides of the overloaded ship sprayed people nearer the ship's edge with water. I felt sorry for those who had to endure the wetness. Thankfully, I was up in my very well-positioned space. Even the biting wind was a bit warmer before it reached me. I wondered how the people close to the ship's rails managed.

The ship was greatly overloaded, and every tiny space was occupied. Therefore, it was lower in the water than it would normally be when carrying the appropriate weight of cargo. Every wave-caused sway was gut-churning. Before long, people began to throw up. The tragedy was that people were so tightly packed that trying to get out to the bathroom or the perimeter of the ship in time to let out the vomit was difficult. By morning, the boat and those on whom the vomit landed stunk. This was just the beginning of sorrows, the first night of a three-night journey.

Luckily for me, I had dry crackers and hard candy to combat the sea sickness. Also, the fact that I had this awesome spot by the big pillar near the crew quarters was very helpful. I could lean against the pillar. That the spot was by the crew walkway meant it was not overcrowded with people. I was relatively comfortable, despite having experienced the "extreme cold" during the night. My early boarding had also enabled me to use the bathroom when it was still clean and useable. After chewing on a few crackers and candy, I wetted my tongue with as little water as possible to reduce the need for bathroom use.

That night, I thought about what my brother Mfon, who had traversed this ocean in a tiny fishing boat must have endured. This ship was hundreds of times bigger than the tiny fishing boats, yet the ocean waves pushed it around like a toy. What did it feel like to be on the same ocean in a tiny fishing boat traveling at a very fast speed to get to Federal territory before daybreak to avoid being seen and shot by soldiers? It's amazing what the human mind can endure when its back is forced against a wall. I felt more appreciative of God's protection and for taking Mfon safely to his destination.

We were happy to welcome the morning and the sun with its warming rays. However, I was very seasick and had a difficult time standing up. I wanted to brush my teeth, but the line was too long and the bathrooms, filthy. Still, it was all that we had. The foul odor from vomit and overflowing bathrooms made the misery excruciatingly torturous. My prayer was that I would still be alive when we arrived at Lagos.

As I looked at the waves tossing the ship around, I was reminded of a song from the Methodist Hymn Book that I loved to sing. I had sung it so many times that I knew the words by heart. I now sang it silently in my heart. The words provided comfort and helped me return to thankfulness. It was written by Priscilla Owens in 1882 and speaks about our anchor in life. The lyrics asked people if their anchor would hold during life's various storms—threatening clouds, strong tides, wild winds, reefs that threatened the ship, and fear that immobilized the heart. In the refrain, the writer said she had an anchor that kept the soul steadfast and sure through every imaginable storm because it was fastened to the rock that cannot move and was grounded in the Savior's love. Experiencing the winds and waves that night and reflecting on the various storms I'd endured over the past three years in the war zone provided a better understanding of the song and gratitude to God who had kept us safe through it all.

The third day finally arrived. As we were approaching Lagos, the crew member friend came to find me. Despite my putting on a brave face, whenever he talked to me during the journey, he knew I was a sorry sight—dehydrated and with no energy whatsoever. He told me we'd soon be docking at Lagos, and if I wanted, I could come to his quarters and brush my teeth and clean up. He promised I'd be perfectly safe. As soon as I was safely there, he would leave. I accepted his kind offer.

He brought one suitcase over and left. I washed my face, brushed my teeth, changed my clothes, and packed for disembarking. After making myself more presentable, I slowly made my way to the place he said I would find him. He took a look at me and asked if he could give me some medication that would help calm my stomach and a drink that would give me a little energy. I agreed to both and thanked him. After taking these, my stomach calmed down, and some energy returned to my body. This kind man helped me offload my luggage from the ship. I don't know how I would have managed without him, being that I had no energy. It appears that God provided him to help and take care of me.

As we went ashore, my brother Edet was waiting. What a happy reunion! If the devil had its way, I would never have seen this beloved brother again. Moreover, if he had died, I wouldn't have sailed to Lagos at all, and my life would have taken a very different trajectory from the one ready to unfold before me. Can I ever thank and praise God enough for His goodness to us as a family?

11

Miracles at St. Anne's School

Lagos is a huge city, the largest city I've ever seen. It appeared never to sleep, lights and sounds were everywhere. I was excited beyond words. The countryside where I grew up had tiny cities which were quiet and "organized". Lagos seemed boisterous and "chaotic" as everyone seemed to be in a hurry. Cars drove at faster speeds and one had to dodge them to cross the street. This was frightful for me because I just came from an area where there were hardly any cars on the streets for an entire year (during the war, only soldiers could access Gas) After liberation, very few people could drive because of Gas scarcity and exorbitant prices.

I knew my brother, Edet, was searching for a school for my A Levels. He wanted me to study science, but there was no way to do that since I had attended a high school that had not offered science. In my mind, the topic was dead, finished, too late—but my brother believed that I could still study science in my A Levels. I reminded him that A-level science students normally would have studied the subjects at O Levels and since my high school didn't offer science subjects, I had lost that privilege. However, he insisted that I could still study science.

He said there was a school at Akure (300 kilometers northeast of Lagos but still in the West) with a three-year A Level program for students who wanted to improve a science subject, usually physics. This program was for students who wanted to major in a field in university where physics was a prerequisite but hadn't done well enough to allow them to continue with physics at A levels. The first year of the program was spent reviewing physics in depth and also a little overview of chemistry. I tried to point out to my brother that these students had already studied physics and chemistry at O Levels and had done poorly at physics. That situation was very different from mine, a person who had never studied chemistry or physics. I felt it would be impossible for me to learn and master five years' worth of the subjects in a year. I didn't want anything to do with such impossible-sounding ideas. All my arguments and pleadings fell on deaf ears, my brother Edet had already made up his mind that I was going to learn science and I could not convince him to see things from my perspective.

After a few days in Lagos, we were on a school-hunting expedition. We traveled to Ibadan, another huge city about a hundred miles from Lagos. Until we arrived at Ibadan, Lagos was the biggest city I had ever seen. Ibadan was less densely populated but bigger than Lagos. It was the largest Nigerian city by size at the time, with a population of just under a million people. Ibadan had the exclusive distinction of having the best university in the country and one of the best universities in the Commonwealth and the world. It was founded as a college of the University of London and although it eventually become its own bona-fide university, it retained the same academic standards as the University of London.

Ibadan was also the location of the best hospital (University College Hospital) in the country and indeed, West Africa. Medical students from the University of Ibadan (UI) practiced and perfected their clinical skills at UCH. The University of Ibadan was the center of learning and excellence and was right in the heartland of the Yoruba people, a joyous people who loved music, and celebrations. They were jovial and more relaxed than the super success-oriented people of the East from whence I hailed.

It was uncanny to hear music frequently playing, even blasting from car radios and in shops. I was thankful for being able to enjoy music again; the war had robbed Easterners of so many things. Ibadan had a bustling market, the likes of which I'd never seen or imagined. This market was probably several hundred times bigger than the "big" Oruko market that my Mom traded at in my homeland. There were also small kiosk stores along the streets offering snacks and other wares. Life was on from morning till dusk.

We had a relative, a fourth cousin, who lived in Ibadan with his family. Our intention was to visit them for a day or two and then continue on with our journey to Akure to sign up for the three-year A Level re-embrace science program. They had three girls and two boys. The oldest girl was a year younger than me. It just so happened that our cousin's two oldest daughters were attending the most prestigious high school in the country, St. Anne's School. My cousin had a meeting with the principal of St. Anne's for something concerning his daughters the afternoon we arrived at his home. My brother asked if we could tag along.

St. Anne's School, Ibadan

St. Anne's School, usually just referred to as St. Anne's, was founded in 1869 by the Church Missionary Society. It was the first girl's high school in Nigeria and indeed, all of West Africa. Thus, the first generation of well-educated Nigerian and West African women were all Alumni of St. Anne's. When these Nigerian women became parents, they wanted their children to attend the same school. Thus, it was the school for the children of the well-educated, the rich, and the famous. It was very expensive and had a reputation for academic excellence. St. Anne's, like all other high schools in the country at the time, was a boarding school. It had six houses, and each house had its own color. These were St. Catherine (red), St. Claire (yellow), St. Faith (green), St. Hilda (brown), St. Mary (blue), and St. Margaret (orange). All the houses were named after female saints.

We arrived at the principal's office. She was a pleasant English educator, who, like my previous high school principal, Miss Skipsey, had spent most of her life educating girls in Nigeria. There had been a three-year physics improvement A Level course at St. Anne's, similar to the one in Akure. It appeared my brother had spoken to the Principal about me joining that three-year A Level program, but she'd informed him that the program had been discontinued at the end of the previous school year due to poor outcomes. However, that did not dissuade my brother from wanting me to study science and attend St. Anne's. He is a very tenacious man when he believes strongly about something.

After our cousin finished his transaction with the principal, my brother suddenly took over. He said to the principal, "This is the student I talked to you about."

Before she could say a word, he handed her a stack of papers he'd pulled out of his briefcase. They were my high school report cards. She accepted them reluctantly. However, as she examined each one, she looked at me, and her facial expression seemed to change. After examining all of them thoroughly, she put them down on the table and seemed to be in deep thought. I wasn't expecting this and didn't even know what was going on. Previous to this, just like any teenager in the company of adults who were discussing something with no relevance to her, I was not paying attention. Now that the focus had suddenly shifted to me, I did not know how to react. I tried to look as relaxed as possible. She finished looking at the report cards, put them down on the table, and was quiet for a while. Then she said, "I will take her. If anyone can do it, it's her."

I must say that my report cards were impressive. God has given me (in fact, all my family members) the ability to excel at academics. Though I worked hard at school, academia came easily to me. I was almost always at the top of my class. So, my report cards were filled with A's and A+'s. When the principal looked through the reports of five years of high school and saw only solid, excellent performances throughout, she wanted me in her school.

I was bewildered. What did her words mean? My brother had mentioned this school to me and I had checked it out. I decided it was not suitable for me, as it did not offer the subjects I needed at A Levels to pursue the accounting degree I desired. I wanted to continue my studies focused on arts courses; I was sure I would utilize my love of math well in accounting. Ever since I'd arrived in the West, I had been trying hard to convince my brother that it was five years too late for me to change to science. I'd suffered enough trauma during the war; I didn't want to do anything that would be physically, emotionally, or psychologically exhausting. I needed a break. I needed to experience school again the way it's supposed to be, without all the suffering of the past eighteen-month post-liberation, when I'd attended school under onerous circumstances.

The opportunity to chase science had long passed. Mom had always thought my calling was in the medical field. I believed that too, but unfortunately, the high school I attended and the subjects it offered were not compatible with a career in the medical field. Where I grew up, there were few professional women role models, no one to advise on what fields were open to women, and what the educational prerequisites were for different career paths. Most of the professional women I knew then were either nurses or teachers; I was not interested in either of those careers. Even if I had been, I wouldn't have known what the prerequisite courses were. Due to Mom's allusions, I was open to a career in the medical field. However, nobody informed me that my choice of high school would play a huge role in attaining that goal.

Do eleven and twelve-year-olds ever think about career pathways? That's the tragedy. You choose your high school at that age. Unless someone educates you about the correlation between high school subjects and career paths, you are likely to make an uninformed choice about high school. It is only when one is more than halfway through high school that she discovers that the subjects her high school offers determine her career path later in life. Because my high school didn't offer Chemistry and Physics, the door to a career in the medical field seemed completely shut and bolted.

I had chosen my high school because it was the only one in my homeland, and it was close to my hometown. I didn't know about the importance of offered courses in determining future carrier paths. Its proximity to home was what mattered to me then. Attending that high school meant I would have the chance to be home more often to see Mom and my younger siblings. My elder sister, Adiaha, had attended a high school far away. It was the nearest Methodist girls' high school to our hometown at the time. During the holidays, it took her a full day to get home. I could get home in less than two hours. Therefore, this school was attractive to me.

Later on, when I was already a few years in high school, and just before the war, my brother Edet wrote to me from London, asking what profession I was interested in. I told him I didn't know. He started discussing all the possible professions open to me and suggested I should study medicine. As the discussions progressed and I informed him of the subjects offered at my high school, he suggested I change high schools, but this was something that was not done at that time. When one started high school, she remained there with the same cohort and completed O Levels at that school.

However, my brother wanted me to change to a school that taught science subjects. From London, he managed to convince a Catholic school sixty miles away from my home to interview me with the aim of me changing high schools. I was just starting my fourth year of high school. The principal of the Catholic School was not convinced that I could catch up on the three years of science that I had already missed. Furthermore, this was a Catholic high school.

Several years earlier, I had been invited for an interview there when I was applying to high schools from my elementary school. They had asked me then if I would be willing to convert to Catholicism if they admitted me. Knowing where my parents stood when it came to faith, I said I would ask my parents. However, from the family history form I had completed, they knew my Dad was a Methodist teacher and lay Minister. Then, if one was not willing to convert to Catholicism, they couldn't attend a Catholic school. With what they knew about my family, and when I didn't return a signed affidavit to become Catholic, I was not given admission. Almost all high schools at the time were mission schools, tied to specific faiths, therefore, your church affiliation significantly impacted where you could attend school as each denomination gave priority to students of the same faith. A prospective student's church affiliation was one of the first questions on the high school application form.

Anyhow, even if I had been admitted to that school on the second attempt, I would not have attended it, as the war broke out shortly after the interview. Furthermore, even if I had been admitted to that Catholic school at the beginning of my high school career, it may not have been possible for me to complete high school there. When my homeland was liberated, all the high school girls went to my high school, Mary Hanney Secondary School, because it was the only high school for girls in the area. It would have been very difficult for me to travel sixty miles to the Catholic school to continue with science, especially as traveling such a distance greatly elevated the risk of being captured by soldiers.

A year had already elapsed since the discontinuation of the three-year program at St. Anne's. Therefore, there was no longer any structure for it. The principal had said she would plan for a dedicated teacher who would teach me basic chemistry and physics during the first semester, and in the second semester after I had learned the basics of the two subjects, I could attend the O Level chemistry and physics classes with the final-year O Level students. In the second year, I would be ready to start the A Level program. The plan didn't sound convincing to me but I was not allowed to have an opinion. In my last year in my former high school, I had been in a one-person class in the Additional Math class; it wasn't fun. If it were possible to avoid another one, I would very much have liked not to repeat the experience. I also wondered how I could learn four years of chemistry and physics in just one semester to be able to attend classes with the final-year O Level students by the second semester. I shared my concern with my brother. He told me this principal was very experienced. She knew how that would work and would arrange it all for me. I should relax and stop worrying. I wasn't convinced, but there was nothing I could do as I was not part of the conversation, nor was I allowed to voice my opinion about how I felt about the situation.

The War Finally Ends

The day to start school at St. Anne's soon arrived. I was uneasy as I arrived at the school, found my house, entered my dorm room, and met my roommates. Six of us shared the room. All my roommates except one were Arts students. They asked what stream I was in, Arts or Science? I didn't know how to answer the question. I had to go through this long explanation to inform them of my situation. They were a little confused but sympathetic.

A few days later, the news that most people in the country had been hoping to hear came. There was an announcement that the secessionist regime had surrendered, therefore the civil war was over. I was overwhelmed by memories of the war even though two years had elapsed since my homeland was liberated. It appeared that all the painful memories that I had banished from my consciousness now made a breakthrough to my consciousness. Memories of the near-death experiences my family and I had experienced, all the fear, and the suffering we endured. I wept and wept and wept as I recalled and reflected on all that had transpired in my family during that war. I thought about my capture and release by the soldiers without any harm, I reflected on my brother Mfon's escape, and the time my brother Etim and I were snatched from the jaws of death. I thought about my brother Edet and how God had intervened on his behalf to keep him alive; how Dad and Grandma were mysteriously shielded as the soldiers stopped burning houses just before our street. I recalled all the months that I didn't sleep for fear that if I did, I could miss the sound of the car engine if the soldiers came back for me.

I thought about Mom's unfailing health throughout the war period. How her heart never went into crisis during the war when we wouldn't have had access to help. Then, the most scary thought came to me: if there hadn't been divine intervention, all my brothers and I could have perished. The idea made me shudder and tremble. As the radio kept announcing and re-announcing that the secessionist regime had surrendered and the war was over, the tears just kept flowing. They were tears of gratitude, self-pity, relief, and anger for the senselessness of it all. I was grateful that even though we had many close encounters and my brother Edet suffered horrific injuries, we were all still alive. I was very thankful my family and I had all survived.

It appeared the war had tried to eradicate my family, but something kept standing in its way, preventing it from accomplishing its heinous desire. A few months later, after I gave my heart to Jesus, I began to comprehend, just minimally, the width and depth, and breadth of the love of God that had brought about all those miracles. I marveled that, though I did not know God as I should and attributed many horrible things to His character, God was still the love that would not let go of me and was always there for me. I was soon to discover that, if I surrendered my life to Him, He could make it rich, full, and to His glory. These thoughts are derived from the words of one of my favorite songs in the Methodist Hymn Book: "O love that would not let me go" by George Matheson with music by Christopher Miner

As I look back and reflect upon that war, I realize I had experienced some of my deepest worship and most heart-wrenching prayers to God through songs. At many of those times, an appropriate song would bubble up from within me. The songs were particularly meaningful when I was afraid, desperate, or felt helpless. The words would minister to me and give me new strength. Now, I was again at the precipice of another physically, mentally, emotionally, and psychologically exhausting adventure. I had no idea how grueling it would be. But God kept giving me songs of comfort and strength.

An Attempt at the Impossible

Many high schools no longer have A Levels, but in my time, A Levels was an intense two-year preparation course for university after high school.

Rather than refer to the two years as Class 6 and Class 7 because they followed the high school Class 5, they were referred to as Lower and Upper Six. The first year of A Levels was referred to as Lower Six, and the second year as Upper Six. Students only focused on three subjects that were pivotal to the career path they were interested in pursuing at university. These subjects would be ones they'd excelled in at high school. That is why I was skeptical that I could succeed by being in classes with people who had studied science and excelled in it for five years.

I had absolutely zero knowledge of chemistry and physics. I didn't know what to expect, but I knew it was going to be very difficult. if not impossible. I was not familiar with failing, and the thought that it could happen scared me more than I can describe. I could see in my mind's eyes the sad faces of the few students who'd failed in my previous high school—the sense of disappointment, the loss of dreams, and the loss of hope written on their faces as they were asked not to return. The shame of being designated "not good enough" was traumatic as they packed their belongings at the school for the last time. Could that be my fate at St. Anne's? I was familiar with being the comforter, not the comforted. I was acquainted with sitting and empathizing with those girls who were expelled as they packed their suitcases to leave. I was familiar with being only on one side of this equation, the happy side, the comforting side; it had never occurred to me that I could be on the other side—until now. As petrified as I was, I was going to do anything and everything within my power to ensure I did not end up on that dreaded side. I sighed a prayer.

I settled in as classes started. My science student roommate had attended high school at St. Anne's. Therefore, this was her sixth year at the school, and she knew everything and everywhere and was able to tell me where to go for what. We arrived at the classroom after chapel and the textbooks were distributed. I was provided with A Level textbooks. I opened what I had. The books were written in English, but they may as well have been written in Greek because I had no idea what the discourse inside them was about. Then, the chemistry class started. As far as I was concerned, the teacher may as well have been speaking a foreign language as whatever he was saying made absolutely no sense to me.

My classmates did not believe I had never studied chemistry and physics at any level. They asked, "How could you have been admitted to be in the same class as us if you've never studied chemistry and physics when the program for those who were deficient in only physics was discontinued because the students did so poorly?" I told them I'd asked the principal that exact same question but never received an appropriate answer. As classes continued, my stress and frustration levels climbed exponentially. The principal's promise of special classes during the first year did not materialize.

I made an appointment to see the principal. I asked her about the preparatory classes I was supposed to have. She responded that she was having problems recruiting a teacher for those classes. However, she advised that, while waiting for the classes to start, I should continue to attend the lower six classes with all the lower six students. I couldn't believe my ears. I asked my house mistress for permission to use the phone to call my cousin. (I could not call my brother, as that would have been long distance.) I asked my cousin to please inform my brother that the promised preliminary "catch-up" classes have not materialized. So, he should please get me out of St. Anne's to a school where I could take classes for which I was qualified and prepared.

In those days, students couldn't just walk into a high school and ask to be admitted. The reasons were logical. The schools were all boarding schools and the fees were very high. Someone had to guarantee fee payment before the student could be admitted. I needed my brother to vouch for me at any school. However, he completely ignored my appeals. He believed I had whatever it would take to succeed, no matter how impossible the task. It's a very difficult thing when your ancestry includes a long line of very determined people who believe that people can reach the sky if they work at it hard enough. My brother Edet is one of them as was my Mom. So my fate was sealed. I was stuck at St. Anne's.

As the first week turned into a second, my frustration and anxiety continued to rise. I wanted to stop attending classes, but couldn't do that. No student was allowed to stay in the dorm during classes unless she was certified ill. As I contemplated and weighed my options the thought occurred to me to try and get Mom on my side. I knew that would be a herculean task, as she was probably the most intransigent of that long line of determined people from whence I descend. First, Mom would ask if someone had ever accomplished the seemingly impossible task. She did not accept flippant answers. You had to present the research and evidence that led to your conclusion. If you could not, tough luck, she would assume it had been done, therefore you could also do it unless you could present evidence that whoever did it had something extraordinary, such as having two heads instead of one. If whoever did it had one head just like you, then it was within the realm of possibility, and you should be able to do it.

Even if you could convince her that it had never been done, she would then say it was a great opportunity for you to be the first person to ever accomplish it. That would be her final stance, as she would not want to hear "any more whining." She would also remind you that she never gave birth to "a quitter," so you better "live up to your heritage." I knew I was stuck. I had almost no options, no recourse, no way out. But there was still a faint hope that Mom could understand this was not one of those circumstances where that argument applied. My chances did not look good, but she was my only hope.

I grabbed a pen and paper and poured out my heart to Mom. Thank God she was still alive. I knew it would take several weeks before the letter reached her, and even if she responded right away, it would take several more weeks for her response to arrive. No matter what her decision, it would already be too late as the first semester will almost be over. I sat down and wept and then put the letter in the outgoing mailbox. However, the very act of pouring out my hurt on paper to Mom was therapeutic. As I finished that letter, a small inner voice said to me; "After giving you the "two-head" challenge, you know what else she would also suggest, don't you?" I thought about that for a moment, and the words streamed through my mind: *Pray about it and ask God to help you.* Thank God for godly parents. That was the clue I needed. Instead of pouring my heart out to people, I began to pour it out to God. It is amazing how fervently you can pray when you are at a dead end—when everything is stripped away from you, and like Jacob of old, you are left alone to wrestle with God.

That was how I felt; alone. With everything I thought I had going for me stripped away, here I was in Western Nigeria, among a people whose culture, language, and way of doing things were very different from what I was accustomed to in the East. Under normal circumstances, this wouldn't have been a problem as I was eager to learn the language, try the food, and hopefully slowly become acclimatized. However, the one thing I couldn't stand to lose was my academic ability. All my life, I was accustomed to being an A+ student. It was all I knew. Now, that was being stripped from me. I felt like I'd lost my identity. A sense of helplessness and hopelessness seemed to encase me. I felt lost, disoriented, confused, and alone. I was miserable.

The Draw and the Encounter

There is a saying, "Misery loves company." But misery can also be jealous and scornful of happiness, while simultaneously being drawn to it. In my state of misery, I noticed a small group of girls who appeared supper happy. They seemed to love each other very much. Whenever they met each other, they would gush love all over each other, hugging, laughing, and enjoying each other's company. At first, I disliked them intensely. Why should anybody be happy when I was so miserable? What was there to be happy about in this place? It bothered me that they seemed so happy in a place where I was so miserable. However, even though I despised them, I was also drawn to them. During the few minutes that I watched them, I forgot about my own misery. So, I continued to watch them from a distance whenever possible. I longed for whatever they had but was not sure if it was real or how anybody could get it.

Then, one afternoon after classes, I saw many of them moving in a certain direction toward an empty junior classroom. Something made me follow them but at a distance. Before I knew it, I was no longer keeping my distance but was inside the classroom with them. I couldn't understand exactly what was happening. As I stood shoulder-to-shoulder with these girls, I heard the leader saying something, but the only words I remember hearing were, "Repent, repent of your sins and ask God to forgive you."

I had always considered myself a good girl. I had to be good to avoid God's punishment. I didn't think I needed much repentance as I considered myself a good person. If I happened to think that I had sinned, I would immediately repent and remind God of how good I had tried to be all along as the reason He should forgive me. But on this day, before my inner self-righteousness was able to raise its ugly head and tell God that I was not that bad, I heard a voice within me ask, *"Jane, why are you so miserable?"* I was startled. What was that and where did it come from?

I knew a lot of Scripture as my parents often made us memorize Bible passages. However, my relationship with God was that of fear and trepidation. Of all the years I had "known" Him, I'd lived in an unholy awe of Him. Many people regarded me as religious, a good Christian girl. But the problem was that I was trying to earn God's favor and I found myself continually falling short. I was still scared of Him, but I had hung around my parents and other spiritually alert people long enough to realize that the inner voice I was hearing was God's. What? Why was God speaking to me? Was I hearing God? Had I joined the crazy people?

God was at work and did not give me time to theologize and uphold my self-righteousness. He asked me again, *"Jane, why are you so miserable?"*

I pondered the question for a second or two and then responded, *"Why shouldn't I be miserable? Here I am in this place where all that I knew, all that had been familiar have been stripped from me, and the one thing that has always been my strength has now also been taken from me. I don't understand a word of what is taught in class. Who wouldn't be frustrated and miserable in that situation?"*

The voice responded, *"Is that it? Or is the source of your misery actually the fact that your pride has been hurt? Until now, you were usually the one to whom people who needed help with their schoolwork came. Now, you are the one going to others, and even then, you're not able to understand a word they're saying, no matter how simply they try to make it. Isn't the thought that this situation makes you appear stupid the real reason you are so miserable?"*

I knew I was "caught." I knew that was correct, and I agreed.

The voice continued. *"Have you ever considered that the ability to read and comprehend easily is a gift from me? Did you do anything to earn it? Have you ever genuinely given thanks for it? Don't you recognize that acting as if you did it all by yourself is pride and usurping my glory? I share my glory with no one."*

I was undone. I was filled with a sense of deep remorse and repentance. I felt the weight of a ton of sins weighing me down. I dropped to the floor and wept inconsolably. It appeared as if my heart was breaking as I saw myself and God in a very new light. I asked God to forgive me, remove that weight of sin from me and cleanse me. I asked Him to come into my heart. I told Him I would follow Him, serve Him, and walk with Him for the rest of my life. I cannot recall how long I was on that concrete floor or how long the transaction between God and me took. I was oblivious to anything and everything else that was happening in the room that afternoon. All I was aware of was my desperation for God. It was an encounter unlike any I ever had. I saw myself in my most wretched state and cried out for God's mercy and grace.

My transaction with God must have taken some time because by the time I came back to the land of the living, the meeting had long been over. Everyone was gone except for two girls, the leaders, who were waiting for me. They came over and asked if I had just given my life to God. With tears-flooded face, I nodded yes. They hugged me and gave me their names. But since they were not in my class or year (relationships were often built around cohorts in the same class or year), they asked if they could get someone in my year to follow up with me. I gave my consent. It was strange, but it seemed the Jane who'd dropped on that concrete floor that afternoon was very different from the one who rose from it. I cannot describe or explain exactly what transpired within me, but the stress and frustration were gone. A sense of peace enveloped me. I walked to my dorm as if I was walking on air.

That evening, two lovely Lower Six arts students visited me just as night prep classes were ending. We talked, and they asked if the three of us could get together every now and then. I agreed. That began a friendship and discipleship relationship that helped me grow in the Lord. Since life in the school was regimented (though nowhere near that of my previous high school) and their house was across the campus from mine, we decided to meet for prayers and worship on Saturday mornings at 5:00 a.m. in the amphitheater, which was a wooded area adjacent to the school. We had to walk quietly so as not to alert the night watchman.

This became our small group, just the three of us. It was a lifeline. The Holy Spirit was always present in a powerful way. The bond of love between the three of us was strong. We also joined the larger group of believers for Bible study and prayers on allotted days and times during the week, but that group of three was where we thrived.

None of us knew how much danger we faced by going to that amphitheater in the dark on Saturday mornings. About a year later when we had stopped meeting there, we discovered that drug dealers often met there, and if one stumbled onto them, they did not leave alive. God had protected us in our ignorance and desire to find a place to worship Him. It was a time of exponential growth in the Lord for the three of us.

Within a few days of my concrete classroom encounter with God, my roommates began to ask, "What has happened to you?" How come you appear so different from the girl we used to know? Why do you walk around with that silly grin on your face? Why are you so quiet all of a sudden?"

All I could say was that I did not quite understand it myself but that I'd had an encounter with God and had given my life to Christ.

He'd done something inside me that I didn't understand but that had changed my perspective and outlook on life.

Some of my roommates mocked and said, "Oh have you joined the 'Praise the Lord People'?"

That was when I learned that the happy people, whom I used to despise were nicknamed "Praise the Lord people." I thought; *That isn't such a bad name."*

The Lord Provides a Strategy

Ephesians 3:20–21 says: *Now to him who is able to do far more abundantly than all that we ask or think, according to the power at work within us, to him be glory in the church and in Christ Jesus throughout all generations, forever and ever. Amen.*

The Lord almost occupied my mind completely from that day forward. That was one thing that appeared very strange to my roommates. I spoke very little because, even when I was studying, somehow a part of my mind was focused on God. It seemed we had an ongoing conversation all the time, except when I was talking to someone else. So, when I was in the room with my roommates after classes, sometimes I appeared not to be present, as there was this unceasing dialogue going on inside, and I hated to disrupt it. All of a sudden, I began to love chemistry and physics classes because, since I didn't understand what was going on, my mind was fully focused on God. As I yielded my heart, thoughts, and life to Him and asked for His help, He gave me a strategy and a supernatural ability to understand chemistry and physics.

I felt led to acquire the earliest possible beginner chemistry and physics textbooks. Some of my classmates still had theirs and lent them to me. I devoured them with the intensity of a starving man who'd just stumbled onto a delicious feast. I found physics a little easier to comprehend, as some of its principles were exactly the same as those I'd learned in my one-student Additional Math class in my former high school. I saw God's hand in making my high school math teacher choose to teach me even when I was the only student and was reluctant about continuing the class. But God, who knows the end from the beginning, had foreseen how much I would need that class and prepared that teacher to jump through many hoops to teach me Additional Math. If I hadn't had that small foreknowledge of physics, getting through the first year at St. Anne's would have been much more difficult.

I do not think the ability to learn, comprehend, and excel in those two subjects within the time frame I had was mine. I don't think many human beings could accomplish such a feat on their own. It was really the Lord's supernatural doing. I cannot take credit for it. He supernaturally enabled me to grasp and understand what I was studying. All glory to His Great Name. The strategy was: when a topic was to be studied at A Levels, I would quickly learn that topic at the most basic level and then move up to the next level so I could follow at least some of what was happening in class. I was always in the library. I was there so much that the librarian made me an honorary assistant. When I look back and reminisce about my two years at St. Anne's, I find I do not have many memories outside the classroom and library; I just didn't have time to participate in other activities. Things such as sports, which I loved, had to be let go. I had been very good at high and long jump, and distance running, but could not afford the time to participate in them now, even though the school was very involved in sports. I also loved being in the choir; another activity St. Anne's excelled in but I had to let that go also because I could not spare the time.

By the end of that first semester, I had mastered the basics of chemistry and physics up to the Class Three level on my own. I bought and borrowed more of the higher-level texts and devoured them. By the end of the second semester, I was almost caught up with my classmates. However, I struggled with the laboratory aspects of chemistry and physics, especially chemistry. Fortunately, a University of Ibadan professor was from my hometown. His wife was a chemistry Ph.D. graduate student at the nearby University of Ibadan. She volunteered to teach me how to perform a few basic chemistry experiments. My brother obtained permission for me to leave the school on some Saturday afternoons to work with her on those experiments. Practicing those experiments was extremely helpful. There are no comparisons in fostering your understanding of the issue when you only read about what happens when you mix certain chemicals to actually doing it and seeing what happens. Performing those experiments greatly increased my understanding of chemistry.

Toward the end of the second semester, I was an integral part of the class. I was following the lessons and beginning to excel at tests. My classmates were astonished and confused.

Some asked, "Isn't this the girl who had never studied chemistry and physics before she got here?"

"Isn't she the one who could not understand anything we tried to explain to her no matter how simply we tried to explain it?"

"How is she able to understand the subject matter now just like the rest of us?"

Some responded, "Maybe she was lying when she said she hadn't studied the subjects before. It's not possible for someone who had never studied chemistry and physics at the O Level to catch up so quickly."

As the questions and confusion among my classmates grew, some said, "Haven't you noticed she has been studying like a monk and practically lives in the library?"

Others joined in with, "Haven't you noticed she has been borrowing lower-level texts in ever-increasing order?"

But whenever anyone had the courage to actually ask me, I always told them I was indeed the girl who had never studied chemistry and physics before the beginning of the school year. As to how I was able to excel in the two subjects within that short period of time, the only plausible explanation was divine intervention. There could be no other explanation. Many did not believe me, and some even mocked the idea. I felt like the blind man described in John 9:25 as he was being interrogated by the Pharisees. His answer was simple: *"I don't know whether he is a sinner,"* the man replied. *"But I know this: I was blind, and now I can see!"*

My answer was similar. I said, "I know I am the same girl and that, until I came to St. Anne's, I had never studied chemistry and physics. How I am now able to excel in them, I do not completely understand.

The only thing I understand is that God has intervened on my behalf. The result is what you see."

Whatever my classmates chose to believe was their problem. As for me, like Mary of Nazareth (Luke 1: 46–55), my heart overflowed with praise and gratitude to God for the mighty thing He had done for me and in me. My soul was filled with joy. As I review and reflect on this implausible demonstration of God's might, Zechariah 4:6(b)–7 comes to my mind: This is the word of the Lord to Zerubbabel: *"Not by might nor by power, but by my Spirit," says the Lord Almighty. What are you o mighty mountain? Before Zerubbabel you will become level ground. Then he will bring out the capstone to shouts of 'God bless it! God bless it!'"*

The impossible had become possible. My first year at St. Anne's School, Ibadan, in the same class with students who'd studied and excelled at chemistry and physics at the O Level came to an end. When the results of the final exams were out, I was in *awe* and *shock*. I knew I was almost caught up in the subjects, but the operative word was *almost*. What I was not aware of or prepared for was having the second-highest combined score for all the subjects in my class. I couldn't believe it. How was that possible? I didn't understand it, and I couldn't stop crying. These were tears of gratitude and amazement, of worship, thanksgiving, and joy. Who would have believed such a thing could happen? I was recognized and presented with awards at the year-end assembly for accomplishing the unthinkable. I couldn't comprehend how it happened, except that, with God, anything and everything is possible. The question was why He chose me and used me to show His glory. I have no answer except that His grace is overflowing and abundant, and He chose to lavish them on me.

I also participated in the J.F. Kennedy high school essay that year. I hadn't heard of the essay before and didn't know much about world affairs. I'd just emerged from the war zone, where we were cut off and isolated from the rest of the world for more than a year. After liberation, the only thing that mattered was studying so to attain the best possible score in my O Level exams. But I love challenges. When I heard of the JFK Essays, I decided to participate. I reasoned I had nothing to lose except the two hours spent writing the essay. I registered for it. There were no clues as to what the topic would be. Even if there were, I wouldn't have had the time to research it. Those were not the days of the internet and Google. Any research needed to be done manually in the Library.

When the day for the essay arrived, my first shock was the topic. I cannot recall the exact wording, but it was about the Organization for African Unity (OAU). I think I may have heard that name in passing somewhere, sometime before the war. But I didn't really know anything about it. After all, I was a kid then. I had no idea when it was founded, how it was funded, or where it was located. The only thing I could deduce from its name was that it was meant to aid and unite African nations. After staring at the topic for a few minutes, I had to make a decision. There were two options:

1. Stand up and walk out and let everyone know that I could not tackle the topic.
2. Let my imagination run wild about things an organization with such a name could do and what its role on the world stage could be.

I chose the second option and began to think. The Nigerian Civil War had just ended. What role could organizations like the OAU play in bringing about reconciliation between the two previously warring factions? There were conflicts between other African nations also. As an emerging market, Africa had much to offer the world and an organization such as the AOU could play a vital role in such areas. I loved the idea and started writing. As I was the only science student who participated in the essay from our school (the rest were history students), I was sure I wasn't going to win, but I loved the idea of letting my imagination run wild.

Imagine my shock when the results were out, and I had won second place. That was a miracle. I was on the miracle roll. To add to the praise and glory of God, the results of the competition came near the school's year-end awards. So, I was called to the podium for the Academic Excellence Award, the Resilience Award, and the JFK Essay Award. My name called in honor three times? If someone had told me during my first month at St. Anne's that such an honor could be bestowed on me, I would have asked to see what they were smoking. My name was everywhere worthwhile, everywhere honorable. It was like the old high school days again; my name being called in honor. When I had been forced to attend St. Anne's, I'd thought I would never hear my name honored again. I had come to terms with that. My only prayer was that it not be called in dishonor and failure, even though it would have been understandable if it were. Still, it would have broken my heart. Now, the reverse was the reality. How could God perform so many miracles for me? I had no answers, only tears of gratitude.

The year-end assembly and awards was a huge thing at St. Anne's. Parents, guardians, dignitaries, and prominent alumni were in attendance. Students who excelled in different areas were recognized and given awards. With three awards, my name was called three times. Each time as I walked up to the podium, I had to fight the tears welling up my eyes. I was in awe. How great is my God?

My brother Edet attended the assembly. He was beaming from ear to ear. In retrospect, I'm thankful to him for not listening to my plea to be removed from St. Anne's and from science and be placed at a school where I would focus on arts. I grew to love chemistry and physics. I think they facilitate the understanding of how the universe operates. They particularly gave me the foundation to understand wellness, something I've always been passionate about. As I went on to study Biochemistry in university, my love of science grew. Today, I cannot imagine how my love and enthusiasm for health, fitness, and wellness would have progressed without an understanding of the science behind them.

I think all my experiences at St. Anne's illustrates God's great love, provision for, and pursuit of me. He had to bring me to the place where all my crutches were stripped away, where I was desperate, to get my full attention and cause me to realize how much I needed Him. If I had continued to enjoy great success as I had previously, I probably would never have recognized my need for Him. I would have continued to think I was good enough for God as I was. I could have continued to rely on my good works as evidence that I had fulfilled the necessary requirements of God's law. I didn't know that, to be justified according to the law, one had to keep every aspect of all the laws all the time. One had to be absolutely perfect, and I don't think there's any human being who can keep all the rules and laws 100 percent every day of their lives. I am thankful that God brought me to a place where I could recognize my need for Him.

I am also amazed at how God prepared me for success years before it happened, by causing my O Level math teacher to advocate to continue teaching me Additional Math even though I was the only student in the class. The whole thing reminds me of Isaiah 45:2–3, which says: *I will go before you and will level the mountains; I will break down gates of bronze and cut through bars of iron. I will give you hidden treasures, riches stored in secret places, so that you may know that I am the Lord, the God of Israel, who summons you by name.*

It goes to show how much God cares about us. Even when I was not walking with Him, even when I thought I was good enough on my own and by my own good works, He loved me enough not to give up on me. God prepared a solution for the problems long before they were encountered, years before I ever anticipated facing them. How great is God; how amazing, caring, and, compassionate His ways?

If anyone reading this book is in a place of desperation, maybe God is trying to get your attention just as He got mine. Maybe he is trying to show Himself strong on your behalf (2 Chronicles 16:9). If you are in that place, please don't fight Him, rather, allow Him to show you His great love for you.

12

Getting to Know the Bridegroom

High school students (both O and A Levels) spent most of their teenage years (from eleven/twelve to eighteen/nineteen) in boarding schools. The school became the surrogate parent, taking care of all the teen years experiences. Since schools were faith-based, they catered to religious rights as well. These included confirmation classes, usually offered in the fourth high school year, when students were deemed mature enough to understand the history, meaning, and implications of this holy sacrament.

The war delayed my confirmation preparation, as it did for many of the Eastern girls who joined St. Anne's for A Levels. Each of us was asked if we had been confirmed, and if we hadn't, arrangements were made for us to join the confirmation preparation class. I was excited to take the class as I had developed a deep desire to know more about God, the sacrament of Holy Communion, and church membership since the day I had that encounter with the Lord.

I enrolled in the class as soon as it was available. It was taught by the wife of the Anglican Archbishop of Ibadan, who was the religious studies teacher for the school. I devoured the study materials like cheesecake. Bible passages I had read many times previously suddenly came alive. I was filled with wonder and awe about the significance of Jesus's life, death, and resurrection and how they related to me personally and my salvation. The Bible was no longer an archaic book filled with stories and events of long ago. It was now a book that had information, instructions, and directions relevant to me right here and now. I was fascinated by this new awareness and wanted to know more about the work of the Holy Spirit, the significance and symbolism of communion, and the intricacy by which bread and wine represented the true body and blood of Christ. In John 6:53: *So Jesus said again, "I tell you the truth, unless you eat the flesh of the Son of Man and drink his blood, you cannot have eternal life within you."*

What was served for communion was bread or wafers and wine. People ate bread and drank wine every day, so what made this particular bread and wine different from the others? I had heard of people being healed of illnesses and diseases just by participating in Holy Communion. I was intrigued by this sacrament and what made it so powerful.

Confirmation at St. Anne's School

Confirmation ceremonies were significant celebrations at St. Anne's. I was shocked at the elaborateness of some of the confirmand's receptions, a few of which surpassed moderate wedding receptions. My roommates who had attended St. Anne's for their O Levels informed me that what I saw was a scaled-down version of what it used to be.

It is important to note that Nigeria is a class-based society. In the West especially and almost everywhere in Nigeria now, one's social status is appraised by his or her display of opulence. One of the ways wealth and status are demonstrated is by the lavishness and priciness of one's attire and celebrations. In a school where all the students wore the same uniform, ate the same food, and participated in the same household tasks whether their parents were paupers or millionaires, finding a way to flaunt social status was arduous. Confirmation ceremonies then were the one and only opportunity for people to display their affluence.

Before my time at the school, parents were asked to provide confirmation outfits for their daughters. Some of the outfits were extravagant wedding gowns with trains so elaborate that people were tripping over them. But by my time, the outfit was a simple white cotton dress made by the same tailor who made all our uniforms and our veil was a piece of the same cotton broadcloth cut just long enough to cover our hair and drop down to our shoulders.

Confirmation in my former high school was a simple event. Parents were not even invited. Students took the classes, and when it was deemed that they were well-versed in church doctrine, they were confirmed during a Sunday service. The confirmands wore their regular Sunday uniforms. However, at St. Anne's, it was a completely different affair. Although the receptions and dresses had been reduced in their elaboration as already discussed, parents, not wanting their kids to be "out flaunted" by others, were front and center, making sure their daughters' celebrations were as lavish as they could make them.

My roommates informed me of the "protocol" and subtly indicated they would not like to eat cafeteria food that day since their roommate was confirming. They entertained the hope I was planning to have some "good food" delivered. I had to think about how I was going to accomplish their wish since my parents were several hundred miles away, and I had nowhere to cook for them. I explored what other Eastern confirmands were doing. Most were going to get snacks for their roommates. I decided to do the same but make my snacks classy hors d'oeuvres.

It's not that I was intending to prove or ascertain any social status. I already know who I am. My parents were middle class. We had enough for our needs and a little extra to help those in need. That was all we needed and we were thankful. Some people thought we were rich since my parents had enough money to meet our daily needs, could pay school fees for all their children and several relatives, pay for Mom's frequent hospital care, and still manage to have something to help those in desperate need who came to them for help. Such people did not know or understand that generosity and compassion have no relevance to the size of people's pockets, only the size of their hearts. However, whatever the perspective, I'd always been very sure of one thing no matter what the plumbline—we, the children of the Okpoyo-Amana family were very, very rich and blessed.

Let me explain. Before the war started, Dad was planning to retire from his teaching job within a few years. He'd started renovating our house in our hometown for this purpose as once he retired, there would be no employment-provided accommodation. Then the war came, and the small egg nest he had built up for his retirement disappeared with the closing of the banks. Dad had to postpone his retirement and remain at work for many more years. Many people in such situations would have focused on rebuilding their retirement egg nest, but for my parents, their kids always came first. They believed the best gift they could give their children was a good education and a godly upbringing. So, when the war made the tools that fostered good education for me difficult in the East, they teamed up with my brother Edet to send me to the West so I could access the best possible education.

St. Anne's was a very expensive school. They could have placed me in one of the less expensive ones, but my parents and brother did not mind making the sacrifice needed for me to be at St. Anne's. Therefore, even though I faced what I considered an impossible task, I worked very, very hard to reward their sacrifice and tried as much as possible not to ask for anything extra that involved money, unless it was absolutely necessary. I was aware of the sacrifice already being made by the family on my behalf.

My brother Edet, who'd almost died just over a year earlier, was still recovering from his near-death injuries. Some in that situation would have focused solely on themselves and tried to recover what they'd lost during the terrible accident. He didn't do that. Rather, he spared no effort in helping me get into the best school possible, regardless of the expense. I think people who are blessed with parents and siblings who love them so extravagantly that they would stop at nothing, not even great inconveniences to themselves, and who are willing to deny themselves many comforts just to provide the best possible opportunities in life for their family cannot be poor. In fact, I considered such people extremely rich; rich with true wealth, the type that no amount of money can buy. Therefore, I had always considered my siblings and myself to be extremely rich and blessed with amazing parents who taught and demonstrated sacrificial love and the importance of family cohesiveness. I consider these some of the best gifts and legacies parents can leave their children.

For these reasons, I wasn't interested in the status-showing escapades unfolding at St. Anne's. I already knew my status. I had wealth in its truest form, one far superior to showy clothing and profuse edibles. But as a teenager in a school with hundreds of other teenagers, you never wanted to be the odd person out, especially at celebrations. So, when my roommates indicated they were looking forward to a nice dinner, I thought I would surprise them, not with the jollof rice most would be passing around since I had no way to cook or buy that, but with nice hors d'oeuvres

I needed to have an outing to make arrangements for those hors d'oeuvres. I had another need. I had shed many pounds since I arrived at St. Anne's because not only was some of the food unfamiliar or unappetizing to me, my misery and stress due to my chemistry and physics situation were not amenable to great appetite. In addition, my focus on studying day and night to catch up made hunger pangs less noticeable. The end result was the making of a very thin girl.

My brother Edet had bought me some nice outfits when I'd first arrived in the West a few months earlier. They replaced the outgrown and ill-fitting homemade war enclave clothes I'd brought. These beautiful outfits had fitted perfectly when they were purchased, but now they hung on my much thinner frame like an oversized gown on a scarecrow. I needed to have them resized so I could wear one after the confirmation ceremony when confirmands were allowed to change into their own clothing for pictures. During a previous school outing, I'd taken them to a tailor to resize. I needed to go back and try them on to ensure they were properly resized before retrieving them. I was in for a very major shock and disappointment.

Permission Denied

At St. Anne's, the A Level students had the privilege of having an outing for several hours on designated Saturday afternoons. The final-year O Level students had the same privilege but on a less frequent basis. However, students didn't just leave the school. Each student had to request and obtain an *exeat* from the house mistress before she could leave the school. This was more or less a formality for accountability as every entitled student generally received permission unless she was under punishment for doing something very bad. Since the school gate was always closed and with a gateman sitting beside it, there was a time to leave and a time to return. Students had to wear the school uniform and beret the entire time they were out and uphold the "impeccable reputation" of the school in whatever they did.

As the confirmation date approached, this privilege was curtailed for confirmands, except for students who were not from Ibadan (the city where the school was located), and those who did not have close relatives in town. The principal said restricting confirmands' outing privileges was a means of curtailing the planning of elaborate celebrations. I didn't understand how curtailing exeats for confirmands could control this problem. After all, parents of confirmands who lived in Ibadan or nearby visited their children regularly and would have had opportunities to discuss and plan the celebration itinerary with them. As I did not belong to either of the two targeted groups, I didn't give the issue any thought, as I assumed it would not impact me.

My surprise came when I went to request an exeat. It was denied. I asked why. My housemistress said, even though I was from the East and should qualify for one, she remembered I had a relative in town. I explained that my relative was a fourth cousin. Even though they sometimes asked to see me when they visited their two daughters, they were neither my parents nor close relatives, and would not be planning an elaborate reception for me. Also, their own two daughters were also confirming; if they were planning elaborate receptions, it would be for their daughters, not me. Furthermore, I argued that almost everyone in the school had someone in town who vouched for them as students as they couldn't be admitted without an adult guaranteeing the payment of their fees. Therefore, every girl in the school from the east had a relative in town. Why was I the only one selected for exeat refusal?

My parents were in the east, several hundred miles away, and we'd just emerged from a civil war, during which my father lost all his money when the banks closed and the records were destroyed. Why would my parents spend whatever little money they had on an elaborate reception? Where would I cook the food or who would cook it for me? To me, the reason for denying me an exeat seemed incomprehensible. It didn't make any sense. I added that my most important reason for wanting to go out was to retrieve the outfits I'd given a tailor for resizing, as I had lost much weight since I'd arrived at the school.

She said I should ask someone else to retrieve the clothing for me. Whom did I have who could do that? I couldn't ask my cousin or his wife to leave their jobs and kids to retrieve my clothing. Besides, I needed to try them on to ensure they were appropriately adjusted before paying for the work and collecting them. She said those were not convincing arguments.

I couldn't believe my ears. I appealed to the principal and was again denied an exeat—for the same reasons the housemistress had given. I couldn't understand what was happening. I prayed desperately for God's intervention so there would be a reversal of the decision. I reminded God of how important it was for me to retrieve those outfits, but heaven seemed closed, or on vacation. Not a sound or gesture of any kind appeared forthcoming in response to my plea.

I was quite disappointed when it was clear the door against my obtaining an exeat was firmly shut and bolted. The refusal meant I would have nothing to wear for pictures and nothing to give my roommates. However, in spite of all this, I was filled with inexplicable joy. There was a sense of anticipation in my soul, I felt like I was marrying the love of my life. The joy and excitement in my soul were so deep I could hardly contain them. Yet ever so often, when I remembered I would probably be the only one among all the confirmands who would have nothing to give anyone and who would also have nothing to wear for pictures, I was a little sad. How can the same person feel disappointed and yet be so full of joy at the same time? I could not understand it.

There was one thing I looked forward to in the confirmation; it was the section of the ceremony where each confirmand had to respond to the bishop's question about her intention to follow Christ all her life. That was exhilarating to me. I had made the decision to follow Christ wholly just a few months earlier on that cold concrete classroom floor, and since then, my heart had been filled with unexplainable joy. Confirmands also had to affirm their intention to forsake the world, follow Christ, live as His faithful disciples for the rest of their lives, and completely belong to Him. That was my heart's desire, and I could not wait to affirm and declare that to the entire world at the confirmation ceremony.

The Ceremony

The confirmation day finally arrived. I was very excited. I remembered Luke 12:8, where the Lord said: *I tell you the truth, everyone who acknowledges me publicly here on earth, the Son of Man will also acknowledge in the presence of God's angels.*

I wanted everyone to hear and know about what had happened to me and in me. I wanted them to know I belonged to Christ completely. I looked forward to participating in Holy Communion for the first time. The time arrived for the confirmands to march into the chapel and take their seats on the front pews. We all filed in, dressed in our white confirmation dresses and veils. All the families were there, and the place was overcrowded and packed with parents and relatives. My brother had made a long journey from Lagos to be present.

Then the time came for us to go forward, row by row; kneel at the altar; and respond with, "I do," to the Archbishop's question about our desire to be dedicated to Christ and His church. The turn for my pew came, and we went up to the altar. As I knelt at that altar, the person before me was not the Archbishop, it was my Lord Jesus Christ. His clothing was dazzling and radiating with light and life. He asked me, "Do you really mean that you want to be wholly mine?"

"Yes, my Lord," I responded.

The brightness of His presence blinded me. I felt weak and as if I was burning up inside. I have no memory of how I returned to my seat; nor do I have memory of the rest of the service. All I remembered was His presence, the overwhelming desire to worship Him, and the intensity of the worship that was pouring out from my soul.

My next recollection was being outside the chapel. As my eyes adjusted to earthly light, I saw my brother Edet pushing through the crowd toward me. I moved toward him too and gave him a huge hug. He took pictures of me in my confirmation dress and then I found my confirmand cousins and we took pictures with them and their parents.

Then I had to go to my dorm to change into personal clothes.

Instructions from James 1:2–4

As the Lord would have it, I had an old, pleated skirt with belt loops. When I was denied the Exeat, and it was clear I was not going to retrieve my nicer outfits, I resigned myself to wearing the skirt and a blouse. I ironed the boxed pleats well to make the skirt look smaller and fit better. I found a blouse that matched the skirt, and neither appeared overly large due to the style. Belts are amazing, they hold things together and make them appear to fit. I was thankful I had this skirt and blouse to wear

I arrived back at my dorm and changed into the blouse and skirt. They looked awesome. Anything would have looked awesome on me on that day because I was so very happy. I found my brother and we took more pictures with him and my cousins. As we visited, my brother noticed that other confirmands were passing around food, desserts, baking, chocolates, sweets, and on and on. He also noticed that our cousin had brought food, baking, and drinks for their confirming daughters to give to friends. He asked why I had not told him I needed those things. I said they were not important to me, and I didn't think I should bother him with them, especially as he had already done so much for me and had to make a whole day's journey to be there. His presence there meant more to me than anything he could have brought.

He thought for a moment and then said, "I will be right back."

He went into town to buy baking and packaged food to bring back for me to give out, but he could not find a restaurant that had what he deemed appropriate or was willing to package them for him to bring back to the school. He was flabbergasted, as that was most unusual. Ibadan is a bulging commercial city. For restaurants with classy hors d'oeuvres to be unwilling to package some for him was unimaginable. He returned to the school shaking his head.

I was filled with joy and peace, although a little sad that I could not give my roommates anything to celebrate my confirmation. However, I was not going to let that ruin my special day. There was great joy in my soul, and my face radiated peace. After my brother left, I tried to find a place for a little peace and quiet to pray. No such luck. All the classrooms and halls were locked. I had to go back to my room and face my roommates' disappointment. After visiting with their daughter, my cousin and his wife stopped by my dorm for a short visit. They noticed I did not have anything to give away. They went back to their daughter's dorm and retrieved a little bit of baking that had not yet been given away and brought them to me. I gave them to my roommates. They did not think it was enough. That was just a little baking, they wanted food.

Meanwhile, the confirmands from our house were distributing meals, sweets, baking, pop, and all sorts of other edibles. I asked my roommates to have my portion of these, as I was not even hungry. They refused, as they also had the same things. In fact, they could not eat all the food that was being distributed. But that did not stop them from harassing me about not providing them with food as part of the celebration.

I was surprised. Usually, my roommates were very nice, understanding, and friendly. We got along very well. They knew about my having been denied the exeat and how that was the reason I didn't have anything to give them. Before the confirmation day, they were sympathetic to my plight and had not supported the housemistress and principal's decision. One of them had gone out of their way to help me acquire lower-level chemistry and physics textbooks so I didn't have to purchase all of them. I was indebted to these girls because they were so good to me. They were even considerate enough to curtail how much Yoruba (their language) they spoke in the dorm since I didn't understand it, even though I encouraged them to speak it so I could learn it. But they didn't think it was right for me to be left out of conversations. That was how nice these girls were, all five of them. They were the kindest girls until that day of confirmation.

Why the sudden change in attitude? Did loving and following Jesus come with a joy that was intermingled with pain? As I weighed the pros and cons of my decision to follow Him, the conclusion was that He was worth much more to me than the rejection by friends. I considered this a small price to pay for the overwhelming greatness and joy of knowing and belonging to Jesus.

This Thing Is from Me

I was glad when the confirmation day came to an end. There had been more than enough excitement and drama for one day. At last, everywhere grew quiet. I crawled into bed and began to worship quietly in my heart. My heart was so full of gratitude and joy I thought it would explode. I was finally completely His. I had publicly declared my allegiance and devotion to Jesus. I was thankful He had chosen me and preserved me till that day.

Suddenly, my roommates seemed to have disappeared and I was alone with a magnificent presence that filled the room. I found myself enclosed within God's heart. All of me was inside His heart, except for my head, which stuck out through what would be the jugular notch in human anatomy. He seemed to be partially reclined on my bed, with His shoulders leaning against the wall, as people would do if they were leaning against their headboard to read.

Waves and waves of intense fire mixed with fierce love began to gush and sweep over me. The waves were so intense, the fire so hot I thought my heart and soul were burning up. Everything in me longed for more of whatever that was, yet also dreaded it intensely. I could not breathe; I had no strength. I thought my lungs were burning up and my heart was going to explode due to the love and joy that was poured into it. I felt like I was going to die because I could not breathe and felt so very, very weak.

Then I heard these words which I believe were God's. He said, *"This thing is from me. I was the one who caused you to be denied the exeat. I was the one who made your brother not find anything to buy to bring for you to give away. Today, you were betrothed to me; I did not want to share you with anyone. I wanted all your focus to be on me. For many, this was all about the ceremony and the chance to show off their fancy dresses and the wealth of their family. They did not even consider me. Many of them never gave a thought to the words they and the Archbishop were saying. To them, this was all just a process, a means to get to the celebration. For you, it was different. I wanted to be the only one on your mind. You are now dedicated to me. I want you to experience my love and know how deep it is."*

I don't remember the rest of the night. The presence and the words burned into my soul. I felt so exhausted I didn't think I had enough energy to draw air into my lungs. My lungs were on fire, burning up, leaving no room for air. The fire was intense and yet comforting. Again, I longed for more even as I dreaded what would happen if I received more. I felt I was going to explode. How could such extreme joy and extreme trepidation exist so powerfully in one person at the same time?

The voice whispered, *"I want you to experience my love and then show it to others. It is not cheap love; it cost me my son. You need to learn how to give it even amid persecution. That is what causes the world to take notice. You will be facing some extraordinary times, but always remember that I am with you and will strengthen you and enable you to accomplish my will. Be strong, be very strong, for the trial will not last long."*

It was a great relief when morning finally came and I was still in the land of the living.

Then something very strange began to happen. The immediate clue was that the harassing behavior of my roommates intensified. There was something about my face that bothered them. They asked what had happened to me. I didn't know how to respond. I couldn't tell them about the vision. How could I? I didn't understand it myself.

How would I expect them to understand? Was that even what they were asking? Then they became explicit and asked me to "wipe that stupid grin off your face." I didn't even know I had "a stupid grin" on my face.

What was most painful to me was that my closest friend joined in this attack. In the days following, she started distancing herself from me and wouldn't let me walk beside her to and from classes as we previously did. Since I'd arrived at the school, she had been my right hand. We were the only two lower six science students from the house. The two of us did everything together and, within a short time, had become such close friends that we were nicknamed David and Johnathan. She had gone with me to the housemistress for the exeat before the confirmation ceremony. She knew the entire story and was sympathetic to my plight. She was a very gentle and kind person by nature; how could she turn on me on my special day and the days following? It was a mystery and out of character for her.

We had been very, very close friends. At any time day or night, if we weren't together, she always knew exactly where I was and what I was doing, and I knew the same about her. Her decision to have nothing to do with me was painful. I had become accustomed to her presence except when I was in the library. However, the Lord told me that this turmoil in the relationship was just the beginning. He said if I was truly going to be His disciple, there would be many more rejections, many more people who would want nothing to do with me. I should get used to it. He also added that I must learn to love those people extravagantly. The "loving extravagantly" part was too lofty for me to understand.

In all my years of growing up in the church, I had often heard "an eye for an eye, and a tooth for a tooth." "Extravagantly loving those who hate you" was a new and very difficult concept for me. How could I love extravagantly someone who didn't love me and who was trying to hurt me? I told God that was a very hard thing, and I had no idea if it was possible and how it would emanate. He said He knew but He would give me all the grace I needed. He provided me with several opportunities to practice showing love to my roommates, especially my best friend, Helen. I was beginning to learn what it meant to "die to self and pick up my cross daily" to follow Him. My actions began to impact my roommates.

One of them said one day, "Something real has happened to this girl. She is not the same girl we used to know."

A different roommate responded, "Yes, she has changed all right, but she has become an idiot and a fool."

I had the impression that the Lord was saying to me, "No matter what they say to you, never defend yourself, never get angry, and never give a retort. Just let Me handle it all for you."

I said, "Yes, Lord."

The problem was that He did not seem to be doing anything—and I was being dumped on every day. However, He gave me such joy and peace that whatever was being done to me on the outside seemed trivial compared to the overwhelming joy and peace I had on the inside.

Under Divine Tutelage

The weeks that followed my confirmation were physically lonely ones. I had been so accustomed to having Helen around that when she decided to have nothing to do with me, it seemed like a part of me was missing. I would walk the same route we used to walk together to class alone now.

At first, I was a little sad. But then the Holy Spirit began to invade me. He would start singing in me, and I would join in. Together, we would sing and worship in my heart as I walked to class. Many of the songs were from the Methodist Hymn Book. Sometimes we do things without really understanding why we're doing them. I'd memorized several songs from the Methodist Hymn Book during the war, partially as a result of singing some over and over again and partly as a way to occupy time. Then, they were not very meaningful. Now they instigated worship from my heart, His glory filling me from top to bottom within the five minutes it took me to walk from the dorm to the classroom in the morning and from the classroom back to the dorm after classes.

Could it be that the Lord had looked into the space of time and, to prepare me for this moment, caused me to learn and memorize those songs? The words often obliterated the feeling of being alone, as the

Holy Spirit walked with me and let me know that I was not alone. He seemed to be continuously ministering to me. Whenever I focused on what was happening on the inside and shut out the happenings on the outside, I would notice that there were rejoicing, worship, and waves of God's love washing over me, overflowing and filling my entire being.

It is difficult sometimes to comprehend, or correctly appraise what the Lord is doing when it is happening. This is particularly salient when our eyes are focused on our own discomfort rather than on Him as our focus dictates our perception. However, when the task is accomplished, if we dare take a moment to evaluate the outcomes, we would often be flabbergasted at what the Lord has done. We could find what we had perceived to be a closed and silent heaven to actually be a very busy one working steadfastly on our behalf.

We fail to receive this kind of revelation sometimes because we're tuned into the wrong channel, the channel of self-focus and self-pity, the one that renders our treatment of God as an errand boy or sugar daddy, someone there just to respond to and answer our prayers, rather than the Maker of the Universe. I did not quite understand worship and what it meant to live in His presence. The Lord is so good, He caused me to be isolated so He could spend some precious, intimate, and formative time with me, pour into me, and build me up. Even when He had forewarned me in the vision, "This thing is from Me," I still did not understand when it was happening. As I write, I have walked with the Lord now for decades but have never again experienced such close intimacy, such continuous dialogue, such a wonderful friendship, and such a love affair with Him. It is precious to be friends with God. He is an incredible lover.

The importance of carving out that time of peace and quiet personal communication and intimacy with God is not easily appreciated until one surveys the context. In any place inhabited by several hundred teenage girls, with half a dozen girls sharing a room, it is very difficult to find a place or space to be alone, especially when time is all scheduled with specific activities and tasks. Therefore, causing me to be alone and walk by myself from the dorm to the classroom in the morning and from the classroom back to the dorm after school was a deliberate gift. Those were divinely appointed times when the Lord and I were in deep communication, a focused time when He could pour into me.

Within days, the feeling of missing my best friend had diminished significantly. I now had a "new best friend," whom I loved much more and whose company I treasured much more than the previous one. I became very fond of and looked forward to those walks. They were intimate and soul-satisfying. It was a sweet time of worship. I was growing in my knowledge of Him, and He was preparing and training me for the tasks He would entrust to me in a little while.

The First Assignment

Within about a month after the confirmation, I sensed that the Lord was saying to me, "You have to speak to Helen about me."

"What? Lord, how is that possible? As you've seen, she's asked me never to speak to her or have anything to do with her. Have you forgotten that, whenever I try to speak to her, she either ignores me or berates me? Haven't you also noticed that she doesn't want me to be anywhere near her? If she's walking to class and I try to catch up with her to walk beside her, as was our practice previously, she will run. If I were to also run and catch up to her, then she would stand still or start walking in the opposite direction? Have you not noticed that she would do anything to avoid me? How can I speak to someone to whom I cannot be near?" I responded.

"Can you trust Me?" He seemed to ask.

"OK, Lord, I can and will trust you, but you have to be the one to set this up and do all the talking."

Again, the answer was, "Can you trust Me?"

Again, I answered, "Yes, Lord, I am willing. But this is something new to me. I would have no idea what to do or what to say. You have to do this. Please help me."

From that day onward, I looked for opportunities to speak to Helen. None opened up. She continued to avoid me and treat me like a leper.

On weekdays, students went back to their classrooms after supper for a few hours to complete assignments and prepare for the next day's lessons. It was called "prep." The length of prep varied with the class. The junior girls in classes one and two had less than an hour of prep. After this, they returned to their dorms and went to sleep. The A Level students had the longest prep time. We were allowed to stay in the classrooms till 9:00 or 9:30, as long as we were back in our dorms and ready for lights out at 10:00 p.m.

One prep night, I had the impression that the Lord was saying to me, "You have to speak to Helen tonight."

I prayed: *Lord if this is you asking me to speak to Helen tonight, please cause her to leave prep early, so we can have the privacy to talk. Also, Lord, as she is leaving if I say, "Helen please wait for me," cause her to wait.*

Considering the state of our relationship in the past few weeks, I thought the probability of her agreeing to wait for me was next to zero. So, I was almost sure I was off the hook. I had barely finished praying when I saw Helen gather her books and start to walk toward the door. My heart began to pound. Could this be the Lord telling me that this was the right time to connect with Helen?

With great trepidation and heart pounding, I called out, "Helen, please, can you wait for me?" To my utter astonishment and shock, she turned and waited. My heart, which had been pounding since the Lord spoke to me that evening, added racing to the pounding. The pounding was so loud that I was afraid others around me could hear it. I quickly gathered my books, and together we began to walk toward the door. I couldn't believe this was happening. I didn't know what to do or where to start, but I prayed silently and asked the Lord, who had asked me to trust Him, to perform the miracle.

Within a short while, Helen struck up a conversation. I can't recall exactly what it was about because my mind was focused on trying to hear what the Lord was saying to me. However, I do recall it had something to do with religion. She was a very religious girl.

She said something, and I responded with, "Helen, that used to be true of you. Can you say it's still true of you today?"

All of a sudden, she started to weep. She sobbed as if something deep was happening in her. I didn't know what to do but continued to pray silently. I put my arms around her. After a while, she wiped her tears and confessed that the transformation in me had impacted and convicted her. But she'd fought it, as she didn't want to become a "fanatic" like me. She apologized for the way she'd been treating me. We both wept over each other and said how much we'd missed each other. I then began to share the Lord with her.

She repented and asked Him into her heart that night. We were both filled with joy. We hurried to the dorm to pray together before the rest of our roommates returned from prep. We made this a pattern. We would leave prep early so we could have the room to ourselves to pray and share before our roommates returned.

The Jesus Breakout

We found the practice of leaving prep early and spending time in worship and prayer very uplifting. We never invited anyone to join us at any time. But slowly, somehow, other students noticed us and began to come and stand outside our room and watch us pray. Then some started coming inside to pray with us. Before we knew it, our room couldn't contain all the people who wanted to pray with us. I don't recall us ever sharing the gospel individually with any of them. We just prayed and asked the Lord to touch the hearts of the people who needed salvation and cause them to receive Him. We only prayed, and the power of God would fall on the students as they came into the room; many would start to weep and give their lives to Jesus. Some of our roommates wanted to know what had happened to us. We shared with them what the Lord had done in our lives. Some repented and turned to the Lord.

Within a short time, our room became the center of revival at the school. Many students gave their lives to Jesus. Some then wrote to their parents and asked them to repent of their sins. Before long, parents were calling the school to ask what was going on. Some of the activity was traced to our room. We were summoned to the house prefect and then the housemistress's office for questioning. We told them all we had done was pray in our room, that we never invited anybody to join us. All who did, have done so of their own free will. Furthermore, we never asked anyone to receive Jesus; we just prayed, and those who received Him did so entirely on their own.

People who had attended the prayers were also questioned, and their stories were consistent with ours. We had not invited them. They'd come on their own volition. We never gave an altar call. Those who received the Lord had done so freely. So, there was no fault found in us. There were no grounds to find us guilty of any offense, but the principal issued an edict banning prayer or evangelization in the dorm. The only place where prayer was allowed was the chapel, and we were allowed in it only in the morning on weekdays for prayers before classes and on Sundays for service.

That was the law, but some who had genuinely experienced salvation persisted. The Lord gave us wisdom on how to encourage each other without breaking the rules. Our small Praise the Lord group of believers, through whom I'd come to the Lord, continued to meet. But our freedom to meet at will was curtailed. This was an Anglican school, so religion couldn't be completely banned. The church would have been uncomfortable if such a thing were to happen. As far as the church was concerned, it was important to have some religion in the school but not too much of it.

Furthermore, it was important that the type of religion be one that didn't involve bringing people to repentance and experiencing a close walk with God. That was too much religion, and there was no room for it at the school and even at the church. The official religious group of the school was the Scripture Union. So, it was affirmed that it was the only group allowed to hold meetings.

Many of the members of the Scripture Union were just religious and not saved. But when their meetings became the only one believers could attend, and as the number of true believers who joined them grew, the religious people felt uncomfortable. Some came to know the Lord, and others who did not want to do so desisted from the organization. Believers then took over. We formed a strong connection with the nearby University of Ibadan and the Bible College Students' Scripture Unions. As they discipled us, we grew both in the knowledge of the Lord and in numbers. The Lord has a way of turning what the enemy planned for evil into good.

13

Decisions That Impacted Destiny

My time at St. Anne's went by like a whirlwind and at the end of the two years, I wrote the A Level exam in December with my peers. High school was over. I went to stay with my sister Adiaha and her family who had returned from London and were living at Ibadan. With the arduous task of trying to conquer chemistry and physics almost behind me, it would have been nice to relax and put my feet up for a few days. There was no such luxury in my plan.

Not only had I registered to write the West African A Level exam, I had also registered for the London A Level exam in January as well. Since the West African A Level exam was the first comprehensive science exam I would have written, I thought it prudent to also write the London A levels in the hope that I would gain some insights from the first exam that could help me improve my grades on the London exam, thereby enhancing my chances of gaining university admission. The London A level was a worldwide exam. Many students in English-speaking countries all over the world wrote the same exam. So, I reviewed the syllabus carefully to ensure, as much as I was able, that I was adept at every detail of the requirements and processes. Scores from the London A levels were highly regarded; a good score would boost my chances of being accepted at the university of my choice. So as soon as I arrived at my sister's home, I hit the books again with a vengeance.

The ability to gain admission into a university in Nigeria at that time was onerous and competitive. There were only five universities in the country with a population of more than 81 million people. The three-year Nigerian Civil War had ended less than two years earlier and the university in the east was almost completely destroyed during the war. Even if it was an option to attend there, I would not have wanted to return to the East. Two of the remaining four were Western state universities. As I was not an indigent of the West, and these two universities' first loyalties were to the people from their state, being accepted into a program there would be unlikely. Of the two federal universities, one specialized and focused on engineering and the technical sciences. As I was interested in the medical sciences, I was left essentially with just one choice, the University of Ibadan (UI). This was the Nigerian premiere university, and degrees issued by it were very highly regarded. Needless to say, the competition was very fierce.

After a month of intense study, the days finally arrived to write the exam … and then it was over. The thing to do now was to look for a job while I awaited the exam results and the beginning of the university year in the fall. Employers needing short-term /temporary help were most sought after by such students. Interviews were often done in December for a January start. I didn't want to spend my December job hunting. I wanted to focus on studying for the London exam. I had completed three applications for jobs at Lagos before I left St. Anne's, with the intention of staying there with my brother Edet, and working during the eight months. However, he moved to Calabar in the East to start an engineering consulting firm that December, so after completing the London exams, I aggressively began a job hunt in Ibadan.

Starting a job hunt after the second week of January put me at a huge disadvantage, as most short-term jobs would already be gone. I searched the newspapers and found only one suitable vacancy. It was in a law firm and I sent in my application letter and résumé right away. I also sent in an application to the Biochemistry lab at the University Hospital where my friend Helen had already started working even though they had not advertised an opening. The hospital told me right away they didn't have a vacancy, but would keep my résumé just in case something came up.

By the end of the week, I received an interview request from the law firm. I was thrilled but also apprehensive as I'd never attended a job interview before. How should I prepare? This was new territory. *Heaven, please help me,* I prayed. I asked some of my friends who were already working and received their tips with gratitude. The day finally arrived for the interview and I presented myself at the appointed time.

The firm had five lawyers. They had just installed a new, modern telephone system, which was quite complicated, and they'd had problems finding a receptionist who could master it. When they viewed my résumé and noticed that I'd learned seven years of chemistry and physics in two years, they were sure I could master the phone system with ease. They were right.

Two days after the interview, I received a call informing me I'd been selected for the job. The salary offer was good. I was ecstatic

The Retreat with Divine Appointment

The church I attended during holidays from St. Anne's was a makeshift gathering of believers. It only existed on Sundays and on some weekday evenings if there was a prayer meeting or something special happening. Normally, the facility was the lecture auditorium for the UCH nursing students' lectures. On Sunday mornings, it was transformed into a church. Therefore, there was always a need for some people to be there early to set up the chairs and pulpit before service and put them back into storage after. I liked this church because it was "alive."

During my first year at St. Anne's, I attended this church because it was only three blocks from my sister Adiaha's residence and I spent my holidays with her and her family. I continued to attend after my sister and her family moved from the hospital residence to consultant staff residences when her husband became a Consultant.

During the time between my exiting St. Anne's and the exams and before beginning work, the church held a weeklong retreat. The retreat was at a perfect time for me. I needed to relax and refuel in the Lord after all the studying and exams. Since I was not working yet, I had time and decided to help with the setup and take down for the retreat each night. Therefore, I arrived at the auditorium early each night. On the opening night of the retreat, I was the first person to arrive at the auditorium. The storage room was locked, so I could do nothing but wait for the organizers to arrive. Shortly after, Asukwo, arrived. He had been my brother Mfon's schoolmate in high school and we realized the connection one Sunday when Mfon, visiting Ibadan from London, attended the church with me.

Asukwo was part of the organizing committee and as we exchanged greetings, another young man, the prayer secretary, arrived. I had heard this guy's name announced many times during services as the go-to person for many things but had never met him. Asukwo introduced him.

"Jane, this is Chris Ekong."

"Oh, you are the Chris Ekong. So nice to meet you. I have heard your name mentioned several times during announcements when I attend services here. It's nice to put a face to the name."

He returned the greeting, and we engaged in a little small talk.

Then I said, "You know, I have a confession that's really funny."

Everyone's ears perked up.

"I had always thought Chris Ekong was a girl, a lady."

"What?" he exclaimed. "What made you think that?"

"Not anything you did," I said. "It's just that, until today, until this very moment, every Chris I've ever known has been a girl. So, when I heard the name Chris, I just assumed the person was a girl. Now, I will readjust my way of thinking about the name."

"You'd better," he said with a smile.

We all laughed and started taking out the chairs and setting them up.

Other people arrived, and within a short time, the set-up was complete.

At the end of the service, I stayed back to help put away the chairs and pamphlets, as did Chris and the other organizers. When all was done, I picked up my stuff and started leaving. Chris walked up to me and asked where I was heading. I told him. He asked if he could give me a ride. I paused briefly and then politely declined. He persisted, but my "no" was firm. Being alone in a car with a non-close relative male, was absolutely against my Mom's rules. Even though she was a few hundred miles away, and I was sure Chris was a very fine Christian young man, I felt this was one of those rules I should never break. I told Chris I very much appreciated his kindness and offer, but I preferred to take a taxi. He asked if I would be back the next night. I said it was likely. We went our different ways.

The next day, I came early and so did Chris. We chatted as we put out the chairs and placed designated pamphlets and tracts on seats. After the service, a few of us, including Chris, stayed back to put away chairs and tidy up again before leaving. I started heading for the door and Chris appeared and asked again if he could give me a ride. I declined. He asked if he could give me a ride to the taxi park, which was about a kilometer away. I declined that too. I told him I preferred to walk since we had been sitting for quite a while during the service.

This encounter and dialogue continued every night for the rest of the five-day retreat. On the last night, Chris asked if he could ask me out. I said, "No" but explained that I had nothing against him; I'd been extremely busy studying for both my West African and London A Level exams, which had just ended, and I'd be starting a job the following Monday. I needed time to regain my breath. He asked if he could call on me in few weeks after I'd had time to breathe. I said I would think about it. It appeared that since we met, he had found out who I was and what I was doing. I knew nothing about him and was not interested in knowing either. At the time, dating was not on my radar.

Not the Best Timing

When God caused me to survive the war and gave me another chance at life and school, I set up a plan for my life. In that plan, what came after A Levels was not dating; it was getting into university and ensuring my feet were firmly planted there. Dating was much farther down the list. Therefore, when this nice young man appeared interested in me, it wasn't difficult for me to say, "No." Dating was not yet part of the plan.

I knew nothing about Chris. I knew most of the people who attended the church were either medical students, nursing students, medical lab technology students, medical laboratory technicians, or newly graduated doctors doing their internship. I had no idea to which of these groups Chris belonged and was not really interested in finding out. My focus was just on the job I was about to start and gaining admission into the university. In a situation where there were about three times as many qualified people as there were admission spaces in universities, especially in medical specialties, being admitted on your first application was not a given. I had to prepare myself for the possibility of having to wait another year before gaining admission, and if that were to happen, I didn't want to have any entanglements that could derail the plan that I had for my life. I certainly didn't want to be included in the statistics of girls who wanted to, but never attended university because ...

Furthermore, about four years previous to this, Mfon's best friend had made a proposal to me. He had spent a great deal of time at our home during the early part of the war before and after Mfon escaped. On his last visit after Mfon's escape, he told me that when he finished university and I was grown, he would like to date and marry me. He was in his final A-level year when the war broke out. What did I know about dating and marriage then? I was fifteen. But it was an appealing concept and several years in the future, so I had agreed.

After that last visit, I didn't see him again until after the liberation of our area when the schools reopened. The high school for boys was about three miles from the girls' school. He came by to visit me at the girls' high school. Later that year, he completed his A levels and gained admission to a university in Northern Nigeria to study engineering. He went to the North and a year later I went to the West and we didn't see each other for three years. However, we did occasionally exchange letters but never talked about marriage in those letters. I was now not sure if that was a commitment or not. I was young. Nonetheless, I thought it important to safeguard any commitment I may have made, no matter how innocently it was made until it was clarified and/or rescinded.

A Great Job with a Twist

It felt good to be working with the expectation of payment at the end of the month. That would be my first salary, how amazing! I quickly learned how to manage the phone system and the schedules of the different lawyers. My employers were very pleased with my performance, as many previous employees had had difficulty grasping how to manage the complicated system.

I was in Ibadan, the heart of Yorubaland. The lawyers in the law firm were all Yoruba men. I was an Oron girl who had learned just a little Yoruba during my time at St. Anne's. I understood a little more than I could speak, but even that was not sufficient for me to accurately follow a conversation, especially on the phone and with someone who spoke fast. So, whenever a call came in, I answered in English. Many of the clients had no issues speaking to me in English, but there were a few who, as soon as I picked up the phone, would rattle away in Yoruba. They could go on and on and on without giving me a chance to interject and tell them I was not following all that they were saying, as I was not yet fluent in Yoruba. With such clients, whenever they stopped to take a breath, I would quickly interject with an apology and inform them that I was not yet fluent in Yoruba. Could they please repeat what they'd just said in English, so I'd be sure to relay their information as accurately as possible to their counsel?

On hearing this, some would apologize and restate their information in English. However, on the Wednesday of my second week, there was a call that I had a feeling could cause a problem for me. This client was not happy that he had to repeat himself and speak

English to a receptionist in a law firm in Yorubaland. He expressed his opinion bluntly to me. I apologized, but it appeared I was not the only one to whom he expressed his opinion. I later understood he had demanded to know from the senior partner why the firm should hire someone who did not speak Yoruba as a receptionist, thus forcing him to repeat himself in English. He was an important client of the firm.

Nobody said anything to me that day.

That same day, when I got home, there was a letter waiting. It was from the hospital's biochemistry lab. They had not interviewed me for a job in January because they had no vacancy, but a vacancy had suddenly opened up. As the lab supervisor liked Helen, and knew me as her friend, he offered me the job to start as soon as possible if I was still available.

I was miserable the entire evening. I badly wanted to work at this lab. It would provide a good experience for me. However, I was with this law firm that had treated me well and offered me a job almost on the spot. Now my ideal job had become available. What was I going to do? I couldn't just quit my job, that wouldn't be right. The lawyers at the firm had been very, very nice to me, especially having not said anything to me after the irate man's call that morning. This was my first job ever. I wondered whether there was a protocol for quitting a job. What if clients continued to complain about having to speak English to me? Would they fire me? If so, should I quit now? I didn't know what to do.

I prayed all night for God's direction. Heaven seemed silent. I decided to stay with my present job, as that was the right and honorable thing to do. Mom always said, "If God has something for you, He will make a way for you to access it in an honorable way."

On Thursday morning when I arrived at work, I was informed that the senior partner, the same man who'd hired me, wanted to see me. My heart pounded excitedly. Could this be it? Was he going to fire me? Would that not be incredulously amazing? I went into his office. He asked me to sit down. He then proceeded to tell me how very happy they had all been with my performance. They were very impressed with how quickly I'd mastered the phone system and how well I performed my duties. But one of their biggest clients was unhappy about having to speak English to me when he called. Since there was not a chance I could learn, master, and understand Yoruba well within days, he would like to reassign me to the back room to do filing and run other errands. My face told him I didn't like that option. Since they didn't have any other position, he also said I could choose to leave.

I said I had been hired as a receptionist and not as a backroom filer and that, during the interview, fluency in Yoruba never come up. It was not a condition for my employment and, as he had said, they were pleased with my performance. So, if I couldn't remain in the position I had been hired for, I would rather leave. I said I empathized with the situation he was in because of the feelings of one of his best clients. However, it was not my fault the client felt that way. I had served the firm well.

He paused for a while, deep in thought. When he raised his head, he said since it was not my fault, they would pay me for the two weeks I had worked and then give me a month's salary in lieu of notice.

I could not believe my ears. Was God crazy good or what? This was like the Israelites leaving Egypt with Egyptian treasures. Now I was free to start my ideal job and with a pocket full of money. I had to work hard to keep from breaking into a song of praise and thanksgiving. Here I was … not having worked in January, but the Lord was giving me all of January's salary. I wasn't worse off than my peers who started working in January. I was in exactly the same situation financially! How great was that?

I told the office manager I was willing to help with anything she wished me to do that day and the day after, as she now had to manage the phone lines as well as do her normal duties, place an advertisement for a new receptionist, and plan for interviews. I went into the back room and called the lab and asked if I could call on them in person by 4:30 p.m. that day. My new boss agreed. By 3:45 p.m., my cheque was ready. I asked the office manager if she would like me to come in the next day, which was a Friday, to help, as they were paying me for that day. She replied, "No." I left the law firm and went straight to the lab to accept my job offer and confirm I could begin Monday.

Being in the Lab and Loving It

From the first day I set foot in the lab, I loved it. It was a joy to get to work each day. Medical students and their instructors often came to the lab to look at the results of tests and learn. It was then that I discovered that Chris Ekong was a final-year medical student and was graduating in a few months. Within a short time, after I started working at the lab, he made friends with my friends and coworkers, who all began to sing his praises, telling me what a very nice guy he was. I said, "Good for him." I was still not interested in dating him or anyone else— even if that person was the most charming angel from heaven—until my future was secured with university admission.

My parents had always wanted their children to be well-educated. My two older brothers were engineers, and from the looks of it, my younger brother Etim was likely to become one too. My older sister was a nurse, and I was interested in the medical field. Everyone thought I would make an incredible physician.

Working at the hospital, I discovered that first-year medical students were each provided a cadaver to dissect and learn from. That was unsettling for me. I asked more questions and found out more details. Preserved in formaldehyde, these were complete human bodies with the heads, eyes, limbs, and everything still attached. I knew instinctively that dissecting a whole human being was not something I could do with ease. Seeing a dead body by accident during the war caused me so much trauma that I experienced weeks of nightmares. I had also witnessed an accident where people died and others were seriously hurt—there was blood everywhere. The sight of that much blood had made me dizzy, and seeing the dead bodies caused me to have nightmares for several days. Could I spend several hours per week dissecting a human body and remain sane? Some of the medical students I knew said they couldn't eat meat during their first year because it reminded them of the cadavers. Other medical students kept fainting at the sight of serious trauma at emergency. Could I really survive medical school? It appears my mind can't stand other people's suffering. I had wanted to study medicine to help people but had never considered the trauma that could accompany the profession.

A few months into my work at the biochemistry lab, I decided that medicine was probably not the best profession for me. As my desire to pursue medicine began to wane, I kept it to myself, as I knew the family was expecting me to go that route. I was already becoming very fond of biochemistry. I loved research, and I loved working on specimens. I decided to start orienting myself toward studying biochemistry rather than medicine.

In the Nigerian system at that time, the gap in terms of earnings between medical specialty PhDs who worked at university hospitals and MDs was not significant. Both MDs and PhDs who worked at the higher level where I was planning to work would be university employees. Their remuneration was dependent on their level of achievement on the university scale. While physicians could operate private clinics on the side to earn additional money, biochemists could also work with drug companies to help develop and test medications and delineate the pathway of metabolic and genetic diseases. Therefore, biochemists could also earn money on the side if they so desired.

My job at the lab also exposed me to the close collaboration within which some physicians and biochemists worked to provide comprehensive patient care. I was delighted. It appeared I would have the best of two worlds as a biochemist as in some instances, I could help alleviate people's suffering, help them get better, and provide them with information that could help improve their quality of life. So, the more I learned about what I could do with biochemistry without having to face the things I disliked about medicine, the more my interest in the discipline grew. My biggest problem was how to break the news to my parents, especially Mom, and my brother Edet. As I suspected, when Mom learned of what I had decided, she was furious. I then promised her that I was going to be a doctor, not a medical doctor, but one that was closely allied to medical doctors and who still helped alleviate people's suffering in very significant ways.

Harbinger of Good News

Although I had applied to the three universities that offered medical sciences, only one, the University of Ibadan, acknowledged receipt of my application. So, I had just one university to vie for. I knew the competition was stringent, as everyone who wanted to pursue a discipline offered by UI had it as their first choice. I had a rough idea when UI's admission results were usually sent out, and as time went on I became more anxious waiting for an admission letter.

Chris Ekong had been keeping an eye on me and my admission. Since I had indicated that I was not prepared to date anybody until I was sure I'd been admitted to the university, he kept an ear open for when the admissions list was coming out. Having been at the university for almost six years, he knew where things were and where one could secure information. Therefore, when he heard that the results were out, he checked with admissions and found that I'd been given admission.

He came to the lab to congratulate me. I did not believe him, since I hadn't received the admission letter. However, he directed me to someone he knew in admissions who checked the list and confirmed I had indeed gained admission to the university. I was overjoyed. I asked when the letters were going to be sent out. He said the letters were sent out more than two weeks earlier. I said I hadn't received mine and asked him to check to what address it was sent. He did and told me the address. It was not my sister's address, which was what was on the application.

I asked him to check for me if that was the address on my file. He did and came back with the right address, my sister's address. I did not receive my admission letter because it was sent to the wrong address. Not only was it the wrong address, but it was also a non-existent address! How the letter was sent to an address that was not on my file, even though the admissions office had my correct address was a mystery, not only to me but to the Admission office as well.

The Administrator was flabbergasted. He couldn't explain how the address on my application file was different from the one on the admission dispatch file. He did not know where the wrong address came from. He documented the mistake, and I was given a new acceptance document, which I completed immediately and paid the deposit to secure the admission. It was more than a month later that my admission letter was returned to the university as "Undeliverable-No Such Address". By then, the deadline for acceptance of the admission had passed. If Chris had not informed me of the admission so that I could follow up and receive a new document, I may have lost the admission. God used Chris Ekong to ensure that any negative plans to interfere with my admission did not succeed.

As I reflect on that situation, I wonder what may have happened if God had not provided Chris to safeguard that admission. In a place where admission spaces were so limited if acceptance of the admission was not within the allotted time period, the space was given to someone else. I marvel at God's goodness, and how He has always been there for me. I marvel at how He has always made a way for me to bypass tragedies before they were scheduled to happen. I was not particularly deserving of Chris's help, as I had always brushed aside his date requests. Yet, God used him as the instrument for my blessing.

Sticking with the Plan

Some would have thought that, after God had used Chris to secure my admission, I would start dating him. I think he expected that also. Wrong. I was very grateful for the help, but I still had my strategic plan, and dating was not the next item on that agenda. I had put that plan together prayerfully and thought it was best to stick to it. With the admission secured and behind me, I turned my focus on the university culture.

I wanted to be fully prepared. It was after my admission that I discovered that biochemistry was the default field of study for people who could not stand or get into medicine and therefore was a very competitive field. Many who aspired to study it failed to make grades that qualified them to be included in the number the university could admit each year. I saw that as a challenge. I had not come this far to lose out.

The first year of study for biochemistry was general science. This was the critical year, and the weeding ground. Even though people could apply to study biochemistry, they were admitted into Science. Biochemistry admission only came after the first year and was based on the student's first-year performance. There were usually more than double the number of people wanting to go into this discipline than there were spaces.

Even though I had finished top of my class after only two years of study, I had learned those seven years of science mostly independently, so I felt insecure about my ability to compete successfully with students who had studied science the proper way. I sometimes wondered if there were areas where I was not as well prepared as the regular science students. It's difficult to know what you don't know until you're exposed to it, so I didn't know in what areas I had deficiencies. I had no idea what challenges university science would present, so I needed to focus and accurately assess my competition before letting my guard down. That meant no date with Chris. First things first, and that first thing was getting into biochemistry.

The start date for the university finally arrived and I moved to campus. I arrived bright and early and found my room. I was sharing it with two other girls, as the admission demands could not keep up with the accommodation availability. But there were no complaints from me. I was just happy to be one of the students who gained admission on the first try. Within two weeks after the start of classes, some of the girls admitted to UI did not arrive, therefore a few rooms opened up. I was moved to another room where I shared with just one other girl—a perfect match as she was a biology major.

My First Semester at University

I just loved being in the lab. It was great fun to actually do the advanced same chemistry and physics experiments I had previously only read about. I was doing well in all my classes, and was continually assessing my ability and capabilities in university physics, chemistry, biology, and math, my main subjects of study. I needed to know how I stacked up against the competition, my classmates, with whom I would be competing for those all-important spots in biochemistry. With everything seemingly going well, I applied to the Academic Excellence Scholarship, the Rolls Royce of scholarships.

I was looking forward to the first semester exams, which would provide concrete evidence of my capability. Then, a week before the start of the exams, tragedy struck. I fell severely ill with malaria. It was common knowledge that about half the students desiring admission into professional disciplines didn't progress to their desired field of study because of capacity issues. There were just not enough spaces for everyone and I didn't want to study just anything because it was the only thing I could gain admission to. Therefore, I needed to be well and do well so I could be one of the first picks for biochemistry.

At the best of times, being ill during the first semester at the university was not a good thing. Falling ill with malaria just before the exams was like a death sentence. How could I fulfill my dreams if I couldn't write the exams? Furthermore, I would receive little empathy for my illness since first-year students who fell ill during the first semester exams were suspected of malingering. I didn't want to be remotely affiliated with that group.

I took some of the best anti-malaria medication I could find and prayed there would be no side effects. Malaria was extra difficult for me because I usually experienced bad side effects from the medication. The medication made me nauseated and dizzy, making it difficult to tolerate even a drink of water. Being well-hydrated during bouts of malaria is imperative because of the high temperature that accompanies the illness. Malaria is a common illness that people who live in the tropics experience from time to time. It is only dangerous to adults if they cannot keep the medication or fluids down. When the medications that I had didn't work, I prayed harder, claiming every healing promise in the

Bible. Still no relief. I became desperate. This was not the right time for me to face such a problem.

Desperate for help when my fever didn't break by the morning of the fourth day, I went to the university sick bay. I needed to be there because, if I missed any exams, I needed a doctor's note that I was ill during the exams to be allowed to write the makeup exam. I also hoped they would admit me and give me some anti-nausea medication to help me retain the anti-malaria medication.

I was admitted and prescribed the regular anti-malarial medication that made my stomach churn like a washing machine. I was not prescribed any anti-nausea medication even though I pleaded for it. My body temperature was very high and anyone could see that I was very ill, yet, I was still considered a malingering suspect. I took the medication and tried hard to keep it down, but vomited every dose. The nurse said she would inform the doctor when next he came, but because there were only two patients in the entire sick bay, the doctor didn't show.

By this time, I hadn't been able to keep food down for four days. My fever was still very high, and I was experiencing a high level of chills, a common symptom of malaria. I was severely dehydrated and had no energy. I tried to take tiny sips of water to keep my tongue from sticking to the roof of my mouth. I was burning up with high temperatures, and nobody seemed to care. Wasn't the university sick bay a place to care for sick students? Or was the facility just a facade?

Oh, how I wished Mom could be close by at least to comfort me and pray for me. Alas, she wasn't. She was hundreds of miles away. I had nobody, nobody who cared. I was alone, alone with God, and I abandoned myself to Him and asked Him to do with me whatever pleased Him.

A Familiar Face to my Rescue

Chris graduated from med school in June, five months after we first met. He was now a bona fide doctor and doing his internship. When the fall semester of the university started, he would drop by my room at Queen's Hall every now and then. He made friends with my roommate and would visit with her if I wasn't in the room. These visits were becoming more and more frequent. Not wanting to encourage long visits, I often found a reason to leave the room after he had visited for about five to ten minutes. He would then just visit with my roommate. She became one of his chief advocates, extolling his many great virtues. I always told her I had nothing against the man as a person, and if he could just wait until I felt ready to date, I would probably date him. However, what I didn't like was his trying to impose his agenda on me. I needed to follow my own.

On my fourth day at the sick bay, a familiar face showed up. It was Dr. Chris Ekong. This time, I was happy to see him. He had dropped by my room, and my roommate informed him I was in the sick bay. He took one look at me, asked a few questions, and then left in a hurry. He came back a short time later with a package. It contained anti-nausea medication and Lucozade, a drink to give me energy and settle and stabilize my stomach. He also gave me an anti-malarial medication that I tolerated better than the ones I had previously been prescribed.

The anti-nausea medication and Lucozade calmed my stomach and enabled me to keep the anti-malarial medication down. By the next morning, my temperature was down. Chris visited a few more times and brought me food of which I ate a little bit of and kept down. I was beginning to regain some energy and strength, and that evening I told the nurse I wanted to be discharged the next day.

I had developed a regular and consistent habit of studying every day and making summaries so even though I lost a week of study time before the exams, I knew I could still do well. I hit the books with a vengeance after being discharged. I was able to write all my exams except the first, which was scheduled for the day before I left the sick bay. The note from the sick bay doctor qualified me for a makeup exam, which was scheduled for the first week of the second semester.

As I finished each exam, I knew I had done well and the results confirmed the premonition. Shortly after I learned I was awarded the Academic Excellence scholarship I had applied for. This was a top-tier scholarship, a Rolls-Royce among scholarships. It paid for everything including money for transportation from the university back home at Christmastime and the summer vacation, whether one was planning to make the journey or not. It also provided spending money. God is incredibly good. Everything was falling into place for me. I rejoiced.

An Item Moves Up on the Agenda

The first-semester exam results indicated that my feet were firmly planted in the university. If I continued with this level of performance, I would be among the top picks for admission into Biochemistry the next academic year. Now, I could confidently say that the Lord and I most likely had the biochemistry thing under control. I felt euphoric about these successes, but I reminded myself that they were all favors from my heavenly father. Now, it was time to look down the agenda and see what was next. I did, and the item next on my agenda was finding a potential spouse.

This was the big one. How does one navigate that? With Chris already in the picture and my distance "boyfriend" who had graduated with an engineering degree wanting to start a relationship, I had to really seek the Lord. By this time, the Christian medical students, technicians, and fresh graduates who knew Chris well and were all associated with the "church" at the nurses' auditorium were on my case on Chris's behalf. Some of them visited me, touting Chris' virtues and saying what a nice man he was. That was pressure. How do women usually go about this, especially when they had more than one guy vying for their attention? I guess the starting point was to ask the Lord.

The university hospital complex where medical students, physicians, technicians, and other medically associated people lived and/or worked was five miles away from the main university campus where I lived. Their Christian group was different from the group on the main campus. I was involved with the group on the main campus and enjoyed the fellowship and teachings there tremendously. The distance also gave me a reprieve from Chris's friends, who were mainly at the university hospital.

I'd always thought the university undergraduate years were the best time to find a spouse. At the university, one was exposed to thousands of "eligible potential spouses." When practically every student lived on campus, one had the opportunity to get to know many people well. Apart from observing them yourself, you could also get to know their friends and their enemies and add the appraisal from both groups to your own observations. Then, you also had your friends, who would be on the lookout for you and report back to you whatever they saw and heard. So, this was the place where, with God's help, one could make informed decisions.

I decided to go out with Chris just to get to know him while I sought the Lord. When I gave my life completely to Jesus during my first few months at St. Anne's, I had turned over every area of my life to Him. I had also written to my distance "boyfriend" and told him about my faith in Christ. I further told him that all of my future, including who I married, was now the Lord's decision, not mine. So, if the Lord asked me to marry him, I would, but if He did not, I would marry whomever He told me to. Now, I needed to find out what was on the Lord's mind. I started praying earnestly about it. During the months I had worked at the biochemistry lab at UCH, I made a list of what I would like to see in the man who would be my husband and ranked the items on the list in decreasing order of importance.

Mom had told me that choosing a spouse was one of the most important decisions I would make. She said choosing a good spouse could make life sweet (she also warned me that nobody is perfect), and choosing an unsuitable spouse could make life difficult. Where could I find the guiding principles that could help me choose well? After giving my heart to Jesus, the top of that list was a man who was a believer and truly loved God. I established some guidelines and wrote them down to help me navigate this pivotal task.

I knew Chris met the criteria of being a believer. As I went down the list, he appeared to be scoring very highly on many items. I felt I needed to garner some unbiased opinion about him because since he "saved my life" at the sick bay, he had become a sort of hero in my eyes. I decided to attend functions where I would encounter people who knew him well but were not already his agents, so I could chat with them and ask them questions about him. I did, and the more people I talked with, the more they confirmed that he was a very nice person. It was looking good, but I needed to hear definitively from God.

I continued my research to find out more about Chris. I knew he was a physician, a believer, and an active member of the makeshift church at UCH. His tenacity also intrigued me. Many people would have given up after a month. Even the most tenacious would have given up after three, four, six, or even nine months. Not Chris. He hung around and pursued me for almost an entire year without seeing positive results. I began to think that maybe God was at work in the situation, and the answer and confirmation I was seeking was right under my nose.

I prayed more earnestly and asked the Lord to make His voice just a little bit clearer. It was at this time that I learned that many of Chris's friends had tried to persuade him to forget about me when for almost a year, I had not responded positively to his overtures. He was advised to get on with his life and forget about "that little girl," especially as there were many other women, including physicians, nurses, graduate students, and other accomplished women pursuing him. But somehow, he kept his focus on "the little girl" who had just completed high school and who, before August, was not sure of university admission. This really intrigued me. And like Gideon, I began to put out fleeces (Judges 6:36–40) before the Lord.

As I sensed that Chris was perhaps God's choice for me, I asked the Lord what to do with my distance "boyfriend." I wanted to be sure, so I prayed about both relationships. The Lord began to open my eyes in little ways. It was like when John the Baptist sent his disciples to Christ to ask Him, "Are you the Messiah we've been expecting, or should we keep looking for someone else?"

The Lord did not give them a direct answer but said, "Go back to John and tell him what you have heard and seen, the blind see, the lame walk, those with leprosy are cured, the deaf hear, the dead

are raised to life, and the Good News is being preached to the poor."
(Mathew 11:2–5)

The Lord wanted me to observe and come to a conclusion and
decision based on my observations. I turned my attention to Chris'
family. What was his family background? (This information is very
important in our culture since marriages are not just between two people
but two families.) The more I learned about his family, the more my eyes
opened and the more I liked what I was seeing and learning.

Some important members of Chris's family were well known to
and familiar with some important members of my family. For example,
his eldest sister Ekaete and my sister Adiaha had been schoolmates in
nursing school and were now best friends. I had become acquainted
with sister Ekaete during the holidays I spent at my sister's house while I
attended St. Anne's and liked her very much. She is a very soft-spoken,
beautiful lady, extremely nice with a great sense of humor. I had known
her for two years but had no idea she was related to Chris. My brother
Edet was a schoolmate of her husband's from high school, and they
knew each other, even though Edet was much younger and many grades
behind him. My sister Adiaha and sister Ekaete were both married to
men who taught at the university. So, the close friendships continued.

My brother Edet also knew Chris's oldest brother Donald, very
well. Moreover, one of his sisters, Grace (he comes from a huge family
of eleven children) had taught me in high school. (She was the best
history and geography teacher I ever had.) His family background and
pedigree were comparable to mine (something very important as well in
our culture).

Chris's tenacity caused me to wonder whether the Lord was
using this incident to teach me that waiting on Him is never in vain.
Sometimes, we may feel pressured to do something because of the
thought that, if we do not, then the chance may be gone and we will
lose out. Hurry is often not of the Lord. In the Bible, many mighty men
and women of God such as Abraham, Sarah, Joseph, and David, had
to wait for long periods for their promises to be fulfilled. But in today's

society, where people want instant gratification, could impatience be robbing us of God's best?

Hurry and the fear of losing it all if he waited for Samuel was one of the sins that caused Saul to lose his kingdom. 1 Samuel 13:7–11, reads: *Meanwhile, Saul stayed at Gilgal, and his men were trembling with fear. Saul waited there seven days for Samuel, as Samuel had instructed him earlier, but Samuel still didn't come. Saul realized that his troops were rapidly slipping away. So, he demanded, "Bring me the burnt offering and the peace offerings."*

And Saul sacrificed the burnt offering himself, and just as he was finishing with the burnt offering, Samuel arrived. Saul went out to meet and welcome him, but Samuel said, "What is this you have done?" *Saul replied*, "I saw my men scattering from me, and you didn't arrive when you said you would, and the Philistines are at Micmash ready for battle."

Let's reflect on this. Have we missed God's best by failing to persevere when He appears slow in answering our prayers? Or can we like Job (Job 13:15) learn to trust Him and say, "Though He slay me, yet will I trust in Him."

I was still not sure of what the Lord was saying. Was my beginning to like Chris my own doing or was it part of the Lord's plan? I didn't know, I wasn't sure, and I needed to be. I prayed more about this issue, asking the Lord to give me a clear direction. How I longed for the type of answer depicted in Isaiah 30:21 where it says, *Whether you turn to the right or to the left, your ears will hear a voice behind you, saying, "This is the way; walk in it."*

Heaven seemed still silent. There were no buzzing words in my ears. By the end of that university year, I was feeling almost certain about Chris.

I was going home to the East for the summer. I looked forward to seeing Mom and discussing and praying about this issue with her. Also, my distance "boyfriend" had arrived back home in the East after his graduation and was working at my brother Edet's consulting engineering firm at Calabar. He was excited to hear I was coming to Calabar and wanted to see me. He probably still had the picture in his mind of the young teenage girl he last saw. However, during the almost five years we hadn't seen each other, I had grown from a teenage girl to a mature woman who had an agenda for her life and was determined to have some control over how that agenda unfolded.

This would be a pivotal trip. I either had to choose one of these men or dismiss both of them, if I sensed that to be what God wanted me to do. Chris also wanted to visit his mom that summer at the same time that I was going home. He asked if he could give me a ride. This time I felt I knew him enough, so I said, "Yes." We drove down together. It was about an eighteen-hour nonstop drive. When we arrived in the East, even though we had to pass through his hometown to get to mine, I asked him not to stop at his hometown but go straight to mine. He was to come back at a later date to visit me at my parents' home so I could introduce him to them.

14

The Elimination, the Job, the Battle, the Victory

Being home with Mom and Dad was refreshing. So much has happened since I saw them last. Mom was my best friend and confidant, the only person who loved me more than her was God. We had four years of catching up to do and less than a week to do it. After being practically on my own for four years it felt so good to be back home and be someone's child again, to once again experience those feelings of safety and belonging.

Chris wanted to meet my parents, but we agreed that I should have the time to broker the information to Mom and Dad about who he was before he came to meet them. I prayed the Lord would speak clearly and as soon as possible during this trip, and that there would be unity in what Mom, Dad, and I each perceived.

I talked to my parents about both men before Chris returned. They knew my distance "boyfriend" very well. Therefore, they took time to appraise Chris when he came for the visit. After the visit and much prayer, the answer was a firm "no" from my parents about the distance "boyfriend." However, they didn't receive either a clear "no" or "yes" about Chris. But Mom felt he *could* be the one. Was that good enough?

The Shift to Calabar and an Elimination

After almost a week at home with Mom and Dad, I headed to Calabar, the state capital, where I stood a better chance of finding a summer job. I would stay with my brother Edit who was getting married soon. He had a huge house, a part of which was used as office space. The firm was new and needed to be judicious in how money was spent. The structure of the house made it easy to demarcate the area used as residence from the one used for office space.

The Monday after my arrival, my distance "boyfriend" asked to see me during his lunch break. It was wonderful to see him again after more than four years. We had both grown up. He asked if he could take me out for a meal the evening of the next day. I agreed but was feeling quite anxious. In his last letter to me before the holidays, he indicated that he wanted to firm up plans about settling down and starting a family. That was deep. We had not even dated and he was speaking of settling down? Furthermore, after the summer, I would be returning to Ibadan where my studies would continue for at least another two years. Therefore, we wouldn't even be able to date. It seemed to me that he was making many assumptions about our future life together unilaterally, and wanted to move forward quickly with them. I always thought those types of decisions should be made together. If he wanted to be making unilateral decisions, then I was not the right woman for him, but I wanted us to part on good terms, so I prayed for wisdom and guidance and for God to also show me personally what His will was by giving me a sign.

As the time of the meeting approached, a feeling of great sadness came over me. I tried hard to get rid of it but to no avail. He was a friend, had always been a friend. Why was I feeling so sad about seeing him? The feeling of sadness grew. Then it occurred to me that the feeling could be significant and possibly part of the answer I was seeking. I prayed that the Lord would tell me what it meant. Was the sadness indicative of the end to our unusual relationship? I kept praying, and when the doorbell rang and I opened the door and saw him, a voice in my spirit said, *"This will be the last time you will meet with him under this circumstance."*

I got the message, thanked the Lord, and asked Him to give me the right words to deliver the message. God is so good. I didn't have to work hard. As we ate, we chatted and caught up on what had happened in our lives over the years that we hadn't seen each other. Then the conversation shifted to our dreams and desires for the future. We quickly discovered that we were two very different people, each with a very different plan, dream, and expectations for the future. Our plans seemed to be on parallel tracks. There was no way they could intersect or coexist. He was ready to get married and start a family. I wanted to complete my bachelor's degree and start the pursuit of my Ph.D. degree in Biochemistry. We were going to be living in two different parts of the country. There was no way our plans could come together to create a future where we both achieved what we wanted.

At the end of the evening, it was clear that beginning a courtship was not a good idea. However, we decided we would remain good friends and wished each other well. That confirmed what I was hearing from the Lord. I was glad for the elimination process. Now I could focus on just the one. However, just because *this* one was not *the* one did not automatically imply that Chris was. This was not a choice by default game. I wanted a real confirmation from the Lord.

Landing a Great Summer Job

I hit the summer job trail with a vengeance. Within a week, I landed a job as a reporter and writer for the state's weekly newspaper, the Nigerian Chronicle. My main job was to start a children's section for the weekly. My first duty was to gather as many appropriate children's stories as possible, sort them out, and determine how to roll them out. I was also assigned a secondary task of being an assistant and understudy to the woman who was in charge of the women's section—if I could do it without neglecting my main job in the children's section. I needed to learn from her how to conduct interviews. I was eager to learn this skill, so I kept abreast of her scheduled interviews especially those with interesting powerful women, I worked extra hard at my tasks so I would always be free to accompany her to those interviews without having to worry about my section.

Being the editor of the women's section in the only newspaper in the State provided her with access to many important and influential women. She was able to have an audience with and interview the wife of the governor, the wife of the vice-chancellor of the university, and many other women in positions of leadership, influence, and authority. I never wanted to miss any of these interviews, so I always worked hard to be helpful to her so she would inform me of any upcoming interviews in advance. That made it possible for me to always have my work in the children's section ahead of schedule to preclude my boss in that section from preventing me from accompanying her to those interviews.

I also had a second job as a radio station DJ between 11:00 p.m. and midnight. The station had a program named *Midnight Serenity* which featured soft and relaxing storylines intertwined with appropriate soft and sometimes romantic music. I found the job interesting and relaxing, as well as a way to earn extra cash while having fun. This was my first time living in Calabar and I didn't yet have many friends. This job enabled me to learn more about soft and romantic music, while also expelling the evening boredom that often assailed me after work.

My brother Edet lived in a gated community, far from the city center. The area was not known for great taxi service as taxis were reluctant to go there due to the distance and the probability that the taxi was not likely to be hired for a return fare to town after dropping off their hire. I was a student and had neither a vehicle nor a great deal of cash. The radio station provided transportation home for us at the end of the program. So, I would go to the station straight from work, select the music I wanted to play, and then develop an appropriate storyline. I worked there two evenings per week and enjoyed it tremendously. I had worked very hard over the previous five years. It was almost intoxicating to discover life without studying and worrying about test scores. I had almost forgotten how to have fun.

The National Youth Service Corps (NYSC)

After the civil war, the Federal Governor of Nigeria, General Yakubu Gowon developed a program aimed at fostering national unity and reconciliation. The plan was to involve Nigerian university graduates in nation-building. The strategy was for graduates to serve the nation for a year right after graduation in a state that was different from their state of origin and one with which they were not familiar. Since Nigeria is a country with a very diverse population, where people of different languages and cultures coexist, it was hoped that living and working with people of different languages and cultures would help develop a better understanding of the people and cultures of other areas of the country. The university graduates of my first year at university were the pioneers that kicked off NYSC.

During the first six weeks of NYSC, all the graduates assigned to a particular state stayed together in a facility that could house all of them. They attended drills and exercises conducted by the military in the morning. Later on, they attended classes where they learned about the country as a whole and the culture and traditions of the specific state in which they were stationed. After the first six weeks and for the remaining NYSC year, the graduates were deployed to different businesses and organizations in the state, based on their educational specialty.

The great thing about this was that believers found each other during the six weeks of common accommodation and later, even when they were sent out to different parts of the state, kept in touch. They also learned from the local believers which churches were alive and how they could collaborate to encourage each other.

The first six weeks of this NYSC coincided with most of my time in Calabar that summer. The NYSC Christians at Calabar formed a small Bible study and worship group, which met at a school on Sunday afternoons. I found out about this group from my boss at work, joined it, and looked forward to Sunday afternoons. I felt fed and challenged to grow in my faith. We were encouraged to take and live the Word wherever we went.

It was an interesting proposition to live the Word at work. Luckily for me, my boss was a Bible-thumping Christian. He guided me in creating the section for children in the weekly newspaper. When I first arrived, he'd hoped to share the Gospel with me. As it turned out, I already knew the Lord. He rejoiced. Sometimes during lunchtime, if I stayed in, we would share with each other what the Lord was teaching us. So, this was a summer of much spiritual growth for me. God is so amazing. He often prepares us for future events we have no inkling of and in ways that are astounding.

Settling in and Having Fun

Life was good. My brother's wedding was a huge one. His wife was amazing. She was a kind and loving woman. Her family lived in Calabar and treated me like a daughter. My sister-in-law and I often visited her parents on weekends. They lived in the part of town that was more accessible to stores. This was another favor from the Lord, making my life and holiday enjoyable. From all angles, life was good.

At the newspaper, there was another student employed in a different department. We became good friends. Even though she was not from Calabar, she and her family had been living there for a long time, so she knew where things were, and I often tagged along with her to places of interest after work. I also met other students at the radio station, so within a short time, I went from knowing hardly anybody at Calabar to having a group of friends.

As already mentioned, my brother lived in a secluded part of town, quite a distance from downtown, which made it difficult to get a taxi there late in the evening. Having my sister-in-law to talk to in the evening was a gift. Otherwise, the evenings I was not working at the radio station would have been very lonely. The summer flew by quickly. I was having a lot of fun and making good money from all my jobs.

However, it was a short summer for me as I needed to return to Ibadan two weeks early.

The previous year, due to greater admission demands, the university had admitted more students than it was capable of housing. It therefore implemented a policy that made every second-year student ineligible for university accommodation, unless the student had a compelling reason that made living off campus an extraordinary hardship. If they were able to receive an exemption from off-campus in their second year, such students still had to find housing off-campus for their third year. This was not preferred as the third year was the final year and had many demands on students. As there were not many suitable accommodations near the university, students had to scramble to find housing close to the university. I had to be back at Ibadan at least two weeks early to find an appropriate accommodation which made my summer holidays approximately six weeks, rather than the eight weeks that it should have been.

A Strange Attack by the Enemy

Near the beginning of my last two weeks in Calabar, I started feeling unwell. There was no specific thing I could identify as being wrong. I just had this feeling of being very unwell. I experienced a loss of appetite, and the sight of food would make me gag. I couldn't understand what was happening. However, I had an intense desire to pray. My boss at work noticed I wasn't looking great and asked me to take the last week off as sick leave. He said I should take the time to take care of myself, especially as I would be making the long and tedious journey back to Ibadan shortly thereafter.

I took his advice but the situation did not improve. I still didn't have any specific symptoms, just overwhelming feelings of being unwell, emotional dread, and a desire to pray. I felt in my spirit that I was under a great demonic attack, but that was not something I was familiar with or understood. I did the only thing I knew, pray.

Another strange thing that happened at this time was the feeling of a "presence" in my room. I had been staying in that room since the beginning of the summer and had never felt anything like that. Sometimes when I entered my room, my hair would almost stand on end, and my heart would palpitate heavily. At those times, I often had a great desire to turn and flee. But how could I explain that to people? Was I going to be like a three-year-old who would tell his or her parents he or she could not stay in the room because monsters were hiding under the bed? I would sound ridiculous. Yet a part of me knew that what I was facing was very real. What could I do? How could I handle this? A part of me felt that the "presence", not me, was what should leave the room, as it was the trespasser. So, whenever the feeling of dread came over me upon entering the room, I would rebuke it in Jesus' name and command the presence to leave. I always told the "presence" that it knew that He who was with me and in me was greater and mightier than it, so there was no way I was going to cower before it.

After three days, things intensified. The night of the fourth day, I could not sleep and spent the night kneeling beside my bed in intense prayer. Even though the air conditioner was on, I was praying with such intensity that sweat was pouring from my body.

During this time of dread and feeling unwell, I had a series of dreams where I was in combat with enemies. There was a horde of them, firing shots at me. I would dodge their rounds and then fire back. As the battle intensified, I started flying. I flew above them, making my fire more deadly. My weapon of warfare was the name of Jesus. My shots exploded with a flare of light, consuming the enemies, but they kept coming at me. There were hordes of them, but they were no match for my weapon, the name of Jesus.

Sometimes, the battle would be so fierce that I would wake up to the Holy Spirit praying over me with groans, as if travailing. This was very strange to me. I had no idea what was going on and was not aware that the Holy Spirit could intercede for us with groans. Why was I experiencing these bewildering dreams and occurrences? I sometimes wondered if I was going mad.

These battles continued night after night, and somehow my spirit was always in what I now know to be *travailing* prayer. I was a baby

Christian then and didn't quite understand the workings of the Holy Spirit. I didn't understand how the Holy Spirit intercedes for us. I am so thankful that my lack of understanding then did not stop the Holy Spirit from intervening on my behalf.

My brother was out of town on business at this time. I didn't want my sister-in-law to worry about me. So, after she returned from work, I would muster all the energy I could and visit with her. I was not showing symptoms of any illness, but my lack of appetite and energy could not be hidden. She was concerned about my not eating, but there was nothing either of us could do about it, as the sight of food brought on a gag reaction. She suggested I see a doctor, but I argued against it at first, saying it seemed ridiculous to go to a doctor and pay a lot of money without a pertinent reason. What would I say were my symptoms? Was it reasonable to tell the doctor I'd come to see him because of a gag reaction at the sight of food? Or that there was a "presence" in my room that made my hair stand on end? Was it the insatiable desire to pray that I could give as a symptom? She didn't know how to respond to these but still thought seeing a doctor was a good idea.

I told her we should wait a few more days, and if things didn't improve, then I would visit the doctor. By the fourth day, she insisted that I see a doctor. I was given several tests—all of which came back normal. I was not surprised by the test results. I already knew there was nothing physically wrong with me; what I was experiencing was spiritual. I knew I was under attack by demons.

Even though I didn't understand spiritual warfare then, I sharpened my sword. I would declare the Word of God in my room and play worship music. That always helped; the demons would depart but would return, often after I was asleep.

On the Saturday night, the sixth day after all these things started happening, everything came to a climax. The battle was fierce, and the devil was out for a kill. I had a dream where I was again being attacked by demons. Then the scenery changed; there was a large gathering. The Lord was in the middle and the crowd surrounding Him was huge with standing room only. There were no openings to move in or out of the room. The scene appeared very similar to the one described in Luke 5:18–20 where men carrying a paralyzed man couldn't find a way to Jesus because of the crowd, so they went up on the roof and lowered him on his mat through the tiles into the crowd, right in front of Jesus.

I was watching this as I floated in the air, hovering over the place where the Lord stood. I looked down and saw someone lying on the floor at His feet. As I looked closer, I realized the person at the Lord's feet was me. How could I exist in two forms, one lying at the Lord's feet and another hovering above Him? This was a mesmerizing sight. I looked closer and realized the me at the Lord's feet appeared lifeless. Then just at that moment, the Lord turned His attention to the me at His feet. He looked at me and then looked up to Heaven and said, "My Father, even though this life has passed, I ask that it be restored." All the people around said, "Amen." Immediately, the me that was hovering in the air descended and rejoined the me laying at the Lord's feet. I awoke.

This was a very scary dream. I didn't know what to make of it. I had been in intense warfare during the night and had gone into deep sleep in the early hours of the morning. So, when I awoke after the dream, it was bright daylight. The presence of evil was thick in the room. I rebuked it severely and then tried to get up but felt very exhausted. Not having eaten for six full days and engaging in intense warfare night after night ensured I had no energy. Not wanting to cause my sister-in-law any worries, I got up, accomplished my morning routine, and got dressed. She was waiting for me to emerge from my room and had made some tea for me. Tea was the only "food" I could "eat." She was planning to go to church, but when she saw the shape I was in and the fact that I was feeling very weak, she suggested we head to the emergency.

Suddenly, I was having problems breathing. Seeing this, she insisted that we immediately go to emergency. I was at a point I was willing to go to the hospital even if I couldn't clearly identify my symptoms apart from the inability to breathe. But before we could get the chauffeur, the ability to get air into my lungs diminished significantly. It felt like my lungs were blocked or filled with fluid, leaving little room for air. I was short of breath and almost choking. This was scary. Then something even stranger happened; my head began to rotate. It rotated such that when it stopped, my face was above my back. I could see my back when I gazed downward. The back of my head faced my front torso. There was no way I could breathe as my windpipe was twisted and shut.

Weeping, my sister-in-law ran to get the chauffeur and other house help. They bundled me into the car, and we raced towards the hospital emergency. When my head was rotated 180 degrees, I managed with every breath in me to rebuke the devil and command it to depart from me. I also asked my sister-in-law to say the same rebuke. After we would rebuke them, the demons would let go of my neck, and it would rotate back to its right position; then I would be able to breathe again. This happened on and off until we got to the hospital. When the doctor saw what was happening and how both my sister-in-law and I were weeping, he became emotional too. He said he had never seen anything like this and had no idea what to do.

The news that someone had arrived in emergency whose face was facing the opposite direction spread through the hospital quickly. People wanted to see this amazing sight. So, before we knew it, there was a big crowed wanting to see what was going on. The doctor tried to give me bronchial dilators, but that didn't really help. I knew I was under demonic attack. So, I focused all my energy on two things—rebuking the demons and asking God to keep me alive until 2:00 p.m. when the group of Christians would be gathered at the school for prayer and I could go to them for support in my rebuking the demons.

Meanwhile, the doctor tried what he could to help me breathe. As the clock struck 1:15 p.m., I asked my sister-in-law if we could begin heading toward the school where the Christians met. She consulted the doctor about our leaving, and he reiterated that he did not know how to help me, so we were free to seek any other help.

God orchestrates everything for His purposes. Some of the Spirit-filled believers came early to the school that day, arriving a few minutes after we drove up. As soon as they saw me, one of them said, "You are not ill. You are under demonic attack."

I said, "I know."

Just then, the demons decided to show their power. They rotated my neck so quickly and so violently that I cried out in pain and could not breathe at all. But the believers were ready also. With the name and blood of Jesus, the believers commanded the demons to stop torturing me. They closed every access the demons had to me and bound the demon's hands from being able to touch me. A fierce battle ensued between the demons and the children of God. The end was a foregone conclusion, even though the demons put up a strong fight, the children of God won.

By now, the rumor of this strange occurrence had spread in the school neighborhood, and people came to the school to witness this once-in-a-lifetime sight. Many wept as they saw me struggle to breathe, but they soon saw the power of the Cross triumph over the power of darkness.

A brother received a revelation that the demons had filled my lungs with slime and that was why there was little room for air and why I was experiencing such shortness of breath. They started commanding the slime to come out. Within a short time, I began coughing and each time I would bring out a mouthful of white gluey stuff. That went on for about an hour. With each expulsion, I was more able to breathe. By the time it was over, the stuff I had brought up filled a container.

I was exhausted from the fierce battle. The children of God put a hedge of protection around me. Because I was extremely exhausted, they asked me to go and rest but not return to my room at my brother's house.

By this time, my sister-in-law's parents had heard the news and arrived at the school. They took me home with them. That night, they did not allow me to sleep by myself. Rather, they asked me to sleep with them on their bed. God bless them for their kindness to me.

I fell asleep from exhaustion, but in the middle of the night I awoke to a voice that mocked me, saying, *"Aha, your Christian brothers helped you and cast us out at the school. Now you are all alone by yourself, who is going to take you out of our hands now? You are doomed."*

Immediately, I cried out to God for help and covered myself with the blood of Jesus. Then the Lord opened my eyes, and I saw that there were two huge angels walking around the bed, and the demons couldn't even come near the bed. They were trying to intimidate me from afar. I reminded the devil of the loser and liar that it is, and went right back to sleep.

This incident provided an opportunity for the Christians at the school to share the Gospel with the crowd that had gathered and had witnessed the strange battle with the demons. Those who had come out to witness the strange occurrence also witnessed the power of the blood of Christ triumph over the power of darkness. They could not deny what they saw. When the invitation was given, many came to the Lord. The Lord always transforms to good what the devil intended for evil, for those who love Him and are called according to His purpose.

When I woke up the next day, there was a pronounced elevation of skin half an inch high around my neck. It was as if someone had taken a thick cord and tied it tightly under the skin around my neck. This neck cord remained for about a week before slowly resolving. It was as if it was there to attest that what had happened was real, if anyone had any doubts. I stayed with my in-laws for two more days to regain some strength and then headed home to Mom and Dad. When I arrived home, the cord around my neck was still there, and Mom wept tears of gratitude to the Lord for sparing my life.

After a few days at home, I started the three-day journey back to Ibadan to start my second year of university. By the time I arrived in Ibadan, the news of my illness had reached my sister Adiaha and her husband. My sister was a very experienced nurse, and her husband was a pediatrician. They wanted me to see a doctor, as they thought what I had could have been a rare form of meningitis. To please them, I did see the doctor. But when he suggested that lumber puncture be done to establish or disconfirm the diagnosis, I refused to allow the test because of the possible risks and side effects associated with the procedure.

I was warned that untreated meningitis could be deadly, but I told the doctor that I accepted the risk of remaining untreated. I knew I didn't have meningitis or any other illness; I had been attacked by demons, and the Lord had rescued me. When the Lord asked the Father in the dream that my life be restored, I knew it was done, and no one could take it from me. My Lord had the final say, and that was it for me.

As I returned to school and focused on my studies, I had no reoccurrences or consequences from this demonic fight. I did not have any symptoms of anything related to or resembling meningitis. Neither did I experience shortness of breath or any other symptoms remotely similar to what happened to me that fateful day.

One question that perplexed me was, "Why was the devil after me?" Now, I know the answer. Paul wrote in 2 Timothy 3:11–12, "*You know how much persecution and suffering I have endured. You know all about how I was persecuted in Antioch, Iconium, and Lystra—but the Lord rescued me from all of it. Yes, and everyone who wants to live a godly life in Christ Jesus will suffer persecution.*"

What an honor it is that I am a threat to the devil. He doesn't just attack anyone. It's only those for whom God has apportioned a destiny that destabilizes the devil's kingdom that he will fight. He started fighting and wanting to take me out even before I was born. Paul gives us some insights in Romans 8:28–30. He says, "*And we know that God causes everything to work together for the good of those who love God and are called according to his purpose for them. For God knew his people in advance, and he chose them to become like his Son, so that his Son would be the first born among many brothers and sisters. And having chosen them, he called them to come to him. And having called them, he gave them right standing with himself. And having given them right standing, he gave them his glory*"

A part of the reason for writing this story is to encourage other Christians who are facing trials and difficult times. Take courage for the Lord your God has a plan for your life, and no one can thwart that plan. Just like me, the devil is powerless over you, imperfect as we are. God's mercy and love cover all our missteps and shortcomings as soon as we confess them to Him and ask for His forgiveness and cleansing.

The devil could not kill me before birth, it could not kill me during the war, it could not kill me during this episode, and it has no power over my life. My life is hidden in Christ. When I leave this earth, it will be at the will of the Father. He and He alone will be the only one who takes me home, at His appointed time and according to His plan for me.

Looking back today as I write this book, I wonder if the Lord allowed this incident to happen to introduce me to long fasts. Did He, for my sake, cause me to fast without my knowing it? I love food. I love to eat. So why I would gag at the sight of food was a mystery. He also introduced me to travailing prayer without my even knowing or understanding what was happening. Perhaps this could be what Paul was referring to in Romans 8:26–27 when he wrote, *"In the same way, the Spirit helps us in our weakness. We do not know what we ought to pray for, but the Spirit himself intercedes for us through wordless groans. And he who searches our hearts knows the mind of the Spirit, because the Spirit intercedes for God's people in accordance with the will of God"*

Was that why He put on me such a burden to pray? He also knew I didn't know what and how to pray, as I had no idea what was going on. So, He caused the Holy Spirit to intercede for me. Oh, how He cares for His children. He trained me so gently in the furnace. He knew my weakness. He knew that if He had asked me to fast for seven days, I might have dropped dead of fright without the devil even lifting a finger. He is so good and so gracious.

Almost every tool of warfare that God gives to His children, the devil tries hard to dissuade them from using it. The devil uses whatever tactics it can harness. It had put a huge fear of fasting in me. I was petrified of even the thought of fasting for more than a day. I believed I would die if I didn't eat. But this was an unsubstantiated fear in that, whenever I had malaria, I couldn't eat for days and I didn't die. This just shows that fears can be irrational and without basis, and the devil seizes the opportunity to scare people out of one of the most powerful weapons that can be used to defeat it.

God saw through all my confusion and made a way for me. I didn't know much about travailing prayers and wasn't familiar with the Holy Spirit praying for us with groans too deep for words. That did not stop the Holy Spirit from intervening on my behalf and praying for me. Later in my walk with God, the Lord introduced me to the mighty power of fasting and travailing prayer. Then there came a time when engaging in long fasts was routine for me. Together with praise and worship, fasting and travailing prayers are mighty weapons of our warfare. Praise be to God.

15

The Betrothal and Departure

It was at the crack of dawn when I was gently awakened by Mom's gentle voice. "Dear, it's time to get up."

I turned over lazily and opened my eyes. "Good morning, Maamma," I greeted her as I stretched and sat up.

We had gone to bed late as I had stayed up to visit with Dad, talk, and share with Mom as much as possible before my departure for Ibadan the next morning.

"*Your breakfast is ready,*" Mom continued. "You have to hurry so you don't miss the bus."

Your breakfast is ready, I repeated slowly to myself in my mind.

How I savored those words. Where else could I get such a royal treatment? How precious it is to be with loving parents, the only two people in the entire universe I knew would always love me no matter what. I relished that loving feeling for a few more minutes.

Who else can ever love you like your mother? I thought to myself.

I reached out and took her hand and encased it in both of mine. She placed her other hand over mine, and for a few minutes, we held each other's hands without saying a word. This was one of those moments where silence spoke volumes.

During those minutes, I thought about what could have happened if God hadn't intervened for me. Wow, instead of preparing me breakfast, Mom may have been preparing for my funeral. I shivered at the very thought, and a deep, *Thank you, God,* escaped from my soul. He had intervened for me. He had saved me and foiled the enemy's plans.

"Thank you, Maamma," I whispered as I released her hand and got out of bed.

I dressed quickly, hugged my baby sister Imaobong—who was now 10 years old—and we went to the dining room. There was a mountain of food on the table and some packaged for the journey.

"Maamma, how many people are you expecting for breakfast?" I teased as I sat down. "Where are Baba and Etim?" (*Baba* was the name we called our father.)

"They will be up in a moment. I have their breakfast too, but this one is just for you. After today, who knows when I will see you again or be able to prepare you breakfast. I have a little bit of all your favorites."

I looked into her eyes with gratitude, love, and joy. "Thank you, Maamma."

As I delved into my breakfast, Baba and Etim emerged and joined me and Imaobong at the table.

My dad was not big into conversations with me. I can recall though that when I was much younger, we'd had some good conversations. He'd enjoyed telling me stories about our ancestry and how things were when he was growing up, but as I grew into my teenage years and especially after the war, our conversations became more businesslike. Since I arrived back from Calabar, Dad has been more talkative than usual and the previous day, we had long conversations. Today, I was leaving for Ibadan again, and he wouldn't see me for at least another nine months. I could detect just a little bit of anxiety over me in Mom and Dad's voices. Considering the fact I had almost died just a week previously, I could understand and appreciate the anxiety. Parents always feel the need to be there to protect their children no matter their age. Here I was, having escaped death, and now I was traveling far away to where they could not easily reach me. Now that I am a parent, I have a greater and more empathic understanding of how Mom and Dad must have felt that morning. I love and appreciate both of them dearly.

Baba did not eat but kept me company and talked with me. He dispensed advice and some cash. Soon I said my goodbyes, and the taxi departed for the city, where I would board the Armels' Transport bus for the journey to Ibadan. Armels' Transport was then the Nigerian equivalent of the North American Greyhound bus. It was the most popular means of long-distance travel. The coaches were usually air-conditioned and comfortable. They needed to be as the journeys were often at least a day long. So, people sat all day and were only able to get up and stretch their legs when the bus stopped for refueling and for nutrition breaks. Most people's destinations took more than a day to reach. The journey from my hometown in the East to Ibadan in the West took three days.

Everything Falls Into Place

Even though the journey was exhausting, I was happy to get back to Ibadan early so I could search for off-campus accommodation and settle in before classes started in September. I intended to stay at my sister's place while I hunted for off-campus accommodation. Chris had said he would help me locate what was available before I arrived. However, before I could even start looking, my sister and her husband informed me of an unoccupied room on their premises that I could occupy. I was pleasantly and thankfully surprised.

The room was perfect. It was just the right size and with its own bathroom. It was one of two identical attached rooms comprising a small bungalow. (The other room was occupied by the cook for the family.) It was just perfect. This was my first place! Although it was just one room, it was my very own room, not a dorm room with roommates. It was not inside my sister's home, but outside on the grounds. That was a sign of independence, a sign I was becoming a big girl, a woman. I perceived this as a sign of my gradual transition from a teenager to a young, almost independent woman. I liked that visible sign of growing up. During the holidays, I received a letter from the university confirming that I was accepted into Biochemistry. It seemed that all the lines were falling for me in pleasant places.

"Thank you, Lord," I whispered excitedly.

My sister and family lived on the university campus since her husband was a professor of pediatrics at the university. Their house was also close to Queen's Hall (the female students' hostel where some of my friends were), the Biochemistry Department, and the laboratories. I was very happy with this accommodation. I got to work decorating my room. My sister and her husband had furnished the room with a bed so all I needed was a desk and a few chairs. It was a large room, so I could fit in a bookshelf and other necessities. Within a week of returning, I had everything in place and I was ready for the new school year.

When some of my friends who had wanted to study Biochemistry didn't make the cut, they had to look to other specialties that weren't their first choice. I was very thankful that God had enabled me to be among the first pick for Biochemistry. This provoked me to start strategizing on how to accomplish my next goal—getting into graduate studies by invitation. I didn't want to have to apply for admission to graduate studies. Rather, I wanted to be invited to it. That way, I would have a full university scholarship and be able to choose which professor I wished to work with. There was no time to waste. The pursuit was on again.

Blooming Relationship

Meanwhile, my relationship with Chris was gaining momentum. Even though I didn't have a direct "yes" about Chris, he seemed to be the choice. This was another sign of transitions progressively taking place in my life. A part of me was excited, while another part was apprehensive. How do people navigate these transitions successfully? I drew a big breath and offered a silent prayer.

Since I was living on my sister's property, I had to preemptively introduce Chris to her and her husband and explain to them the nature of the relationship as Chris desired to come over as often as he could on the weekends that he was not on call. Weekdays were for school, and I told him he was not allowed to visit unless there was something critical and earth-shattering that could not wait till the weekend.

Right from the beginning, Chris had made it clear to me that he was not just looking for a girlfriend but for a wife. He said he wasn't interested in dating, rather, he was interested in courtship. Within two months of my return to Ibadan, he asked me to marry him. I told him I would do no such thing as I didn't even know who he was. I told him I needed more time to get to know him and his family before I could make that very important decision.

A month later, he asked if I had learned enough about him to make the decision. I said I hadn't. He couldn't understand what more I needed to know. He wanted me to tell him all that I wanted to know so he could tell me and get on with the commitment. I told him it was not that simple. There was a process that needed to be followed, and I didn't want to be rushed. I had to accomplish the due diligence, and that needed time and patience. I informed him that I would let him know as soon as I was satisfied that I had covered every angle that needed to be covered. What was a few months, when one was making the decision of an entire lifetime?

Family Connections

A month later, Chris asked me again to marry him. I said, "No." He then asked if he could at least introduce me to his oldest sister Ekaete and her husband and his oldest brother Donald and his wife. I had disclosed earlier that I knew these people, even though I didn't know at the time that they were related to Chris. Professor Donald and his family also lived on the university campus. He was a professor of chemistry. As I got to know Chris's relatives, they readily embraced me. They didn't even wait for me to say "yes" to Chris first. I have no idea what Chris told them, but right away, they treated me like family.

His sister, in particular, invited me over for meals with her family. She became like a big sister to me. I must say I started feeling the same, as she treated me more and more as such. So, I went from being a little teenage girl who had traveled alone to the West just a few years earlier to attend A Levels, to a maturing young lady for whom life was falling into place and who was surrounded by "family." God is amazingly good.

In December of my second year of university, just over a year from when our courtship began, Chris shared with me his desire to train to be a neurosurgeon. He said he wanted to start the program by the following summer, just about six months to the day. He had his sights on some programs in the United States and Canada, to which he was making applications. One of the reasons he wanted me to make up my mind was because securing a wife was one of the things he wanted to accomplish before leaving Nigeria.

Was that pressure or what? What was it with this guy? At first, it was just saying yes to courtship. Now, after I had made that small concession to getting to know him better, he wanted to get married. Getting married before finishing university was definitely not on my agenda. Even if it were, I couldn't see how it could happen by the time he left Nigeria in the summer. There was no way to plan a wedding in less than six months when we were both hundreds of miles away from home. Besides, I hadn't yet officially said yes to marriage; I had said, "Yes" to courtship. Therefore, we hadn't even officially informed our families of any decisions. Only our relatives in Ibadan knew we were courting.

The process of vetting which commences when two young people express their intention to be married in our culture, usually requires significant time. The families have to investigate each other and ensure the match is a good one for their children. Even if the family investigation process could be accomplished quickly, it would be a huge distraction from my studies to plan a wedding from afar within a few months. I was not prepared to sacrifice my opportunity to finish my first degree well as that would impair my ability to gain admission into graduate studies. One could get married anytime, but how one finished their first degree impacted their ability to proceed with further studies. When I decided to study Biochemistry rather than Medicine, my intent was to continue with it to a PhD. If I allowed myself to be distracted, that dream could easily die. A wedding before the summer was definitely out of the question for me. However, I conceded to notifying our families of our intentions and becoming officially engaged before the end of June, when he would have to leave. Then, after my graduation, we could decide when to get married.

In our tradition, the young man is not the one who asks the parents of the girl for her hand in marriage. It is the elders of his family who do this after they are satisfied that this is the right woman for their son. Since we were both far away from home, speaking to family elders was difficult. Luckily as already mentioned, we both had family members nearby who already knew each other well. At Chris's request, his brother Donald and his wife, his sister Ekaete, and her husband sent a message to my sister Adiaha and her husband that they would like to come and visit. In our culture, everyone knows what such a message means. So, a date was set, and his people went to visit my sister. They informed her that they had informed their family in the East that Chris had found a prospective wife, and they should be ready to get the traditional investigative process started. They also said she should officially relay the message home to my parents and family, that their family would like to seek their permission for their son Chris to marry me. Upon receiving the message, Baba wrote to me to confirm that I had consented to the official process being initiated. He wanted to hear it from my mouth before consenting to anything. I replied, "Yes." With that, the process began.

By the end of May, both families had completed their investigations and given consent for things to move forward. Meanwhile, Chris had applied to programs in the United States and Canada. He was accepted into a program in New York City and a program in Saskatoon, Canada. His second brother, Joe, who was the Nigerian consular officer for the United Nations in New York City at the time, advised him to choose the Canadian program. The program started on July 1, so Chris needed to be in Canada before that date. I had exams until June 16th. The pressure mounted.

The Anchor is Cast with a Ring

The engagement ceremony in our tradition is very different from the ones done in the Western world. It is usually an elaborate ceremony where the two families come together to celebrate the new relationship being established between them. The two children would willingly consent to be married to each other in the presence of their parents, elders, and extended family members. Since marriages are between two families and not just between two people in our tradition, this ceremony is very important. When the two children agree to be married to each other in the presence of their families, they are also committing their two families to be "married" to each other. Before the advent of church weddings, this was the official wedding, the only marriage ceremony needed and necessary. Indeed, even today in our tradition, people are not considered officially married without the traditional ceremony where the families come together and agree to consent, celebrate, encourage, and bless the marriage.

We needed to get home for this ceremony, but as I had exams until June 16, we could not leave Ibadan before June 17. The outfit typically worn for this ceremony is an elaborate gown made with colorful fabric, family colors, and emblems for those from royal or ruling families. There was no time to get one made for me as Chris had to leave Ibadan and depart for Canada on June 26.

We planned to start our journey to the East at the crack of dawn on June 17. Chris was driving. He was determined to make the journey in as few hours as possible. We arrived at his hometown late that night. We planned to visit with his family for two days so they could put a face to the name of the person they were about to welcome into their family. His mother welcomed me with open arms. She was already treating me like a daughter. Several members of the family came to visit and size me up during the two days I spent there. On June 20, we drove to my hometown. Luckily, my parents had met Chris the previous summer when I had first introduced him to them.

Since we didn't have the time to organize the elaborate ceremony that would normally have been part of the official engagement, my dad thought it best for the ceremony to be held at Calabar, away from my hometown where the extended family could demand the normal elaborate ceremony. Dad met with, explained the circumstances to, and invited just two important and senior family members to the ceremony at Calabar. The date was set for June 22 for Chris and me to become officially engaged. The ceremony was simple but not any less meaningful. By this time, Chris' oldest brother Donald had moved from Ibadan to Calabar to start a new university there. He was the Founder and first Vice Chancellor of the University of Calabar. On June 24, just two days after our engagement, Chris left Calabar at the crack of dawn and started his journey back to Ibadan to drop off the car, pick up his already-packed luggage, and depart for Canada.

I stayed at Calabar and started my summer job. This time, I didn't have to look for a position. The job at the weekly newspaper was already waiting for me. l had continued to write and send articles to be published in the weekly, even after my return to Ibadan after the first summer holiday. Because of that, I was treated as staff. That meant I could just continue working there during the summer without having to re-apply. Furthermore, being staff meant I had seniority and earned more than a summer student. Even though I wasn't paid for the articles I sent from September to June, the elevation to staff status more than compensated for payment for the dozen or so articles I had provided to keep the weekly column going.

Staff privileges also entitled me to benefits such as paid holidays and better sick leave privileges. Life was good, and I was very happy. Apart from the few people I met the previous summer, I now had a new friend Akon, the fiancée of Chris's younger brother, Ebong, who was also working at Calabar. We became very good friends. The summer flew by quickly and thanks to my staff status, I was entitled to a two-week paid holiday. I decided to spend one of those weeks with Chris's mom (his dad had passed away seven years earlier). I am very glad I spent that week with her.

16

The Blessing and the Sorrow

In previous years, final-year students were entitled to single rooms. However, because of the large number of students admitted, there were not enough single rooms for every final-year student, especially at Queen's Hall, the female hostel. The solution was to hold a raffle at the end of the university year for returning final-year Queen's Hall students. All the room numbers whether single or shared, were placed in a bucket, and returning final-year students drew for a room. It was the best way to assign rooms without bias. Those who drew shared rooms had to share with the other student who also drew the same room.

I desperately wanted a single room. Having enjoyed a room by myself the previous year at my sister's place, I didn't want to go back to a shared room. Fortunately, I drew a single room. My room wasn't just any single room; it was large and well-situated, but more importantly, it had been occupied by Christian final-year students for the two years that I had been at the university and I understood it had been occupied by Christian final year students for many consecutive years in the past.

I referred to it as "the anointed room" and had prayed that I would be assigned to it in September. I was very pleased that I drew it.

Strange Behavior

I arrived back at University in Ibadan at the end of the summer with a ring on my left hand. (I was eager to show it to my friends, especially those who had journeyed with me through the vetting process.) I settled into my room, and classes started on cue. Final years at the university are usually very busy; mine was no exception. Apart from classes, we had three projects to complete—one for each semester. The experiments had to be performed and results collected, tabulated, analyzed, and reported on, then submitted by the end of each semester. I love research, finding out why things happen and how they happen. The lab was the place where that detective work took place. I was really having fun.

My sister Adiaha, who was staff at UCH Ibadan had arranged for the top cardiologist at her hospital there to be Maamma's doctor. In the past, Mom traveled to Ibadan for checkups often until my sister departed for London. Now that she was back in Ibadan and the war had ended, it was time for Mom to have her long-delayed checkup. Mom traveled to Ibadan to see the cardiologist and also visit my sister and her husband, her grandchildren, and me. She stayed with my sister and was glad for the opportunity to spend time with all of us.

Mom arrived in October and was planning to stay until mid-December. Dad was not a traveler and happily stayed home, attending to the church's business and his administrative duties as Chair of the local Cooperative and the Chief of our hometown. My sister Adiaha and I wanted Mom to stay in Ibadan for as long as possible. She had arranged for the various tests prescribed by Mom's cardiologist before she arrived in Ibadan. Because many years had elapsed since Mom's last assessment, there were lots of tests to be done.

Despite my busy schedule, I wanted to visit with Mom as much as I could. Therefore, I created a plan to visit her on Wednesday nights after my lab and on Saturday afternoons. Wednesdays were hectic days for me, as I was usually on my feet all day in the lab, and when I got back to the hostel at the end of the day, I was too exhausted to do anything but just watch TV to unwind before going to bed. This made it a perfect evening to visit with Mom. After my lab work, I would stop and spend about an hour with her before going to the hostel. Sitting and chatting with her was relaxing. Saturday visits were more than a brief stop; those afternoons were wonderful and I looked forward to spending each of them with her.

Although those times together were wonderful, something very strange and foreboding was happening. Since her arrival Mom often interjected into our lighthearted conversations a comment about death, her death. This troubled both my sister and me. The imminency of her demise as Mom perceived it was contrary to what the test results had indicated. After reviewing the test results and examining Mom, the cardiologist reported that Mom's heart was quite healthy. In fact, he indicated that for all the years he had been looking after her, this was the healthiest her heart had been. Furthermore, Mom had been relatively "healthy" even before the war. From the day I had found her almost dead and she had come back to life, her health had improved significantly. Yet, Mom felt that death was imminent, soon, right by the door. She had brought keepsakes from home that she wanted my sister and me to have, but we refused to take them. We didn't want to validate her death thoughts.

The Matriarchal Blessing

On one of the Wednesday nights in mid-November, I stopped in for my usual quick visit with Mom, but it turned out not to be a quick visit at all. The death issue dominated our conversation even though I tried to steer the conversation away from it. She disclosed to me that night that for years, she had pleaded with and asked God to keep her alive until her youngest child left home for high school. My baby sister, Imaobong, had just left home for high school that September and Mom sensed that her time was up. God had kept His part of the bargain, and she felt He was about to make her keep hers. She was very, very "clingy." She acted as if she would not see me again if she were to let go of me. She also acted similarly to my sister Adiaha. We didn't understand why she was acting that way.

The amazing thing was that Mom was not feeling ill. She seemed to be in great health and as her cardiologist suggested, in better health than she had been in a long time. I pointed this out to Mom and told her that, if God wanted to take her, He would not have made her heart the healthiest it had been in years. Furthermore, even if her barter with God was due, it didn't mean it had to happen the moment her baby girl left home. God is gracious, and I was sure He would give her a little time to catch her breath before coming for her.

I pointed out to her the fact that I was graduating from university in about eight months, and I wanted her to savor my graduation and my wedding which would be taking place sometime later. I was sure God would not have a problem with either of those desires. She brushed my arguments aside and insisted that doctors only know in part and only see the visible, but the invisible is also present and is often the more tangible and important part of the equation. There was no way of convincing her to consider the possibility that she could be wrong.

Mom offered me the keepsakes again that night, but I again refused to even look at them. After a while, she stopped talking about death. It seemed something different was on her mind. Mom started telling me things she wanted me to know. It seemed like a trip down memory lane. She talked to me about my birth and childhood, how she was so ill and her heart so weak when she was expecting me that the doctors were not certain I would be born alive or that she would survive the pregnancy or childbirth. But God kept us both alive, and I was born healthy.

She also shared with me the story of her growing up an orphan, how difficult things were for her, and how God had come through for her. She told me about the many things God had done for her as a person and for us as a family. She reminded me of the many times God had performed miracles for me and snatched me from the jaws of death. She concluded these long stories by saying the reason she was telling and reminding me of all these things was to let me know that God is always with me. He had a plan for my life, and if I stayed close to Him, no power on earth could foil those plans. She encouraged me to be strong and stay close to God. I felt overwhelmed by all these—maybe because I was extremely tired as I had been on my feet all day at the lab. It could also be that I was afraid that the death "talk" could be real. I found the conversation draining. It was now close to midnight; all I wanted to do was get back to the hostel and go to sleep. I was exhausted.

I didn't appreciate or understand what Mom was doing and saying to me that night, but a few weeks later, it became clear. She was giving me her final instructions and pronouncing her final blessings on me, similar to what Moses did for the children of Israel as recorded in Deuteronomy chapter 33 or what Jacob did for his children as described in Genesis 49. By the time Mom was done, my little stopover, which usually lasted for an hour, had ballooned to over four hours.

I will backtrack a little to give context to the story. At about an hour and a half into the visit on that Wednesday night, I stood up and tried to leave, as I had already overstayed my usual Wednesday night one-hour visit. As I started walking toward the gate of my sister's house to start the journey to the hostel, Mom followed me. She talked as we walked slowly toward the hostel. As we reached the front door, Mom was still talking. I turned around and told her I was going to walk her back to my sister's house, as I wasn't sure she could find her way back in the dark by herself. However, when we arrived at the gate and I turned around to return to the hostel, Mom turned and followed me, still talking. At the hostel, I turned to walk her back and she turned with me, still talking. This walking and turning continued several times. I was getting frustrated; it was close to midnight, and I was very tired. Wednesdays were all-day laboratory days and I had been on my feet most of the day. I impressed on Mom that I really, really needed to go to sleep. Apart from being extremely exhausted, I also had an early morning class the next day. I told her I would walk her back to the gate to my sister's house one last time, and she should please, please not turn around and follow me again.

Just then, a saving strategy occurred to me. I asked Mom when she was planning to leave Ibadan. She said she didn't have a date planned but thought she still had a few more weeks. I asked if those few weeks were going to be over before the next Saturday. She gave me one of those *Oh-you-think-you-are-very-smart* looks.

I told her I had to go to sleep, but would come early and stay later than usual on my visit the next Saturday, just three days ahead. I promised to listen without interruption to anything and everything she desired to tell me on that Saturday. And I would also take her out to a quiet place she would enjoy, where we wouldn't be interrupted by the grandchildren. The Saturday would be the day for just the two of us. If by the end of that Saturday, she still had things to tell me, I was prepared to repeat the procedure the Saturday after that. I asked if that was acceptable to her. She was quiet for a while, then said, "Yes." She then stood still for a few minutes.

When she started to speak again, they were no longer instructions. Mostly, she pronounced many blessings on me, and at the end, she said, "When you hear that it has happened, don't come to the East. I don't want you to attend the funeral. Stay here. Work hard on your studies, and the God who has always been with you will continue to be with you and give you good success."

Then she prayed a blessing on my marriage and future family. She turned and we both walked to my sister's house in silence. I opened the gate, she stepped inside, gave me a huge hug, turned around, and walked right into the house without looking back. I watched in silence as emotions I could not quite comprehend stirred inside me. I turned, and as I walked back to the hostel, I tried to squash the emotions of fear, dread, and foreboding that were stirring inside me by strategizing how I could reorganize my schedule to fit in the extra hours I had promised to spend with Mom the next Saturday.

It was already November, a busy time as the first semester exams were starting in about two weeks. I didn't recognize then how lucky and blessed I was to have spent those hours with Mom that night. If I had known how significant those hours would turn out to be for both Mom and me, I would have sat with her for a much longer time, listened, and taken notes as she spoke. I would even have asked a few questions. Alas, hindsight is always twenty-twenty.

The next Saturday, I hurried and did everything I had to do so I could keep my promise to visit Mom early and spend more time with her. I arrived at my sister's house; Mom wasn't in the sitting room. I thought she was probably in her bedroom. I went to her bedroom; she wasn't there. There was also no sign of her luggage. A little concerned, I went to the kitchen to find my sister. After greeting her, I asked, "Where is Maamma?"

"She left for home early this morning," my sister responded.

"What? How come? What happened at home?" I queried.

"The news came on Thursday that Mrs. Essang's mom had passed away. Mrs. Essang made plans to get home as quickly as possible. She bought a lot of the necessities for the funeral here. As you know, she is the firstborn of the family, so she'll be in charge of organizing the funeral. She bought so many things that she had to rent a van to accommodate them. After packing everything, there was still room in the van. Mom wanted to attend the funeral, and since there was room in the van, she decided to hitch a ride with her, as it was a more convenient option for her than going back by public transport in a few weeks. I tried unsuccessfully to dissuade her from going. They left early this morning."

I was stunned, concerned, afraid, and disappointed—disappointed that I could not visit with her that Saturday and disappointed that the many fun things I had planned to do with her were no longer going to happen. Her visit to Ibadan had been at a busy time for me, the weeks just prior to examinations, so I hadn't really taken her out or spent much quality time with her. I was planning for us to have more time together after my exams since her visit was supposed to last till mid-December. Remembering her clinginess the previous Wednesday night and how she'd talked and acted as if that would be the last time we would see each other, I was troubled and afraid. Did she know something the rest of us didn't know? Had something been revealed to her?

I was concerned because one of the emotions stirring in my heart that Wednesday night when I turned to walk back to the hostel for the last time was fear. I feared that something may have been revealed to her. I was anxious that her death story could actually come true. I was afraid that I might not see her again, and had tried very hard to squash that emotion. The fear that what she was saying could come true was one of the reasons I had determined to spend some quality time with her the following Saturday, exams or no exams. Now she was gone. What could I do? Fear assailed me. No, it couldn't happen. I was just months from graduating from university. I needed her to be there to celebrate that milestone with me. She had to be there. I couldn't let myself think otherwise.

Mom and I had a very close relationship, but her behavior during that last visit was unusual. Though she often said she was living on borrowed time, she hadn't said those words in a few years. Our visits, especially since I had moved to Ibadan, had always been cordial. Even though she had always enjoyed spending time with me whenever I visited home, she never tried to hold on to me so tightly. Why had she tried to hold so tightly onto me during that Wednesday night visit? A shot of guilt fired across my mind, accusing me and my sister of having been too busy to spend quality time with her. We had things to do, work, kids, school, exams, and more. Besides, we didn't think we should indulge in or encourage the death conversation. Until that morning when she left with Mrs. Essang, we had expected her to remain in Ibadan for many more weeks; she didn't need to go back home until mid-December when Imaobong would be home from high school for the Christmas holidays. So, why did she act that night as if it would be the last time she saw me? That was the question that troubled me.

I whispered a prayer. "God please, please give me another chance. Please, please, don't let this be it. Please do not take her yet." I worked hard to push aside the troubling thoughts. I had exams just around the corner, and the first semester's project to report on and submit. Even though I had completed the experiments and tabulated the results, the analysis and write-up still remained to be done. I couldn't afford to be distracted. I said goodbye to my sister and returned to the hostel.

The Dreaded News

Two weeks later, exams started and lasted just over a week. I worked hard and was pleased with my performance after each paper. When the exams were finished, I turned my attention to the project's analysis and report. Finally, one joyous afternoon, everything was completed and I submitted my report. How nice it was to have everything done. I was pleased with myself, and as I walked from the department back to my room, I felt as light as a feather. Now, I could relax. I was looking forward to a well-deserved, refreshing siesta. I had just one more task to complete before I could curl up in my bed for that well-deserved nap—laundry. I hadn't had time to do laundry for a few weeks leading up to the exams, but now it was time to catch up. When I arrived back at the hostel, I soaked the laundry before heading back to my room for my nap. Just as I was getting under the sheets, there was a knock on my door. I wondered who had the audacity to knock on my door at this time when I was just about to enter the siesta I had been looking forward to for almost a week. I thought it was probably one of my classmates wanting to chat.

Tough luck, I thought. *I'm just going to ignore whoever is out there.*

I pulled the sheets up and over my head. But the knocking continued. Exasperated, I got up and opened the door to see who this importune visitor was. Behold, standing there in front of my door was the nanny of my sister's children, Victoria. The look on my face must have indicated that I wasn't happy to see whoever was knocking on that door.

She said, "Sorry Auntie, but Mummy said I should come and get you."

I asked, "Vicky, Is anything wrong? I am quite tired and was just going to take a nap. Can it wait until I wake up? Is it urgent?"

"Mummy said you should come now, Auntie," she responded.

"Victoria, is there something wrong?" I asked again.

"It will be good for you to come now, Auntie. Mummy said I should come back with you. I think you need to come with me now."

"Vicky, please tell me, is there something wrong?"

"You need to come with me now, Auntie," she responded.

I sensed she was withholding something important from me. "Okay, I will come now. I just need to change from my nightie."

After she saw that I had changed and was definitely going to go the house, Victoria started on the journey back, saying, "I will see you at home, Auntie." She walked swiftly, leaving me trailing behind her.

I was beginning to have a sick feeling in my stomach. I knew something was very wrong. Could it be Mom? I fought hard to keep my mind from entertaining that thought. My steps quickened as I neared my sister's house.

Dark Days with Tiny Rays of Sunshine

I arrived at my sister's house, dreading, desperately hoping but not really believing that whatever the reason for my summons could be handled quickly so I could go back and have that long-coveted sleep. I entered my sister's sitting room to find her there, along with my cousin's wife. They were both crying. Instinctively, I knew that Mom was gone. This was about three weeks from that fateful Wednesday night. My legs felt weak and wobbly. I sat down quickly.

Have you ever encountered something you have dreaded all your life? Can you imagine what it feels like to finally come face-to-face with a dread that has been part of your life for as long as you can remember? This was the day I had dreaded all my life. Here it finally was. What should I do? How did one manage such a day? My mind was bombarded by a multitude of emotions, and for some time, it appeared both my mind and brain were so overloaded, they just froze.

I couldn't think and I couldn't feel. It was as if my body was paralyzed. I think I might have tried to pray, but no words could get into my mind. I just sat there numb. After what appeared to be an eternity, some emotions began to return and tears started to roll down my cheeks. They were tears, but they were not all tears of disappointment, although there was some of that. They were not tears of anger. No, there was none of that. Were they tears of sorrow? Yes, there was definitely some sorrow in my heart. I had just lost my best friend. But overwhelmingly, the one emotion that dominated my mind was gratitude.

I didn't quite understand it. When the woman who had been everything to you passes away, are you supposed to be grateful? Why was I experiencing gratitude? Why did I have this strange emotion on such a fateful day? I did not know the answer, but I felt grateful that this news had not come two weeks before this; that would have impacted my ability to perform well in my exams—if I were able to write them at all. I was grateful it hadn't come last week as that would have impaired my ability to analyze and write up my project's report appropriately. I was thankful it had not come two days previous to this, as that would have impacted the presentation of my project report. I was thankful that God and Mom, even with this, took me into consideration and chose the least negatively impactful time if there could be such a thing at a time like this to break the news to me. All the exams were finished and the project report submitted just that afternoon. How they both love me so very much to orchestrate the time to fit my schedule so precisely.

Maamma, you are the best. You even arranged with God such that this transition did not impact me more negatively. Thank you, God. Thank you, Maamma. Your love for me is incredible.

Those were the thoughts that invaded my heart and mind. They did not stop but continued. Memories of that Wednesday night flooded my mind. I was thankful God had kept Mom alive till then. I was grateful for the great privilege of that Wednesday night. I was thankful for all that Mom shared with me. I was thankful she had blessed me and prayed for me for the last time in my presence that night.

Continued Attitude of Gratitude

How many children are that fortunate to receive a blessing from their parents before they depart? How many children have life-giving words spoken over them by their departing parent? How many children have the awesome privilege of hearing and being reminded of their life history and all the great things the Lord has done for them from their mother before her departure? We heard about Isaac planning to bless

Esau before passing away. Also, Jacob blessed every one of his children before he passed away. But those were millennia away, not in modern times. I pondered that for a moment and was again filled with gratitude and thankfulness.

I thought about June, a few months earlier, when I got engaged. I was thankful Mom was there to witness the engagement. I was thankful that, on that last Wednesday night together, she had blessed my future home. I was thankful she had been there throughout my life to guide me to this point when I was just about to be able to stand on my own two feet. I was thankful there was no one left at home for me to worry about. My baby sister was in high school, and she could spend her holidays with our oldest brother or sister, or even me, as I would be graduating from university in about seven months.

I was thankful for being blessed with a mother who taught me that a life focused exclusively on oneself was impoverished and joyless while doing our best to help those who needed our help was where fulfillment and blessings resided. She taught me how to care for those less fortunate and to be a giver. Best of all, she and Dad modeled a life that honored God, thus giving me an example to emulate. I seemed full. What other blessing could I desire? Mom had lived well. I was so happy that she had been my mother. I was so happy that she had left this world peacefully knowing she had fulfilled her mandate. What else could a child ask for?

I was grateful for all God had done for me through Mom, but her death created a huge void in my life. Now that I had emotions back in full flow, I gave way to them. Oftentimes, tears accompanied the gratitude. Even though I had much to be thankful for, I also was very disappointed. I was disappointed that Mom wouldn't be at my graduation or my wedding. I grieved that I would never be able to buy her anything, despite the fact that she and Dad had denied themselves many comforts so that we, their children, could have the best education possible. I was grieved that she would never see or hold any of my children and that she wouldn't be there when I came home from the hospital with my babies, especially the first, to show me what to do and how to care for my child.

I was heartbroken that I would no longer have her to confide in, to discuss the important issues of my life, and to benefit from her wisdom. I was devastated that my best friend was gone. She had told me that life was unpredictable. Parents teach and train their children to the best of their ability, and then they pass on, hoping and praying they have given their kids all the tools they need to lead a successful life.

I hoped I had been a good student, and had learned well and as much as possible from her. Life would definitely not be the same without her. However, I had these precious memories tucked deep in my heart. They were jewels that not even death could take from me. Oh, how grateful I was for that Wednesday night. That was a precious gift. Mom had told me that Wednesday night not to come home to the East for her funeral, but when it happened, I wanted to go. But my sister Adiaha advised me to honor her last wish. I acquiesced.

So, all my images and memories of Mom are those of a lively, loving woman. I am thankful that my last encounter with her was a huge hug and her looking me in the eyes and telling me how proud she was of me, asking God to bless me, my future family, and my children. I felt full. I felt she had given me everything she could give me. Now, what I needed to do was use those treasures wisely.

Reflections and Recollections

After sitting in my sister's living room for about two hours, pondering all my thoughts of gratitude and sorrow, I told her I needed to return to the hostel. Both she and our cousin's wife told me it was not a good idea for me to be alone. However, I needed to deal with my soaking laundry. Besides, I needed to have some time by myself to ponder what had just happened. Even though I knew Mom was gone, it hadn't yet sunk in. I needed time by myself to process that information. I told them I needed to go, but I wouldn't sleep there. I would return to my sister's later that night.

Back at Queen's Hall, I calmly finished my laundry, went to the communal fridge to collect what perishables I had there, and then returned to my room. I lay on my bed and pondered what had happened.

I tried to imagine what life would be like without Mom. I couldn't. It was difficult for the reality to sink in.

As I lay there, I began a conversation with her as if she were in the room with me. I would ask a question and imagine what her answer would be. I recalled some of our conversations over the years, the way she often teased me, and how I teased her. I tried to recall our joyful times, the many times she or I would tell funny stories and jokes that made us laugh. The more I did this, the more my spirit was elevated. I was glad to be able to recall those memories on this particular day. I had heard somewhere that what mattered most in life was how one finished her life on earth. I examined Mom's life. I tried to recall the number of unrelated people who called her "Maamma" because she had cared for them like a mother, the number of people who respected her because she had impacted their lives positively, the number of people who sought her counsel repeatedly because she was a wise woman and those who came to her when they needed help because they knew they could count on her. I thought of her faith and example in Christian conduct and of those she mentored in the Lord. Her six children were all excelling in their diverse fields of endeavor and our family had an honorable and prestigious reputation. These were some of her legacies, her fruits. Matthew 7:16 says, *By their fruit, you will recognize them"* She bore good and great fruits that outlived her, fruits that did last, as described in John 15:16a: *"But I chose you and appointed you so that you might go and bear fruit—fruit that will last"*

I was thankful to have been her child. I was grateful that this amazing woman had brought me up, taught me about faith in God, and encouraged me to walk with Him. I was thankful she had finished well and had now departed in peace. My heart was full of thankfulness and gratitude once again. I drew a big breath, got up from my bed, and called my best friend, Nike. She had a room on the floor above mine. She came down, and I calmly told her about my mom's departure. She couldn't believe I could be so calm under such circumstances. I told her it was not about me or my own doing but a fulfillment of Philippians 4:6–7, which says, *"Don't worry about anything; instead, pray about everything.*

Tell God what you need, and thank him for all he has done. Then you will experience God's peace, which exceeds anything we can understand. His peace will guard your hearts and minds as you live in Christ Jesus"

I thanked God for what He had done for Mom and for me. That brought peace to my heart and soul. She hugged and held me for a long time. We both cried. I gave her all my perishables and told her I would probably be gone until the beginning of the new semester. I wished her a Merry Christmas and sent my love to her folks and then packed up and left for my sister's house.

At my sister's house that night, there was not much sleep. She was busy making a list of all the things we would purchase to take with her to the East for the funeral. My sister had not been aware of Mom's final instructions to me as I hadn't yet told anyone about our conversations on that last Wednesday. She therefore was planning that I would be traveling with her to the East. A part of me wanted to keep it from her so I could go, but the other part alerted me that it had never been a good idea to go against Mom's wishes, especially one so important to her that it was part of her final instructions. I knew I had to tell her.

As soon as she heard it, she told me I couldn't go. I needed to respect Mom's wishes. She said we may never know why, but both of us knew her well enough to know she must have had a good reason to advise against my attending the funeral. I was sad that, apart from my second brother Mfon, who was now in the United States working on his doctorate in engineering, I would be the only child not there to pay my final respects. But then, I had already done that on that fateful Wednesday night. Peace returned to me.

A Peace That Surpasses All Understanding

I helped my sister purchase some of the things needed for the funeral over the next two days. At the crack of dawn on the third day, as my sister and her husband drove off and started the journey to the East for the funeral, I whispered my last adieu to Mom. I stayed at my sister's house while she was gone, playing surrogate mom to her children and overseeing the household. It was just the alone time I needed to further process the news and think about Dad. If I was feeling that lonely, how did he feel? I whispered many prayers for him.

My sister and her husband were gone for eight days. When they returned, she brought pictures of the funeral. It was a huge funeral, as many of the people whose lives Mom had touched had come to pay their respects. We both had a good cry. It was now officially over. Mom was no longer on this side of heaven. It was up to us to put into practice all she had taught us.

Christmas that year was quiet. I spent it with my sister and her family but then went back to the hostel early as I needed solitude to continue to process my new state of aloneness and become more accustomed to the fact that Mom was no longer around. I spent a few days in my room by myself before the new semester began. By the end of that time, I had made peace with heaven and my heart. If there was one thing Mom would want me to do, it would be not to waste time mourning over what I could not change. The thing she wanted me to do was to study hard, graduate with honors, be invited into graduate studies, and marry that young man who was waiting for me in Canada. Yes, I was going to make her proud by doing well in my studies. Having this goal to pursue helped.

Gratitude for a Second Mother

I began to thank God that Chris's mother was still alive. She was soon going to become my new mother, so I would still have a mother. In our tradition, when you marry into a family, the mother becomes your mother. Judging from how she'd received and treated me during the two times I had visited with her, especially the one week I had spent with her, I was sure she would be a great mother to me. I was thankful that, even though I had just lost a mother, I would soon gain a new one. My in-laws already treated me like family so I considered myself blessed.

Some of our dreams do not become realities. Six weeks after my mother's death, Chris's mom passed away suddenly in her sleep. This reopened the death wounds in me. I was sad that the mother I looked forward to getting to know better had also left. What was going on?

I refused to dwell on the negative side but searched for a reason to be thankful. I found one readily. I was thankful I had gotten to meet her. I was thankful I had spent that one week at the end of the summer with her. That was not enough time to really get to know her, but it was better than nothing. How did God put it in my heart and mind to go spend that time with her even though I was not yet fully married to her son? It was all God's doing. He delights in giving amazing gifts. The one week spent with Chris's mom was a very precious gift. She gave me a scarf during that visit. I still have it.

A Devastating Sense of Loss

My fiancé Chris, who was now in Canada, was devasted by the news of his mother's death. His father had passed away five years earlier during the war while Chris was in the West, at Ibadan. He was unable to attend the funeral. Now, his mother has also passed away at a time when he couldn't attend her funeral. Furthermore, most Nigerian children looked forward to the day they would finish their training and start earning money, so they could give good gifts to their parents as a show of appreciation for the sacrifices they had made to provide for their education. At the time of her death, Chris's mom had been a widow for five years and Chris was looking forward to being in a position where he would earn enough money to take care of her. That is our tradition. Now that she was gone, he would never be able to do that. He was devastated.

When his father passed away, Chris had been in medical school. It was distressing to him that he would never be able to do something for his father. However, he took solace that his mother was still alive. The news of her death was devastating to him, as it made all those plans and dreams of no consequence, and without warning.

Unlike those of us in Nigeria who could mourn together and console each other, Chris had no one with whom to mourn, and he had no time to appropriately mourn because he was in a very demanding and intensive residency program. There were just two residents in the program for the entire province, and they worked practically around the clock. If one was away, the other worked 24/7. The most time he could take off now was two days. He felt all alone.

This triggered something in him; he wanted to get married as soon as possible. He explained that, while his mother was alive, he always felt he had a home. Now that both of his parents were dead, he felt he belonged nowhere. He wanted to reestablish that sense of belonging, and the solution was for us to get married as soon as possible.

17

Navigating Through Difficult Waters

Chris' desire to get married as soon as possible was problematic for me. I was in my final year of university, and with all the demands such a year brings, there was no way we could be married before the end of the university year, which would be the middle or end of June.

Would the wedding take place in Nigeria or in Canada? I did not have a passport so it wouldn't be easy for the wedding to take place in Canada. At that time, getting a Nigerian passport was a Herculean task; I had tried unsuccessfully the previous two years to get one. I had applied for one through the university student's union office but never heard back from the passport office. The student's union tried unsuccessfully to follow up on the application. I applied again the next September on my own, but still no response. There was a rumor that the passport office wasn't issuing passports to students in general and final-year students in particular, as they suspected that, if the student left the country, he or she wouldn't return for the National Youth Service Corp which was mandatory for every university graduate. How was I going to navigate the passport issue under these constraints? There was a significant possibility I would be refused a passport on a third application.

What were the alternatives? None of the different options were great. First, we thought of Chris coming back to Nigeria for the wedding. That would be too hectic, as he was entitled to just three weeks of holiday per year. He had already taken a week to attend a course earlier in the year. Then after the news of his mother's death, he had taken off two days to mourn. So, he had just twelve days of holiday left. It took two days to fly from Canada to Nigeria and the same number of days to fly back. He would need to have at least a one-day cushion on the return just in case a flight got delayed and another day to get over the jetlag. That meant six of the twelve days were off for travel. It seemed he would almost have to go from the airport to the altar for the ceremony and then turn around and leave. That was not the type of wedding either of us wanted.

The only viable option was for me to join Chris in Canada, get married, and then return by mid-August to start my NYSC posting. Though this seemed like a good option, there were two issues. The first was the passport issue already discussed. Furthermore, it was also rumored that the names of all NYSC-eligible students had been provided to the airport authorities so that if anyone whose name was on the list tried to leave the country, he or she would be stopped and taken off the airplane.

The second issue was that even if I managed to circumvent the passport and departure issues, how could I get married in a strange land where the only person I knew was the groom? How would preparations be made? It is difficult enough to plan a wedding when one has a full year and plenty of family and friends to help. How then could I plan a wedding in Canada from Nigeria in the middle of my final year at university? These were exactly the types of distractions from my studies I had always wanted to avoid. Doing well enough to be invited into graduate studies was a one-time shot, and I didn't want to jeopardize my chances in any way.

I felt as if I was caught between a rock and a hard place. But one thing was clear—I had to find a way to tackle the passport problem. The only option was to go to Lagos and apply in person and hope I would be lucky and not branded a possible NYSC deserter. Even if I applied in person, it could take several weeks of personal follow-ups at the passport office to have it processed. I could not afford such time away from my classes, exams, and projects. The maximum time I could afford to set aside for this was a week. Could it all be accomplished in a week? Lagos was an overcrowded city rumored to be difficult to navigate because of congestion that caused long delays to get anywhere. I had visited Lagos twice, but both had been short stays. The first time was to see an optometrist and I had stayed with someone from my hometown and his family. He had arranged for me to see an optometrist near his office. The only other outings I experienced during that visit were with his wife to shops. Even then, I knew it took forever to get anywhere. I didn't know what to do. I turned to my refuge, shelter, and miracle worker, God. I prayed that He would make a way for me where there seemed to be no way.

A way became clear. Chris's youngest brother, Ebong, and his wife had just moved to Lagos. I was overjoyed and contacted them right away to share my problems. They said they would be happy to help. (Ebong's wife and I had become very good friends the previous summer when she was also working at Calabar.) They would investigate what was involved in the process and let me know so I could schedule appropriately. Ebong offered to help me navigate Lagos—something not for the fainthearted.

I asked Ebong to send me the forms and requirements so I could do all that could be done remotely before I arrived in Lagos. I completed every document and had my passport photograph ready prior to starting the journey

The first day, Ebong and I were up before dawn and on our way to the passport office. We were one of the first people at that office that day. The Lord gave me favor. Within three days, I was approved for the passport. Nobody asked whether I was a student or not. Thank you, Lord. Not wanting to take any chances, I asked if Ebong could collect the passport for me when it was ready, rather than having it mailed to me. Now that it appeared I had a lock on the passport, I would let the quest for a visa wait until after my final exams.

Setting Sights on a Remote Shore

Getting married that summer was not going to be easy. After finishing my exams, I had only seven weeks before I was scheduled to start my NYSC, a year-long program. My success with the passport office emboldened me and made me suspect that maybe God was at work and could make a way for us. I accepted Chris's suggestion that he should begin making the wedding plans without my input until after my exams. Before I secured the passport, I was reluctant to give that approval, as it would be very embarrassing for him to plan a wedding and send out invitations without being sure I could leave Nigeria. However, Chris is an eternal optimist, and even before I secured the passport, he was prepared to take the risk. That is the exact opposite of me. I don't like to take precipitous risks. I needed to be sure I could get the passport before he sent out invitations. Even after getting the passport, there was still the possibility I could be taken off the plane. But that was a risk I was willing to take, as waiting until I could leave the country would have made it too late to send out invitations. I reasoned that if God wanted us to be married in Canada that summer, He would remove all obstacles. He has already removed a big one, getting a passport.

However, some negative thoughts were never far from my mind. They were questions such as: *What is the penalty for people caught trying to leave the country just before their NYSE? What would happen to me if I was taken off the plane and branded an NYSE deserter? How could such an event affect my future? How would it impact all the plans I have for my life?*

Both God and I knew I didn't have any intentions of deserting the NYSC. I fully planned to be back to complete that service before continuing with whatever life had in store for me. But would anyone believe me if I were caught and falsely branded a deserter? Was this a chance worth taking or should I just hold tight and tell Chris to wait until I finished my NYSC?

Being able to leave Nigeria was not the be-all and end-all. The whole idea of going to Canada, a country where I knew no one except my fiancée, to get married was preposterous. How would a wedding in a strange land where the bride arrived a week before the big day look? What were the usual preparations needed for successful weddings? I had never been part of planning one. Even if I had, it would have been a Nigerian wedding. What did Canadian weddings look like? What needed to be done? Who was going to do them? Would Chris really be able to plan the wedding by himself?

Her wedding day is usually one of the biggest and most important days of a girl's life. So many important details, even the most minute vital to the success of the event. Could I take such a gamble with mine? Would Chris be able to adequately plan it? Would he even know what details needed to be attended to? He swore he would take care of every detail and all I needed to do was show up and say, "I do," but I knew that was just all talk. There were just too many details to attend to—could an overworked young man possibly know, remember, and take care of them all?

Having reluctantly conceded to getting married in Canada that July, I knew I was giving up the right to have control over the wedding planning and execution. The wedding day was set for approximately two weeks from the day I finished my exams. Chris planned for me to stop over at New York City on my way to Canada, so that his brother's wife, sister Lucy, could help me determine what we would need for the wedding and help me purchase them there if possible. The few things I knew we needed were a wedding gown, shoes, rings, and other wearables. Sister Lucy could help me purchase those items in New York.

Stopping over in New York meant I needed to get a US visa as well as a Canadian one. I got all the forms in advance and, as soon as the exams were finished, I completed them. My plan was to make just one trip to Lagos and, as soon as I got the visas, depart from there for Canada. I also set up plans such that, when I returned from Canada, my journey to my NYSC posting would be smooth.

The day I finished the exams, I purchased all I would need for NYSC and packaged everything in several big boxes. I sorted my belongings into three piles—those that were going with me to Canada, those that were going to the NYSC boxes, and other things (such as books) I would not need until after the NYSC. I packed them accordingly and stored the boxes that contained the NYSC things at Chris' sister's house and the ones containing items I would not need until after the NYSC at my sister's house. Within a few days of finishing my exams, I moved the boxes to their different storage locations and then set off for Lagos to start the process of getting a visa and then departing for Canada.

The Winds and Waves Still Obey His Will

I completed the forms for both Canadian and American visas. The Canadian visa was quick. When I arrived at the Canadian High Commission, I was informed that Commonwealth citizens did not need a visa for a short-stay visit to Canada. Since I was planning to be in Canada for less than six weeks, I didn't need to apply for a visa. Wow, that was easy. Praise God. I crossed that off my list. Then I was off to the American embassy. I submitted the forms, and the agents asked me to come back in two days.

I arrived back at the embassy bright and early on the day. I was invited to meet with the consular officer at his office. I sat down on the chair he motioned me towards. Then he pushed my passport toward me and informed me that my application for a visa was denied. I asked why. He said he refused to issue me a visa because he didn't believe I was just stopping over in New York City for a short time. He indicated he believed that, if got into the United States I would not leave. I asked him what made him think that. He didn't have an answer. I asked him what he thought I would be doing in the United States. He couldn't answer that either. I asked what made him think I would abandon my fiancé in Canada and not show up for my wedding. He had no answer. I asked why I would want to forgo a great future with a man I loved in Canada or in Nigeria where I had my family, including my father, to become a fugitive in America. He had no answer but said he had made up his mind and that his decision was final.

I could not understand his reasoning. By this time, we had already bought the ticket that showed me stopping over in New York for five days and then going to Canada. I showed the officer the ticket in an attempt to allay his concerns and convince him I had no intentions of staying in the United States. That did not dissuade him. The flight was in two days.

I reiterated to the Consular Officer that I was getting married in Canada in less than two weeks. My fiancé was already there in a neurosurgery residency program. Why would I want to stay in the United States? Stay there as what and do what? Chris's brother Joe, with whom I would be staying in New York, was the Nigerian Consular officer to the United Nations. Would a man in his position be part of a plan to harbor a fugitive? Why and for what? If I was not getting married to his brother, what relationship would I have with him and his family? Furthermore, I had NYSC in approximately six weeks. The whole thing seemed so preposterous it didn't make any sense to me.

I didn't understand what was happening. I was a very innocent young lady who had not yet been exposed to racism. I had no idea that racism-based decisions didn't have to make sense. As I encountered more and more racism during my years in North America, I came to learn and realize that racist actions often defy rational explanations and do not often make sense to unbiased, rational minds.

I was bewildered. If I could not stop in New York to make the purchases that I needed, where would I make those purchases? Would I be able to change the ticket to go straight to Canada? There were a hundred and one concerns bombarding my mind. The Consular officer must have noticed the concern and frustration on my face. He looked at me with a smirk on his face and then began to laugh. I asked him why he was laughing and his response was, "I can see that you are very frustrated."

That did it. I was going to let him have it. What type of a person was this man that he would cause someone to be so utterly frustrated and then sit back and laugh in her face? He seemed to be enjoying the fact that I was very frustrated. At that point, I thought he had pushed me too far, and every ounce of diplomacy left me.

I said to him, "So, getting people 'very frustrated' is funny to you? Is that your job here? Does being in this position, which gives you a tiny bit of authority over people who want to travel to the United States, make you think you're somebody, that you're God, and that you can entertain yourself at other people's expense? Let me tell you something, you must be a very miserable man, and I feel very sorry for you."

I was not yet finished. I continued, and in a nutshell told him, "I respect your decision to deny me a visa; it is within your right. However, there is one thing you have to do. You have to call Chris's brother in New York and explain to him why I will not be on the flight that will be landing in New York in two days. He is the one who is supposed to pick me up at the airport, so he is expecting me."

"I will do no such thing. That is your problem," he retorted.

"Oh yeah? It's your problem now; you just created it. If you had a viable reason to deny me the visa, it may not have been your problem. Since your reason is just to boost your ego by making me frustrated, it is your problem, and you are going to fix it," I explained.

By this time, I was very upset and didn't care who he thought he was. I was just going to let him have a piece of my mind. I began to tell him a few things about people like him. I asked him if he had ever heard about King Nebuchadnezzar, the person who tried to make himself look like a 'god.' If he hadn't heard of him, I was going to tell him the story and I did. I reminded him of what happened to Nebuchadnezzar the king of Babylon when he created that type of image for himself. I told him also that I didn't find the US so appealing that I would sacrifice my dignity to be a fugitive in it.

He seemed surprised, but I wasn't yet finished. I gave him a few more reasons why he should not be so arrogant. Finally, I said, "Nigeria may not be as developed as your country, but it is my country, and I love it. The only reason I need to stop by New York is to have the help and advice of my fiancé's sister-in-law on what I need for the wedding. So, don't feel you have something that I cannot live without. Always remember that the world is a small place and that you are on Nigerian soil."

I continued, "Today, I am sitting in your office asking you to do your job with fairness and integrity, and you are acting as though you are a god, an unfair one. You are in Nigeria. You never know, maybe tomorrow you could be in a situation where you need help from a Nigerian. Just imagine if he or she treated you the way you are treating me now. Never forget that the world is a very small place. However, today and in this visa issue, you have two options: you can either issue me a visa or make the phone call to New York. The choice is yours."

With that I sat back in the chair, relaxed, and took out a small book I had in my purse and started reading it. I was praying silently in my heart for God's intervention. The officer sat there and stared at me for several minutes. He appeared confused and flabbergasted. He probably wasn't expecting such a reaction from me. Maybe people he'd encountered previously had stroked his ego too highly, which enabled him to cultivate the idea that he could inflict misery on others as he pleased and then have fun at their expense. As I read, I observed him out of the corner of my eyes. He suspected I was resolved to stay there for as long as it took for one of my two options to be enacted.

I am glad I was naïve and innocent then. I wasn't quite aware of the extent of the power that consular officers or anyone in such a position had inside their Embassies. Even if I did, I probably wouldn't have cared at that point. Nobody, irrespective of who they think they are, has the right to treat another human being so rudely and make them feel insignificant. As far as I was concerned, I was somebody, and nobody had the right to treat me like a criminal-to-be without a good reason. However, I believe that whatever I did was inconsequential to the outcome that ensued. The real difference-maker was God. He was with me, and even though I didn't quite appreciate how devastating not passing through New York would have been in terms of my being able to purchase a wedding gown and wedding rings, He did. That made all the difference. Again, God made a way where there seemed to be no way.

Finally, the consular officer picked up my passport, which was still on the table in front of both of us, stamped a visa on it, signed it, and pushed it toward me. He said, "I have changed my mind and decided to give you a visa. I only have one condition. When you come back, come back here to the embassy and visit me."

I took my passport and looked at it; he had just given me a double entry. I had applied for a single entry. "Thank you very much, but I do not live in Lagos, and when I return, it will be just two days before the start of my NYSC posting. So, I may not have the time to come and visit you. Besides, by then I will be a married woman and will have to ask my husband if he would approve of such a visit. Thanks again."

I walked out of that embassy as if walking on air, with hallelujahs and songs of praise pouring from my heart. That was another miracle. I know it was not due to anything I said or did, it was just another favor from God. It turned out that Saskatoon, where Chris lived, was at that time a very small city. Not only was there less choice of shops for wedding dresses (only two in the city at the time), they also didn't stock wedding dresses. I later discovered that no shop actually stocks wedding gowns—be it in Nigeria or Canada—but that they always are pre-ordered and made for the bride.

I knew that brides-to-be in Nigeria would either have a tailor create a gown for them (which usually took several months) or order one from a catalog. What I didn't realize, since I had never been part of planning a wedding, was that even the ones ordered from overseas were not bought "off the rack," but rather the style was chosen from the catalog, and measurements sent for one to be created. I didn't know all these details, but God did, and He caused the consular officer in Lagos to give me the visa for the United States where He had already planned another miracle. I have a God who never stops intervening for me. He never stops working on my behalf. He loves me that much.

18

The Transition

The day before my departure was hectic and full of activities. I needed to exchange some money; Chris had said I didn't need to as he was going to send money to New York for me, but I thought it prudent to have some dollars just in case I needed to make a phone call or pay for something at the airport. Doing even the simplest thing in Nigeria, and particularly Lagos, is never simple, so exchanging currency took almost the entire day.

The next day was D-Day and I was excited! I checked all my documents and made sure I had everything I needed for the journey and my time in Canada. Quite a few people had warned me that Canada was a very cold country and that I should buy warm clothing in New York so I wouldn't freeze upon landing in Canada. I wondered why Chris had not informed me of this. I thought maybe he didn't want to scare me. The time arrived for me to leave Lagos. I said all my goodbyes and headed to the airport to check in for the Nigerian Airways direct flight to New York City.

Soon the boarding announcement for the flight came and the passengers lined up to board. I was both thrilled and apprehensive. Forty minutes later, the attendants locked the doors. I felt fluttering in my stomach, or was it my heart? The plane started to taxi down the runway, joining the queue of planes awaiting their turn to become airborne. More knots formed in my stomach. The thought in my mind was: This is the point of no return. Are you sure you are doing the right thing?

I watched through the window as the engines accelerated; faster and faster the plane went until the wheels left the tarmac. As the plane gained altitude, the ground receded, growing smaller and smaller until it finally disappeared and was covered by clouds. There were more knots in my stomach; some from exhilaration and some from dread. I was exhilarated that the fear of being taken off the plane didn't materialize. I was excited to be going to see this man with whom I had fallen in love and whom I had not seen in a year. I was going to be married to him. Our courtship had been exciting and sometimes stressful. What would marriage be like? Would it continue to be exciting? Would I be able to maintain some individuality within this new relationship? How did people navigate this new territory? I would be in a new country where I didn't know anyone. Who would I turn to for help if I needed it?

Since I was admitted into university, I had been my own master, deciding what I wanted to do, choosing how I was going to do it, and whether it was good for me or not. I knew that had to change, as all my decisions from henceforth wouldn't be made by me alone. Chris would be a part of every decision from this point forward. Was I losing something or gaining something? Some parts of life are complicated, with no clear or easy answers. This is where faith comes in. Hebrews 11:1 describes it this way: *Now faith is confidence in what we hope for and assurance about what we do not see."*

I had faith in God's providence and goodness. He had performed miracle upon miracle for me. Now, I was leaving behind almost everything that had been familiar—my country, my family, my friends, and the support system I turned to when I found myself in a tight spot.

I was leaving all these behind for just one person. Even though I loved this man very much, was this wise?

Millions of women have done it. For some, it had been a beautiful thing. But for others, it had turned out to be a nightmare. What would living with Chris look like? This was a point of no return. I had crossed the Rubicon. What awaited me on the other side? I had heard of wedding day jitters. This day, indeed, was like the wedding day for me because it was the day I left all that was familiar behind. I was on a plane and at the destination was the wedding. I was sure this man was the one God had appointed for me. Did that mean there would be no problems?

As, I whispered a silent prayer, 1 Samuel 7:12, came to my mind. It says: *Samuel then took a large stone and placed it between the towns of Mizpah and Jeshanah. He named it Ebenezer [which means "the stone of help"], for he said, "Up to this point the Lord has helped us!"*

I didn't have a large stone, but the God who had orchestrated and brought all these together was still on the throne. He was still in control. Would He forsake me now? I doubted that. I closed my eyes and inwardly bid goodbye to all that had been familiar up to this point in my life. I opened my heart to all that the future held, determined to embrace each and every day and each and every task, opportunity, issue, and eventuality with faith, grace, and God's guidance. I closed my eyes and settled into the flight.

The Arrival

The flight to New York was uneventful. It was a sold-out flight that was packed to the brim. The New York airport was massive. The processing lines for immigration and customs were miles long. The first lineup was for immigration. The officer asked me almost the same questions the consular officer had asked me in Lagos. Why was I in the United States? How long was I going to be there? Was I planning to work there? Where would I be staying? What was the relationship between me and my host? However, unlike the consular officer in Lagos, he didn't make any unfounded insinuations or appear distrustful. At the end of the questions, he stamped my passport and wished me a pleasant stay in

New York City. Then, I was off to the customs line. Despite the long line, this actually went very quickly for those of us who had nothing to declare. The officer asked me a few questions, including whether I had anything I was going to leave in the United States that I should declare. I did not. He waved me goodbye.

With all the formalities over and my luggage on a trolley, I moved toward the exits—of which there were many. I didn't remember which one Chris's brother had said he would be waiting at. Had that been mentioned in the letter? I pulled out the letter and re-read the instructions. Yes, it said which exit, and I was already near it. I walked over to it.

It was then that a panicky thought struck me. Chris' brother and I had never met. I had seen pictures of him in Chris's photo album, but those pictures were at least ten years old. Did he still look the way he had looked in those pictures? How would we recognize each other? I'd been so busy with exams and preparations before my departure that I hadn't had the time to ask Chris to send me a recent picture of him. This was going to be tough. It would be difficult enough for two people who knew each other well to find each other in the massive airport crowded with thousands of people, let alone for two strangers.

I couldn't think of a solution. The phone number I had for him was that of his residence, so, even if I could call that number, I was sure he would have already left his house to come to the airport. I turned to the one resource that has always been there for me. I sat down on a bench, put my head down, and began to pray silently but I kept my eyes open. As I prayed, I saw out of the corner of my eyes a pair of feet that moved exactly the way Chris's feet move when he is walking. I looked up. Instantaneously, I knew that the man who just walked by me was Chris's brother. I stood up and walked towards him. I greeted him in our native tongue. We knew we had found each other. His chauffeur loaded my stuff into the car, and we drove to his residence in Manhattan.

Shopping for the All-Important, Sacred Gown

New York City was mesmerizing—and crowded. It was almost like Lagos in terms of the crowds on the streets, except that the traffic actually moved. There were many skyscrapers. I had never seen so many tall buildings. The streets were lit up with advertising signs—blinking constantly. There was a lot to take in.

His Excellency Ambassador Joe Ekong had a lovely family and I was warmly welcomed by his wife, Sister Lucy, and their three young children. My soon-to-be-sister-in-law welcomed me with open arms, ready to help me with everything I needed for the wedding. We didn't waste any time, as I only had five days to accomplish all that needed to be done in New York.

Those five days in Manhattan were full of activities, with Sister Lucy devoting as much time as possible (considering her young family) to helping me shop for the things I needed. The first item on our agenda was the wedding gown. There were some we liked but they were all samples, and the store wanted us to place an order for one to be made with the usual turnaround time being about three months. I had four days. Time was my enemy.

We went from shop to shop until we found the dream wedding gown. It was made of beautifully flowered snow-white lace, elaborately adorned with beads and pearls, and lined with a velvet fabric with a satin finish. The bodice was an A-line which flared out from the waist into a flowing large skirt with a majestic train. The back of the dress had satin-covered buttons from the high neckline all the way down the entire length of the zipper. The back skirt flared out into a four-foot train with a hook appropriately located so the train could be pinned up for the dance. The gown came with a twelve-foot veil, attached to a six-inch-long curved headpiece, covered with the same beautiful lace fabric as the gown. This headpiece was adorned with large white lace daisies attached to ribbons and cascading down to the temples. It was absolutely stunning. Furthermore, this dress was a perfect fit for me.

We wanted to buy it there and then. But just like all the others, it was a sample, and the shop wasn't interested in selling it. They wanted us to place an order for them to make us one which would take at least three months. We explained that we didn't have even a week, we only had a few days, three to be exact.

The store owner explained that she had just created that design and displayed it the previous month, and even though it was an expensive gown, it had attracted considerable attention, drawing people into the store, so she couldn't let us have it. We told her of our plight. We needed a wedding gown; one I could take with me when I left New York in three days. She said it was impossible for me to have it. And we told her nothing was impossible, as where there is a will, there is always a way. But she would not budge and we would not leave. Since the gown seemed to be a big seller, she didn't want to part with it without a replacement. We couldn't help her with a replacement, but we entreated her to explore plausible alternatives, such as creating a new gown, so I could have this one. She reiterated the impossibility of recreating a replica of the gown in three days, even if she worked day and night. We kept talking and exploring alternatives, none of which she said was possible.

From the moment I set my eyes on this gown, I knew it was the one I needed to have. It fitted as if it had been custom-made just for me and we were not going to leave the shop until we had it. I might have embarrassed my poor sister-in-law by refusing to leave the store without some arrangement about the gown. When I think about this incident now, it reminds me of the story of the persistent widow of Luke 18:1–8. Just like the widow, we wore the shop owner down.

Finally, we struck a compromise; she would let us have the gown—but only on the last possible day, as she would need to work hard to make a replacement. We were overjoyed and lucky that the owner of the store was also the designer of the gown and a seamstress. She took the next two days off and sacrificed her evenings to work on the replica. Even though overjoyed, we were still a little anxious—afraid that, if she didn't make enough progress with the new gown, she might refuse to allow us have the one on display. Adding to our discomfort was the fact that she wouldn't let us pay for the gown or even take a deposit. She asked us to wait until we could take it with us. I had a gnawing fear that she might change her mind about letting us have the gown. She assured us the gown would be ours on my last day in Manhattan. We had no other option but to trust her and God. I prayed that things would go well for her in creating the replica, so she would let us have the display.

With the gown planned for, we turned our focus to other things. We ordered the rings, and we were now shopping for the shoes and the bag to match my wedding dress. It was exhausting but fascinating. My host also advised me to buy at least one warm outfit to wear to Canada as "it is always freezing up there." The hunt was on for a pair of woolen pants, a heavy sweater, and a winter jacket. These were difficult to find in Manhattan at the end of June when it was so very hot. But she was reluctant to let me "freeze on arrival." So, we kept looking. When we were convinced we had exhausted our search, we settled for a pair of lined pants, a long-sleeve shirt, and a heavy sweater that we were lucky to find.

Our shopping mission was accomplished, except to collect the wedding gown. On the afternoon before my departure for Canada, we went for the gown. To our surprise, the shop decided to give us a discount since we were taking the floor model. Floor model? They had packaged the gown beautifully for me. I was overjoyed and overwhelmed. How could that be? They should have charged us extra for having to work day and night to create a replica. They didn't quite finish making the replica, but the front and the skirt were sufficiently complete that they could pin it on the mannequin. For all that work and inconvenience, instead of charging a surcharge, they gave a discount. Wow, God was extravagantly good and kind to me and I was thankful.

The Final Destination

At last, it was time for me to continue my journey. The five days in New York had been hectic but exhilarating and had flown by like a whirlwind. Now, I had all my wearables for the wedding. I said goodbye to my most hospitable hosts and headed to the airport. It was so warm in New York that I couldn't wear the "warm clothing" I had purchased for the journey. However, I had them on the very top in my carry-on luggage for easy access.

The first leg of the flight was to Toronto. After we boarded the flight, I noticed that most of the people were lightly dressed. Indeed, many were in shorts. Before takeoff, I checked with the flight attendant to make sure I was on the right flight. I knew Toronto was in Canada, and if Canada was "always freezing cold," why were these people in shorts, sandals, T-shirts, and other summery clothing? I thought maybe it got colder as one went west. I knew Saskatoon was in the west.

The flight to Toronto was short, only about an hour. I went through immigration smoothly. Then it was time to go through customs. They asked if I had something to declare. I told them about the things I had purchased in New York. Since this was my first international travel, I wasn't familiar with customs and duties. By this time, I had spent most of the money sent by Chris. I was wondering whether I would be asked to pay duties on the wedding and other items I had purchased. Luckily, I was informed my purchases did not incur any duties, as I was a visitor, had a return ticket, and was not planning on leaving those things in Canada. That was one load off my shoulders. When all the entry requirements were completed., I made my way to the waiting area for the flight to Saskatoon, my final destination.

As I waited to board the flight, I wondered whether I should change into my warm clothing. However, I noticed that many of the people in the waiting area wore shorts and other light clothing, just like those on the flight from New York to Toronto. Again, I wanted to be sure I was in the right place. I asked the attendant by the boarding gate if that was indeed the waiting area for the flight to Saskatoon. She said it was. I was a bit confused. If it was so very cold that people could freeze on landing without heavy warm clothing, why were these people not appropriately dressed? I began to wonder who was misinformed. Was it my advisers or the people on the plane? I assumed that at least some of the people boarding the plane must live in Saskatoon. As such, they would know better what the weather was like. They would be the ones with firsthand information, and unlikely to be the ones misinformed. I concluded that my advisers were more likely the ones who were wrong. I reasoned that within a few hours, I would find out once and for all who was right and who was wrong. The mystery will be solved, and I will know for sure if Canada was indeed the land of the frozen.

The flight from Toronto arrived in Saskatoon at about 7:30 p.m. It was very hot. However, that was not my biggest surprise. The big surprise was that it was still bright daylight, the type of daylight brilliance that I would expect at 2 p.m. in Nigeria. How could that be? I was accustomed to it being quite dark by 7:00 p.m. How could 7:30 p.m. have no sign of dusk?

The Saskatoon Airport was very small. Flights landed on the tarmac, and people walked inside to retrieve their luggage from the one baggage carousel. I picked up my luggage and stacked the suitcases in a corner and then stepped outside to see if Chris was there. He was as close as nontravelers were allowed to come. It was nice to see his face again for the first time, in twelve months. Finally, this journey had come to an end, and a new but different journey was beginning.

19

The Reunion and the I Do

With the wedding less than a week away, the days immediately following my arrival in Saskatoon were extremely hectic. There were bridesmaids and flower girls to meet, dresses to buy, a cake to order, and food to plan. Even though the meal was catered, Chris had also promised people there would be Nigerian food and expected me to cook it. How was I going to do all the things that needed to be done and also cook the meal? I didn't even know what would be available in the supermarkets in Saskatoon and whether it would be possible to find the ingredients to cook Nigerian food. I tried to convince my fiancé that it would be impossible for me to cook on that day, but he said nothing was impossible if we put our minds to it. Luckily, the wife of one of his Nigerian friends agreed to cook the food.

There was so much yet to be done before the wedding that it was bewildering. I wondered what happened to the guy who had said he would take care of everything and all I needed to do was show up and say, "I do." I was not surprised though. I knew he wouldn't be able to even think of half the things that needed to be done, left alone do them.

Poor fellow, he had no idea he was in deep waters until he started talking to Mrs. DeBlock, the pastor's wife. He was overwhelmed. Planning a wedding alone in less than three months, in a strange land with no relatives and advisers would be overwhelming for anyone, let alone a young man in a hectic residency program. He actually thought the one week after my arrival would be plenty of time to do whatever needed to be done.

The invitations had been printed and guests invited. I was probably the last person to see the wedding invitation. However, I knew what was on it, as we'd discussed the wording together over the phone and co-constructed the words. I particularly loved the inscription in the middle with the words of Psalm 118: 23. It said, This is the Lord's doing; it is marvelous in our eyes" It was indeed the Lord's doing. There had been so many obstacles and many adjustments over the three-year period since we had first met to make this wedding a reality. It was indeed the Lord's doing. If this had not been part of His plan, it wouldn't have happened. Finally, it was here, within reach, just a few more sleeps away.

Chris had, indeed, taken good care of the big things. The invitation was beautiful. At the time, raised printing was just emerging and our wedding invitation had this beautiful effect. He had booked the hall, selected the music, the caterer, and had a rough copy of the program set up, just awaiting my approval before printing. God was gracious to us. The University of Saskatchewan had a Lutheran student chaplain and a small church on campus. Pastor DeBlock, was the Chaplin of the Lutheran Students' Center. He was also affiliated with a bigger Lutheran church in town. Chris attended the church on campus. He had become friends with the DeBlock family and was especially close to one of their four sons, who was about his age.

The pastor's wife, Mrs. DeBlock, was a wonderful woman and God's special gift to us. Having seen many weddings, she had a better idea of the needs than we did. She came to our rescue and was my resource officer. She informed us of what needed to be done, helped us make many arrangements, and reminded us of the little things we hadn't thought of. God bless her.

Finding the same dress in the right sizes for the two bridesmaids was a Herculean task and we had to settle for approximate shade and as close in style as possible. The flower girls' dresses were just as difficult to find.

Then there was the wedding cake. There weren't many bakeries in Saskatoon at the time that made wedding cakes. But just like gowns, wedding cakes were usually ordered months in advance and we had less than a week. However, Mrs. DeBlock knew the owner of a bakery. She explained our situation to the owner. God intervened. The baker agreed to bake our cake: another miracle. A four-tier wedding cake within our color code in a beautiful design.

We didn't have time to go to the flower shop until two days before D-Day and then were told, "You will have to settle for local flowers, whatever we can get."

I said, "That will be absolutely perfect, as long as they are flowers."

They were just perfect, beautiful daisies tied up with a gorgeous ribbon—nothing fancy, but in my eyes, absolutely stunning.

The Countdown

One of the most difficult problems we encountered that Mrs. DeBlock couldn't help with was finding someone to do my hair. There were very, very few black people in Saskatoon at that time, and not one was a hairdresser. My hair needed a lot of help and tender loving care from someone who knew what to do with black hair.

But God is a miracle worker. He led us to a lady, who, had worked in a salon previously and had a hot iron straightening comb. She didn't have many of the products for black hair, but using what she had, she did an amazing job. My hair looked gorgeous. However, it had to be done on the wedding day and as close to the ceremony as we could make it, as black hair straightened and styled with a hot comb would try to return to its natural state as soon as it was exposed to air, friction, and time.

My second brother, Mfon, was at MIT in Boston at the time, just finishing his Ph.D. in engineering. He was planning to come to

Saskatoon to walk me down the aisle, but there was a problem getting the visa. It was not the visa to Canada that was an issue, as a Commonwealth citizen, he didn't need one. The problem was with a US visa to get back into the US. No one had anticipated a problem with that, but there it was. He already had a student visa, but it seemed it had to be endorsed by the Immigration Department to enable him to re-enter the United States. Until the Thursday before the wedding day, the endorsement hadn't come through.

We didn't know what would happen. But God is always gracious. The visa came through on Friday afternoon and he arrived only an hour and a half before the start of the ceremony. God is never late, His miracles are always just on time. I was overjoyed to have my sibling, my special brother be present, and be the one to walk me down the aisle on this special day.

Mrs. DeBlock had advised me to get dressed at the church, so she could help me. She was an amazing "Mother of the Bride". Finally, I stepped into my stunningly beautiful wedding gown. All the stress and tiredness of the day evaporated. This was the day, the moment. All the obstacles had been overcome. God had made a way time and time again where there seemed to be no way. Now, I was ready to walk down that aisle. Mfon had come straight from the airport to the church. He changed at the church too. When he was ready, the bridal march song announced it was time to go. Mfon put out his arm, and I placed mine in it. We started the march towards the narthex where the bridesmaids and flower girls were waiting. Everyone was in their rightful place. The entries began. One by one, each member of the bridal party marched to a preassigned position. The church was full. We had 150 invited guests, plus the bridal party and our out-of-town guests.

After a few songs, the pastor started his charge. He explained what marriage was all about, and then asked that all-important question. "Chris, do you take Jane to be your lawfully wedded wife, to live together in holy matrimony, to love her, honor her, comfort her from this day forward, for better, for worse, for richer, for poorer, and to keep her in sickness and in health, and forsaking all others, keep you only to her for as long as you both shall live?"

He responded, "I do."

Then it was my turn. The same questions were asked of me.

I responded, "I do."

After a few other exchanges between us, including the exchange of rings, the pastor finally said, "By the power vested in me, I pronounce you husband and wife. What God has joined together, let no man put asunder." With those words came the culmination of a three-year love affair and an almost two-week hectic schedule that started the day I finished my exams in Ibadan, Nigeria, and ended with "I do" in Saskatoon, Canada.

The wedding party filed out of the church and we lined up to greet and thank our guests. We took pictures and then moved on to the reception. Everything was mesmerizing; it was like a dream. My only regrets were that Mom was not there and Dad could not be there because of the tight timeframe, and the uncertainty about my ability to secure a passport or leave Nigeria. I drew a big breath and whispered internally to myself, *"No one ever gets everything they want, girl. Just be thankful for what you have been given and enjoy this euphoric day."*

At the reception, many people spoke and I was so glad Mfon was there to tell funny stories about my childhood. At the end of the evening, my hair was still holding beautifully. Thank you, Lord. This had turned out to be a perfect day. When we went outside at 10:00 p.m., it was still daylight with dusk just coming in. I was still in awe of the long days and short nights. What was this place where there was still light from the sun at 10:00 p.m.? This was a phenomenon I had never experienced.

We got into the car, and my husband was excited to show me around Saskatoon. During the week I had been there, we had been too busy to go anywhere or do anything that didn't relate to the wedding. Now, the pressure was off, and we could begin to breathe. Everything had worked out wonderfully well. I was thankful for the many people God had placed in our path, who'd helped us so wonderfully. I had met many people eager to help upon hearing I was only there for a week before the wedding. The world has many kind people, and God sometimes places them strategically in the path of those He wishes to bless. Praise be to Him.

The two days following the wedding were spent returning everything we had borrowed or rented and paying any outstanding bills. We only had only a few days—three to be exact—for a honeymoon before Chris had to return to work.

The first week after the honeymoon was busy, as I opened the gifts, recorded them, and wrote thank you notes. Many of them were very thoughtful gifts, things people who were just starting out needed. As the days ticked by, both Chris and I were increasingly aware of my need to return to Nigeria to start my NYSC duties. My husband didn't want me to leave and as much as I would have liked to stay, I felt a duty to return and complete my obligation to my country. I thought that someone like me (who went to university on an Academic Excellence Scholarship, the Rolls-Royce of scholarships), was particularly obligated to provide the service to the nation. I didn't think my return was a huge commitment. It was only one year, and just as the year since Chris left Nigeria for Canada had gone by quickly, this other year would too.

Added to my feeling of obligation was the consequence of not completing NYSC. The government had enacted a decree, which stands till this day. It stated that any employment in the country that requires a university or polytechnic graduate must have on file every applicant's NYSC completion certificate. Any university or polytechnic graduate who did not have an NYSC certificate was not allowed to be employed. If they somehow managed to gain employment, the employer who hired the person faced very severe penalties. Therefore, there was no way around not completing NYSC if I ever wanted to be employed anywhere in the country. The consequences of NYSC avoidance were deliberately severe to deter noncompliance. I did not want to be put in jail on my return to Nigeria. Additionally, even if I surrendered myself voluntarily with a good explanation on our return to Nigeria after six or seven years and escaped the punishment, it would not be fun to serve my NYSC year with a cohort that graduated many years after me.

Also, by then, we would probably have children. Being away from my prospective children for an entire year was a thought that was very troubling to me. I deemed the present inconveniences much more palatable than the ones that would exist in the future if I didn't return as scheduled. My husband didn't share my perspective. He didn't want me to return and mounted a vigorous campaign in which he got the pastor, the head of his department, and anybody else of influence to write to the NYSC secretariat to plead his case. Meanwhile, he also got his friends and anyone else he thought could persuade me to change my mind, to talk to me about how unorthodox and unfair it was for newlyweds to be separated for a whole year.

Meanwhile, my results from the university were out. I had done extremely well and was eligible to be invited to graduate studies. Chris immediately took my results to a professor at the Biochemistry department to whom he had already spoken before my arrival in Saskatoon. I was given admission for graduate studies at the University of Saskatchewan. This only complicated my decision to stay or leave.

How I wished Mom was still around for me to consult. She was the one person on the planet to whom I could unburden myself and know she would pray things through for me and with me. I didn't even have my Christian friends to ask to pray for me. Many voices spoke against what I considered the right thing and I was being pulled very strongly to that side. However, the consequences were only on one side—my side. I would be the one to go to jail. I would be the one to have my reputation ruined as an NYSC evader. I would be the only one who would bear all the consequences.

I knew being married made things complicated, but I didn't expect the complications to arise so early or the consequences to be so ominous. I was torn. I wished the people from the NYSC secretariat to whom several letters had been sent would respond one way or the other. They didn't; they were silent. They didn't agree or disagree with the postponement and the assurance that I would report to the secretariat the moment we returned to Nigeria. What was the silence indicative of? Was it a quiet consent or a foreboding threat?

20

The Ponder, the Verdict, the Implications

Why is this book titled "Loved Beyond Compare"? It opened with a terrifying dream. There were bombs, fear of death, a desperate cry for help, and a voice with a promise. Throughout the book, there are stories of narrow escapes from death, a shooting resulting in tremendous suffering, very difficult circumstances at schools, and the deaths of mothers. One may ask, "Which one of these depicts love? What love? Whose Love?"

Those are legitimate questions, but just for clarification, the love definitely does not refer to the love affair between Chris and me even though that love is real and has endured for more than 45 years. The love affair referenced in this book is that between Jesus and me. It began before I was born. If He had not intervened for me in utero, I may never have seen the light of day. Now that we know who the lovers are, let's delve into the questions.

I have never been on Jury duty, but I understand that one of the instructions usually given by the Judge is that the Jury suspend their preconceived ideas and prejudices, keep an open mind, and follow the evidence wherever it leads them. I am asking the same. Let's suspend our beliefs and prejudices and just follow what the happenings recounted in this book lead.

One could dismiss the dream as just a dream that had nothing to do with God, and others may laugh at the thought that there is even a God, that He speaks to or is interested in people, and that He does intervene in people's lives and affairs. Whatever people's perceptions or beliefs about God, His existence, and character, I had invited everyone to join me in exploring all that happened to my family and me throughout the war and a little beyond. Now, we have read the stories, pondered over the circumstances, and marveled at some of the outcomes. What is our verdict?

Some may say, "Jane it is easy for you to know God because He has been good to you, even though you experienced some hardships, He answered all your prayers and blessed you in many ways." Anyone who says this would be both right and wrong. Right, because I believe God answers all my prayers, but wrong if he/she thinks an answered prayer is one that God says "Yes" to whatever is asked. I believe there are three possible answers to every prayer. "Yes", "No", and "Not Yet". If we see answers to prayer in this light, then God answers every prayer.

In the narratives of this book, there were many instances where God didn't answer my prayers the way I wanted. But there are always two sides to every story and every situation. What you see in any situation depends on where your focus is. In any of the stories recounted in this book, if one flipped the focus, we could be looking at a very different story. Let's take for example the story of Maamma's illness which spanned the entire length of the book. I could have looked at that and said, "Why me?" "Why did I have to grow up in fear of losing my Mom and not have a carefree childhood like others?" In fact, someone who knew me as I was growing up told me he felt sorry for me because he thought I didn't have a "normal" childhood, that my childhood was "stolen" because of my Mom's ill health.

That certainly is one way of looking at the situation, but I beg to differ. I think the opposite is true, as my Mom's illness was the catalyst that made me the very person that I am today. That illness introduced me and my entire family to faith in Christ. After I came to know the Lord more fully, He opened my eyes even wider to see the incredible joy and peace He offers even in the midst of suffering. Suffering is never a pleasant thing, but suffering that yields rich rewards is palatable. First and foremost, the greatest gift of knowing God is the incomprehensible peace He offers His own in the here and now. This is followed by the gift of eternal life. As the Lord said in Mark 8:36: *"For what shall it profit a man if he shall gain the whole world, and lose his own soul?"*

Furthermore, because Mom always thought she could die any day, she didn't wait for us (her children) to grow up before learning many things she considered important for life. She taught us how to love God, live responsibly, care, and watch out for each other from a very young age. That has resulted in a tight bond between us. As you would recall from previous chapters, my siblings went out of their way to help me and do things for me. We go out of our way to help each other. We are a very tight-knit family.

When I was growing up, many middle-class families had maids. Even though we frequently had one, Mom often sent her away when I was home or prevented her from doing chores that she wanted me to do so that I could learn good housekeeping, childcare, and all the other tasks she perceived as essential for good healthy living. That training became vital since I have lived almost all my adult life in North America, where I couldn't have a maid and had no relatives to help me with childcare or household chores while I pursued higher education. There are many positive effects on my life because of Mom's ill health.

If I could choose what happened to Mom, would I have chosen differently? Absolutely. But we often don't choose what life throws at us, do we? The only part we get to choose is how we respond to what happens to us. We can choose our perception of it, our attitude, and our reaction to it. However, what we choose, why we choose, and how we choose to react to our circumstances are what determine whether the circumstance sinks us or strengthens us. Our focus can dramatically change what we see, how we see it, how we react to it, and how it impacts us.

Our Focus Determines What We See

Are there situations in your life that at first glance appear devastatingly bad? Can you look at the flip side of it? The problem with human beings is that we tend to focus on the negatives. On any given day, we can have several positive things happen to us, but we soon forget them. However, if there is one, just one negative thing that happened, we would remember that and ruminate over it in an ever-increasing negative spiral until we make ourselves utterly miserable. What would our days look like if we chose to focus only on the positives and ignore the negatives? If we choose to focus on the positives which, on any given day, far outnumber the negatives. Would we be happier, less depressed, less angry? Because focusing on the positives would be against our natural tendencies, doing it will definitely be difficult. We would have to work at it, determined not to let failures deter us. If we persist, we will get better at it. We may never perfect the skill, but we may make significant progress and effect positive changes in our lives.

I have recounted the many experiences that happened to my family and me during the war that would not be classified as "normal." The "miracles" happened time and again when our backs were up against the wall. In the first chapter, I recounted how a "Voice" spoke to me in a dream/nightmare when I faced a desperate bombing situation; the Voice promised protection for me and my entire family throughout the war. The question is, *Was that God speaking to me or was it just an ordinary dream? If it was God, did the promise materialize?* The corollary to these questions is: *Does God exist? If He does, does He speak to people? Does He interfere and intervene in people's lives and affairs? If He does, why do we not hear much more about those encounters?* These are questions that many of us ask from time to time. Can we infer some answers to these questions from the things that happened to my family and me during the war?

Coincidences or Divine Interventions? The Review

The first big happening to my family when the war started was Mom being able to purchase a huge amount of salt, sugar, and other essentials at hugely discounted prices the day the Oruko market was bombed. On that day, Mom was at that market, but the bombs fell far from where she was. Instead of that occurrence being detrimental it was a huge blessing to us. The bombing was the reason merchants, whose customers didn't show up to claim their merchandise because of the chaos and confusion, offloaded the wares at ridiculous prices. Mom was one of the people who bought those items at those prices. At the time, she didn't know what she was going to do with it all, but she wanted to help the city merchants who were desperate to get rid of their unsold merchandise.

We did not understand at the time how having those goods would be pivotal in providing funds for the many issues that would assail the family during the war. Issues such as paying for Mfon's escape, my school fees after our liberation, Mom's trip to find my brother Edet, and my trip to Lagos. Was Mom's decision to buy that huge inventory of merchandise shortly before their prices soared God's strategy for providing for the needs of the family? Did God foresee the bank closure which resulted in the family losing all our banked money, and then provided this merchandise as a way to help us to meet our needs? It would appear so. God made a way for us to have the money we would need for the many future eventualities long before they happened.

Was my brother Mfon's safe escape from the war zone an exceptional occurrence? In a situation where most of the people who attempted the crossing drowned, was he just one of the lucky few, or was there an invisible hand protecting him?

Was my being captured by the soldiers a divine intervention? Instead of my capture resulting in my hurt, it turned out to be a great blessing as it enabled me to retrieve my books and other belongings without any harm to me. None of the people who experienced that war and knew the reality of what usually happened to girls captured by soldiers believed I could have been captured, taken to the soldiers' barracks, allowed to retrieve all my belongings, and then returned home unscathed. They said it was impossible for that to have happened. Why would they have been so skeptical if that was something within the realm of possibilities? How do we describe, reference, or allude to happenings that are beyond the realm of reality?

Then there were the ten adults and two children who left the village of refuge to retrieve essentials. All the adults perished, but the two children survived by choosing a strategy the adults did not think of. Was that a coincidence or divine intervention? How could a child, a young teen devise a strategy the adults did not think of? From where did such a wise strategy emanate? Could it be attributed as part of the fulfillment of the promise in the dream? I believe the capture, which caused me to develop a phobia for open spaces was pivotal to my choosing not to follow the adults and thus save the lives of my brother Etim and me.

When my hometown was being liberated, the final act of the retreating soldiers was to burn homes. Why did the burning stop on the street just before ours? If the houses had continued to be torched, and ours was set on fire, my dad and grandma might have perished with the house. How would we have fared without our dad and our home? If that was another coincidence, how many coincidences can one family experience?

The greatest war-time miracle of them all was the shooting of my brother Edet. First, the aim was for his head but somehow, they missed the head and hit his pelvis, breaking several bones but missing all his vital organs, his spinal cord, and his major blood vessels. How can we account for the missed shots when the soldiers shot him with the intent to kill? How about the senior officer recognizing him just in time before the soldiers would have incinerated him with a grenade? How could someone with injuries so heinous and who had lost so much blood that doctors regarded treating him as "a waste of valuable medication" survive? How could his recovery and rehabilitation be so fast? Why was Mom so adamant that he was alive and went to find him when everyone who reported the news said he was dead? These were the questions that boggled my mind and kept me wondering if all these events could really be regarded as coincidences. How many unusual coincidences can one family experience?

Then there were the miracles at St. Anne's. First, the admission. My brother had already spoken to the principal about me and received a definite, "No." How great a coincidence was it that our cousin had to call on the principal the day we visited him and he allowed us to tag along? What made the principal change her mind when my brother reintroduced me? Then how was I able to learn five years of chemistry and physics on my own in one year while at the same time, learning and keeping up with the 6th year's syllabus with my classmates? How was that possible? How could one little girl succeed in learning by herself two subjects she had never studied? Was I sent to St. Anne's just so that I could be stripped of all the pride and self-reliance that had kept me from seeing my need for Christ and inviting Him into my life?

Then there was my decision to go to the church retreat early. That one simple decision resulted in a chance encounter, an encounter that significantly impacted the course of my life, my being introduced to Chris. Should we examine the strange illness or attack by demons that almost took my life? What about the consular officer? The wedding dress? The many people who helped with the wedding? If these occurrences happened in isolation, or to different people over a long period of time, it would be easy to write them off as coincidences. However, when they all happen to the same family within a few years, a pattern begins to emerge. A pattern that appears to have pre-destination written all over it.

We must not forget the biggest miracle of them all—the prognosis given to Mom and Dad when they were expecting me. The odds of my being born alive were slim by human standards, but God had a plan. How could one person/family experience so many unexplainable negatives turned positives within such a short period of time? Could they all have been coincidences? If they were not, then could they have been God encounters? Could they have been ways that God was wooing us and letting us know that He is alive and able to intervene in the lives of people if He chooses?

Our Attributions

One of the problems that human beings have that could preclude us from recognizing God's involvement is that we like to take credit for the good things that happen in our lives. We like to think that the positive things that happen to us are all due to our own ingenuity and that they happen because we are smart, creative, or lucky. Not giving God a thought, we take the credit for ourselves, and often cannot stop bragging about it and patting ourselves on the back. We don't even remotely think that God could be playing a role in what happened. No, we take all the glory and credit. We fail to see, attribute, and recognize God's hand, his love, care, and intervention in our successes. However, when bad things happen, our reaction is quite different. We are very quick to blame God and question His love, availability, and concern for us.

How would we like to be that "god"? The person who is blamed for all the bad things that happen but who is given no credit for the good things that happen? If someone did that to us, would we be running to help them when they are in trouble? In spite of all the ways we disrespect and ill-treat God, He still shows up when our backs are against the wall. However, even then we often don't recognize His presence because our focus is firmly on the problem and to whom we can assign the blame.

We also often don't consider the long-term effects of the trials and tribulations we encounter. James 1: 2 -3 says: *Consider it a sheer gift, friends when tests and challenges come at you from all sides. You know that under pressure, your faith life is forced into the open and shows its true colors. So don't try to get out of anything prematurely. Let it do its work so you become mature and well-developed, not deficient in any way"*

I have already referenced how my mom's ill health could be seen to produce many positives in our family. Could it be that God sometimes allows us to go through difficult situations to enable us develop character and become better people? We have all experienced setbacks in one way or the other. If we take a look at the long-term outcomes, can we sometimes see positives that were not obvious at the time when we were going through the trial? There have been many situations in my life that I had pleaded with God to take me out of because they were difficult and painful, but after the fact, I was very thankful that He hadn't answered my rescue prayer because what I learned from the situation far outweighed the pain. Could it be that we sometimes make attributions based on limited and immediate outcomes which may appear negative? If we examine the situation in hindsight, could we identify some unexpected positives that were not obvious at the time of the happening?

Our Short-Sightedness and Limited Knowledge

Whenever I think of reactions made out of limited knowledge, I am reminded of an incident with one of my children. I had taken my toddler for his immunization booster shot. At the immunization office, when he saw the needle coming towards him, he wanted to flee. But I held him tight and close as the nurse administered the shot. He screamed in pain as the needle pierced his skin. When it was all over, he looked up at me with tears running down his cheeks. When I tried to hold him close and comfort him, he pushed me away and looked me straight in the face as if to say, "How could you allow them to hurt me?"

I know immunization is controversial these days. I am not interested in being part of that controversy; I am just making a point. All that my little boy saw was the few seconds of pain from the needle. He could not understand why I would let someone inflict such pain on him. But as a biochemist and a parent, I knew the pain from the immunization was temporary and minuscule compared to the pain that would ensue if he was not immunized and contracted rubella, diphtheria, mumps, tetanus, whooping cough, or polio. My decision to allow him to experience the needle pain was based on my more expansive knowledge of immunizations and the protection they provide against painful and life-impacting diseases. However, to the toddler whose knowledge of what was happening was very limited, my action appeared to be a betrayal. There was no way that I could explain to him what I knew about immunizations that convinced me to subject him to the temporal pain. He was a toddler and just did not have the capacity to understand the logic behind immunizations. I know this is a simplistic illustration, but could our understanding of some of the things God allows to come our way be similar to that?

If God is who He says He is, and He can see the end from the beginning, could it be that His vision is like that of the parent in the immunization story, while ours is similar to that of my toddler? Is it possible that God could be speaking to us and intervening for our good but we lack the capacity to understand what He is doing? Could it be that because He sees things in multiple dimensions while we see them only in one, we only see a little part of the picture at any one time? In hindsight, there have been times I have been thankful for some setbacks because the lessons I learned from it were so important that I consider whatever distress and/or inconvenience I had experienced minuscule when compared to what I learned from the situation. Could our shortsightedness allow the enemy opportunities to fill us with fear?

Did My Childhood Fears Materialize?

The childhood fears that threatened to act as a barrier between God and me had power over me as long as I was not talking with God. From the day I completely gave my life to Christ, and God became my confidant, those fears evaporated. Lies and truth cannot co-exist. Christ is the truth and when He enters into our lives, the lies and their advocate have to flee.

I was afraid that if I gave my life to Christ, I would have to forgo a good education, have to leave in rural areas, do weird things, and be unsuccessful. None of these materialized. After my homeland was liberated and even before the war ended, I moved to the largest city in Nigeria, Ibadan. I am highly educated and have enough to meet my needs and the needs of my family plus a little extra to help those in need which resulted in my founding and running Amakon Women Empowerment, a charity that promotes women's success by providing disadvantaged women and girls access to success-enhancing tools. Therefore, none of those fears materialized. It is not surprising because they came from the devil. Here is how the Bible describes him in John 8:44(b), *He was a murderer from the beginning. He has always hated the truth because there is no truth in him. When he lies, it is consistent with his character; for he is a liar and the father of lies."*

Is Fear Robbing You?

What about you? Is fear keeping you from saying "Yes" to God? It is the same old trick that the enemy used in the Garden of Eden when he tempted Adam and Eve. He made them think that God didn't have their best interest at heart. He caused Adam and Eve to doubt God's sincerity, integrity, care, truthfulness, and love. He has continued to do so ever since. Maybe that's why the word "Fear Not" appears 365 times and the word "Fear" more than 500 times in the Bible. The Apostle Paul said to Timothy in 2 Timothy 1:7: *For God has not given us a spirit of fear and timidity but of power, love, and self-discipline.*

God knows how debilitating and limiting fear can be, and He doesn't want that for His children. Furthermore, even secular research acknowledges the debilitating effects of fear and indicates that the majority of our fears do not come true. So, if fear has been keeping you from experiencing life to its fullest by inviting God into your life, learn from me. He loves His children too much to deprive them of life, rather, as articulated in John 10:10(b), He said, *I came so they might have life, a great full life."* Don't let the enemy's lies impoverish you and rob you of the abundant life that God has in store for you. In Acts 10: 34-35, Peter said, *I see very clearly that God shows no favoritism. In every nation, he accepts those who fear him and do what is right.*

This indicates that God shows favor to everyone. Nobody has everything, and nobody lacks everything. We can sometimes deceive ourselves by thinking that some people have everything and wish we could be like them. Big mistake. It is difficult to truly know someone without living with them and spending quality time with them. Some people may have flaws where it is easily noticeable; those are the people we like to denigrate because their flaws are in the open for all to see. However, we applaud those whose flaws are not easily visible, but with time, some of the hidden flaws become visible and we realize that nobody has it all; nobody is perfect.

I am not saying that if we follow Christ our life will become easy. If I were to say that, I would be preaching a false Gospel because Christ himself said in Mathew 16:24(b) *If any of you wants to be my follower, you must give up your own way, take up your cross, and follow me.* The cross he is referencing here is not a piece of jewelry, rather, it is the real cross, the type that Christ was crucified on. It is an instrument of torture, shame, and death. Therefore, Jesus is saying that if we want to follow Him, we should be prepared not for a life on a bed of roses, but one on a bed filled with thorns. That is not a very palatable call, but it's the truth. Christ further spells it out in John 16:33(b) which reads: *Here on earth you will have many trials and sorrows. But take heart because I have overcome the world."*

He says here on earth His followers will have trials and sorrows and yet they will also have peace. Does that seem contradictory? It does, until you experience it, and when you do, the trials and sorrows seem trivial in comparison with that peace that defies understanding. That is what Jesus offers. You need to experience it to believe it. It is real. That's why God keeps inviting us to come and talk with Him because it is during such conversations that He downloads the peace to us. It is during such conversations that we get to "hear" His heart and receive His counsel.

I think God is more interested in our character development and maturation than in our comfort. He will allow us to go through situations that cause us to see our need for changes that can result in the maturation of our character and bring us closer to Him. However, some of us do not often see things in that light, instead, we get angry at God and raise our fists at Him. But gently and lovingly, He continues to invite us to talk with Him.

So, did the promise in my dream come true? What is your verdict and why? Which occurrences were pivotal to your decision? Whatever your opinion of the role of God's work in my life, I hope it encourages you to examine your own life and see if there are miracles that you have not recognized or overlooked.

The Invitation; God's Invitation

When things happen in our lives, most of the time, even for believers, the first person we run to is often not God. Rather we run to friends, family, counselors, healthcare providers, or even a stranger sitting beside us on a train or plane. It is when we have exhausted all the earthly resources that we have the novel idea that maybe we should probably talk to God about it. I am very guilty of this but the Lord has been gracious and patient with me and He continues to gently whisper, "Jane, come and talk with me, come and talk with me about the issues of your life. Don't be concerned that you fell on your face, I still love you and want you to come and talk with me about it."

Such an invitation is not for me alone. I believe that invitation goes out to every human being irrespective of who we are and what we have done or have not done. David, the man after God's heart, received this revelation when he was in deep distress. King Saul was hunting him down to kill him even though he had done no wrong. It might have been difficult for David to understand why God was not intervening on his behalf. But when he quietened his heart in God's presence, he was able to hear God and what he heard, he recorded in Psalm 27: 8. He wrote: *My heart has heard you say, "Come and talk with me." And my heart responds, "Lord, I am coming."*

God still extends that invitation to us, whether we are believers or not. He knows that our vision is very limited and our viewpoint very narrow, these would make it difficult for us to understand the true meaning and outcomes of what is happening. It's only in Him that we find true love and compassion. He knows that no human being has it all together because we are all fallible. Even though the church could help, He doesn't say run to the church, or the pastor or the priest, because they are all human and fallible. He says come talk with me. It's only in God that we can find true compassion and understanding. People, no matter how good and righteous will fail us. That's why it's so important that we do not equate people and/or institutions, no matter how benevolent with God. If the church, pastor, or priest hurts us, let's not equate that with God. Just like any parent, He is heartbroken when someone hurts one of His children, and if we go to Him, He will comfort us as nobody else can.

Therefore, making God the first go-to person when in distress is very wise. Asaph, a Levite, and one of the worship leaders commissioned by King David to lead worship in the Temple struggled with what many of us struggle with today. Some of the questions that we struggle with from times immemorial include: *Is there a God? If there is, is He just? Does He reward good and punish evil? Why do evil people appear to prosper while good people seem to have hard times?* We have all struggled with these in one way or the other. However, we have records of what some of the people in the Bible who struggled with the same questions discovered.

Asaph expressed his frustration about this issue in Psalm 73. It is quite long but reading all of it will help us understand Asaph's frustration and what happened when he talked with God about it. He wrote: *Truly God is good to Israel, to those whose hearts are pure. But as for me, I almost lost my footing. My feet were slipping, and I was almost gone. For I envied the proud when I saw them prosper despite their wickedness. They seem to live such painless lives; their bodies are so healthy and strong. They don't have troubles like other people; they're not plagued with problems like everyone else. They wear pride like a jeweled necklace and clothe themselves with cruelty. These fat cats have everything their hearts could ever wish for! They scoff and speak only evil; in their pride, they seek to crush others. They boast against the very heavens, and their words strut throughout the earth.*

And so the people are dismayed and confused drinking in all their words. "What does God know?" they ask. "Does the Most High even know what's happening?" Look at these wicked people—enjoying a life of ease while their riches multiply. Did I keep my heart pure for nothing? Did I keep myself innocent for no reason? I get nothing but trouble all day long; every morning brings me pain. If I had really spoken this way to others, I would have been a traitor to your people. So, I tried to understand why the wicked prosper. But what a difficult task it is!

Then I went into your sanctuary, O God, and I finally understood the destiny of the wicked. Truly, you put them on a slippery path and send them sliding over the cliff to destruction. In an instant, they are destroyed completely, swept away by terrors. When you arise, O Lord, you will laugh at their silly ideas as a person laughs at dreams in the morning. Then I realized that my heart was bitter, and I was all torn up inside. I was so foolish and ignorant I must have seemed like a senseless animal to you. Yet I still belong to you; you hold my right hand. You guide me with your counsel, leading me to a glorious destiny.

Whom have I in heaven but you? I desire you more than anything on earth. My health may fail, and my spirit may grow weak, but God remains the strength of my heart; he is mine forever. Those who desert him will perish, for you destroy those who abandon you. But as for me, how good it is to be near God! I have made the Sovereign Lord my shelter, and I will tell everyone about the wonderful things you do.

Asaph had the same struggles in understanding life as we do today. When he sought the answers from elsewhere, he only got more frustrated. It was only when he took the issue to God that he received the revelation that made sense. That is why God still invites us to make a chat with Him our priority. You may think that a chat with God is "crazy talk." How can a person hear God?

It is a matter of familiarity. My mom had a friend who was deaf and mute. However, they would be "talking" and laughing whenever they got together. Mom used to say that her friend "spoke more eloquently and was more funny" than those who could hear and speak. This lady did not learn or know official sign language. However, she made up her own sign language and because Mom was her close friend and spent time with her, she understood her gestures and signing. They could hold great conversations. I was always intrigued and in awe as to how Mom could understand what each gesture meant especially as this lady made them at such a very fast pace. Mom's answer was that when you spend quality time with someone, you get to know them well and you understand them better. The more quality time you spend with them, the better you know them, and the greater your understanding of their language will be.

Could it be the same with God? Could it be that some of us do not hear God or understand His language because we don't spend enough time with Him? Could it also be that even when we want to spend time with Him, we fail to follow His protocol?

The Protocol

For many things in life, there often is a protocol. Even computers and appliances have procedures that we are supposed to follow if they are to work well for us. We gladly follow those procedures because we want our pieces of equipment to accomplish what we want. We try to follow as closely as possible the instructions set out by the manufacturer. However, when it comes to God, we don't seem to take the same due diligence. Why? I know this illustration seems odd and insulting. I am not really comparing God with equipment. Not in the least. That would be sacrilegious. I am just trying to make a point with the illustration. I hope you see the point.

There is a very clear protocol for visiting and talking with God. It is simple, does not cost any money, and is not complicated. If you follow the protocol, you will surely find Him. The first step is found in Hebrews 11:6. It says, *Anyone who wants to come to him must believe that God exists and that he rewards those who sincerely seek him.* Every step is very important. To go to God, you must first believe that He exists. We can't just be flippant about seeking Him. We need to believe that He exists. Makes sense, doesn't it? The next step is found in Psalm 100:4. It says, *Enter his gates with thanksgiving; go into his courts with praise. Give thanks to him and praise his name."* Gratitude is very important. Even human beings like and are more open to those who are joyful and grateful rather than those who are bitter and vengeful. Lastly, in Jeremiah 29: 13, God says, *"You will seek Me and find Me when you search for Me with all your heart."*

The Apostle Paul expounds on the protocol. He tells us what to do after we get into God's presence in Philippians 4: 6-9. He says, *"Don't fret or worry. Instead of worrying, pray. Let petitions and praises shape your worries into prayers, letting God know your concerns. Before you know it, a sense of God's wholeness, everything coming together for good, will come and settle you down. It's wonderful what happens when Christ displaces worry at the center of your life.*

Summing it all up, friends, I'd say you'll do best by filling your minds and meditating on things true, noble, reputable, authentic, compelling, gracious—the best, not the worst; the beautiful, not the ugly; things to praise, not things to curse. Put into practice what you learned from me, what you heard and saw and realized. Do that, and God, who makes everything work together, will work you into his most excellent harmonies."

There we have it, a few easy steps for getting rid of anxiety and worry, and enjoying God's company and peace. A protocol discovered by people well-known for walking with God. Let's recap: If we want to have an audience with God:

1. We should believe that He exists and that He rewards those who sincerely seek Him with all their heart.
2. Then enter His gate with thanksgiving and His court with praise.
3. Have a conversation with Him about what's on our minds, and thank Him for what He has already done for us.
4. If we do these, our anxiety and worries will be replaced by the peace of God.
5. To retain the peace, we need to watch what we allow into our hearts and minds. We need to focus and meditate on the good, the positive, the praiseworthy, the beautiful, and the noble.

There we have it. As the saying goes, "Garbage in: Garbage out". If we don't want garbage in our lives, we have to keep it out by centering on God, and the good and positive. We need to forget the one negative thing that someone said to us or about us but remember and celebrate the hundreds of positive and good things that people have said to us and about us. It is a learned behavior, a difficult one to make a habit of, but with practice and persistence, everything is possible.

The Practice of Talking With God

The practice of talking with God is as simple as talking with your best friend. Now that you have the protocol, find a quiet place where you will not be disturbed. Sit and make yourself comfortable. Follow the protocol. Begin with thanksgiving. That can be as simple as saying, "Thank you God for inviting me to talk with you. It feels weird but, here I am. Thank you for … . I am grateful for that, but I am wondering about … ." You can keep going, but remember that this is a conversation, not a monologue. So, have times when you are quiet and are just listening to God's responses. Remember, He speaks in various ways but mostly to your heart, not your ears.

One way that God talks to us is through the Bible. Do you have the habit of reading the Bible? If you read it with the intent of hearing from God, He will certainly speak to you from it. He has not asked us to do anything difficult or tasking. All he has done is invite us for a conversation. Something as easy and natural to us as breathing. Throughout this book, we have seen what having a conversation with God can accomplish. Now, it's your turn. What are you going to do? He has issued the invitation and is waiting for your response.

If you are a believer, have you had your conversations with Him today? How many? Remember there are no limits. If you have not yet believed in Him, that shouldn't be a deterrent, the invitation is for everyone. You are still invited. What are you waiting for? Remember He is continuously inviting you and saying; "Whatever the issue, come talk with me about it." He will not judge you, rather He will give you good counsel and comfort. He says in John 3: 37(b): *".… and I will never re*ject them."

There is the promise that you will not be rejected no matter what your situation and what you have done. He is waiting for you. What have you got to lose? Remember, there are some things that may be difficult for you to handle on your own. Accept the invitation that keeps going out to you: *"Come talk with me; come talk with me."*

Have you talked with Him today?

Gratitude

Recently, I started to practice something new. I started doing this one thing that has positively and dramatically revolutionized my sleep. Before I fall asleep each night, I examine my day and pick out two things from the day that I am thankful for. I meditate on these two items from different positive perspectives. I chew on them and inform myself of all the positive things that accompany those two things and how they have blessed me. I tell God how thankful I am that He allowed me to experience these things. As I continue in that attitude of gratitude and thankfulness, waves and waves of peace begin to gently wash over me, and I float into sleep in a sea of peace.

You may never realize how many positive things happen in your life each day unless you stop and take time to think about them. Even on a day you may consider your worst, you still have something to be thankful for. Even if you experienced a tragedy or disaster of some kind that day, that you are still alive is a reason to be thankful. How about going out and returning home safely? Some people who went out that day never returned. They encountered one disaster or another and were killed, injured, or maimed. That you went somewhere and returned safely is a reason to be thankful.

Did we have enough to eat, water to drink, a roof over our heads, and people who love us? These are things that some people around the world and even in our own backyard may lack. That we have any of them is a reason to give thanks. Try it. Let your last thoughts of the day before your eyes close be those of gratitude and thankfulness. Give it a try and notice how it changes how well you sleep. Doing this is the practical side of what Paul talked about in Philippians 4 which we have already discussed. Practice makes perfect. Therefore, practice, practice, and practice.

You didn't know the Bible has an antidote for insomnia, did you? Try it. It may be difficult for you to keep your mind focused at the beginning. But if you persist and practice, your concentration will improve and you will become better at it with time. Then you will see your sleep pattern take a dramatic positive and peaceful turn. This could be one way of beginning to talk with God every day. What a wonderful way to end each day! What a wonderful way to banish sleepless nights but float into a peaceful sleep on a sea of gratitude. Blessings.

Appreciation

Many people gave very generously of their time and resources to proofread, review, and provide valuable feedback to this book. Your acts of kindness were very much appreciated and greatly treasured.

To those who made time to review the manuscript and provide feedback—Gene and Judy Packwood, Gwen Frederick, and Laurelie Martinson—thank you so much.

A huge thank you goes especially to Fred Hill, who spent a ton of time and energy reviewing, proofreading, and providing valuable feedback for this book.

About the Author

Dr. Jane Amana Ekong earned her B.Sc. and M.Sc. in Biochemistry from the University of Ibadan, and the University of Toronto, respectively. Later, she earned her Ph.D. in Psychology from the University of Calgary. She has utilized these skills in many areas of the medical field.

She volunteered extensively with many charities that help women and children. Upon retirement, this mother of four founded Amakon Women Empowerment, a charity that helps disadvantaged women and girls succeed. She is a joyful person, a worship warrior, and a fitness enthusiast.

www.ingramcontent.com/pod-product-compliance
Lightning Source LLC
Chambersburg PA
CBHW051004140626
46546CB00016B/228